Z
716.45
.L932

W9-BWL-702

DATE DUE

DEMCO, INC. 38-2931

Reading
and the
Adult New Reader

Z
716.45
.L932

Reading
and the
Adult New Reader

HELEN HUGUENOR LYMAN

American Library Association
Chicago 1976

KVCC KALAMAZOO VALLEY
COMMUNITY COLLEGE
LIBRARY

41382

Library of Congress Cataloging in Publication Data

Lyman, Helen H   1910–
    Reading and the adult new reader.

    Bibliography: p.
    Includes index.
    1. Libraries and new literates. 2. Reading (Adult education). I. Title.
Z716.45.L932   025.5'4   76–44431
ISBN 0–8389–0228–6

Copyright © 1976 by the American Library Association

All rights reserved. No part of this publication
may be reproduced in any form without permission
in writing from the publisher, except by a reviewer
who may quote brief passages in a review.

Printed in the United States of America

*To Librarians
and Library Science Students*

CONTENTS

FIGURES

TABLES

Preface

This work has been undertaken because of a strong belief that reading and library reading services and programs can be dynamic factors in the lives of adult men and women. It is a logical outgrowth of the research on reading materials for the adult reader and library science courses conducted by the author. It has some foundation in its predecessor, the report *Library Materials in Service to the Adult New Reader* (ALA, 1973).

It is intended to serve as a stimulant and guide for those persons— librarians, teachers, editors, library science professors and students—who are involved in the evaluation, use, and creation of adult reading materials. It strives to combine theory and practice.

An effort has been made to place at their disposal the knowledge and experience of others, who, like the author, have a profound respect and pleasure for, and a lifetime of use of, the communications that are contained in the print and reading resources of libraries.

I wish to acknowledge the contributions of those contributors who represent the six reader groups discussed in chapters 5 and 6: Gladys Alesi, Dr. Samuel Betances, Dudley Randall, Rarihokwats, Elizabeth Martinez Smith, and Dr. Cratis Williams. I am grateful for the support of the U.S. Office of Education, which made possible those separate reports. I am also grateful for the support and encouragement extended to me by Henry T. Drennan, Research and Demonstration Branch, Office of Libraries and Learning Resources, Office of Education; by Charles E. Bunge, Director, Library School, University of Wisconsin–Madison; and by Herbert Bloom, Senior Editor, Publishing Services, American Library Association. I thank all those who have permitted the use of their material.

Books and reading, along with the other communication media and viewing and listening resources, are the bases of library service. Libraries and librarians have a direct, public responsibility for developing resource collections which are acquired through discriminating judgments. They have responsibility for interpreting and promoting those resources, based on their recognition of the power and value those resources may have in the lives of adult men and women. Thus they have responsibility for helping adults become discriminating, independent, and mature readers.

Reading
and the
Adult New Reader

1

Purpose of the Book

WHY READING SERVICES?

Why do librarians address themselves to services for adult readers? Upon what basic assumptions may fundamental agreement be reached?

The informational, recreational, educational, and research functions are common to all library systems, to a greater or lesser degree. Service is an important function at every level and in every type of library. Libraries are well organized, with technical and bibliographical aids from the simplest to the most complex. Libraries place at the disposal of the residents of a community all the knowledge and information contained in multimedia resources. Resources and programs are organized and promoted to assist users and potential users.

When service goes beyond the bibliographical, organizational, and reference services to more direct individual informational services and a variety of reading guidance activities, problems arise. In the first place, limited resources impose limited services, or may result in no service to parts of the community. Librarians who are engaged in direct service to residents quickly recognize this handicap.

Librarians, either consciously or unconsciously, also *impose* limited services and resources by the subject areas and kinds of materials they emphasize or reject, neglect or ignore, promote or recognize. They may do this because of choice, demand, policy, lack of demand, ignorance, prejudice, or limitations imposed by narrow selection criteria and rigid budgetary allocations.

By the choices and decisions made in developing library collections, librarians broaden or narrow the choices for residents of the community. By the range of their professional knowledge, understanding of the clientele, and familiarity with reading materials, librarians are able to create opportunities for continuing education and pleasure reading for adults. By the development of special skills, personal talents, and interests of the staff, librarians increase the possibility of providing appropriate service and programs. By the kind of criteria they apply in the evaluation of materials, librarians narrow or widen the type and character of the materials they collect, organize, and interpret.

Various conditions set obstacles in the way of service to individuals and groups in a community. The size of the library frequently isolates librarians from active personal contact. Reader groups within the library's community frequently include one or several ethnic groups with life styles and information interests and needs which are unfamiliar within the established library system. Obstacles arise when the staff is predominantly unrepresentative of the ethnic groups who are to be served; when the users or nonusers and the librarians are unable to relate to each other, are even hostile and fearful; when concentration is on administrative efficiency, centralized organization, automation, systems development, and expressed information needs. Governing bodies may be unsympathetic or ignorant of the need for service to persons of different cultures. Philosophies of service may support services exclusively to a selected part of the population. Studies show that services and collections have been, and frequently still are, primarily directed to students in the process of being educated, to educated adults, and to adults in continuing education who are primarily from the white population with higher incomes.

TRENDS IN SOCIETY

The diversity and change which permeate the society of the United States in the last half of the twentieth century affect every individual and group. Every public agency must take the changes into account. A knowledge of life styles and diverse cultures is essential to effective service. The diversity in life styles, the crossing over from one style to another, the transitions and changes in attitudes and values are potent forces. Mobility is everywhere apparent, not only in movement of individuals and whole populations from one place to another but also within the occupational and professional world and classes of society. Most persons today will have at least seven different jobs during a long lifetime. The high school graduates of 1975 probably will begin a second career by 1980.

Racism, prejudice, and violence are strong forces. New ethnic identity is creating new demands among ethnic and nationality groups. Opposing forces create various problems—big versus little, the destructive versus the constructive, mass culture versus experimental, conformity and sameness versus differences, freedom versus restrictions, the affluent versus the poverty stricken, the educated versus the uneducated, the literate versus the illiterate.

Although change itself is recognized and stressed, it is also ignored, and frequently what seems more evident is how little change takes place, how much remains the same. The fragmentation, tensions, and uncertainties which are generated, as well as the new knowledge, the cohesive elements of communication, transportation and electronic media, affect everyone. In this diversity there is a worldwide range of culture. Men and women search for identity, survival, information. The search for tradition, cultural heritage, and new values generates tension and conflict, and at the same time creates new understandings and peaceful cooperative efforts.

The library profession states clearly that the present, postindustrial society, in which information created by research and development increases as never before, is dependent on codification of theoretical knowledge and continuing educational opportunities for all adults at all levels. Alvin Toffler, the prophet of "future shock," emphasizes the need to encourage a more future-focused orientation. The time bias formed in response to the rate of change, whatever the characteristic attitude toward the past, present, and future, must be identified. In the literature of the last three or four decades there is evident a preoccupation with problems of the population in cities and urban areas, and findings of the studies are restricted to the "crisis of the cities." In 1971 the Committee for Economic Development predicted an increasing economic specialization of the central city and a marked shift in population. The CED report envisioned a "suburbanization of the poor," with many of the central-city problems transferred to the suburbs. What is known about problems and solutions in the central city may have implications for the suburbs.[1] Similar situations exist in rural communities.

Impermanence, not permanence, becomes characteristic of various facets of life. Places, friends, schools, housing, and family relationships change. Change is pervasive in nearly every aspect of life, except for

[1]*PLA Newsletter*, 10:1 (1971).

the very young and very old. Mobility of individuals, families, and whole population groups, whether voluntary or involuntary, creates impermanence. Automation takes away jobs, and advancement in jobs requires new training and new knowledge and skills. Multiplicity of products creates multiple choices which necessitate difficult decisions. Consumers need detailed, accurate information in order to choose everything—food in the supermarkets, the make, model or color of an automobile, a title in a bookstore or library. Basic survival needs and coping skills require learning skills and learning resources for mere survival in a social system more intricate than ever known before. The complexity of political events creates innumerable questions for which decisions are needed, varying from local town elections to international war and peace efforts.

A concerted effort is needed to assure economic, social, and educational mobility in addressing these complex problems. Resources recorded in various communication media can assist in closing the gap adults face when confronted with multiple choices and decision making. Career choices and continuing education solutions confront more and more adults. Ironically, situations and events may conceal such choices, and solutions seem impossible. The librarian and the resources which the librarian selects for a library collection can assist in meeting this complexity. The benefits and rewards of modern living, as well as the problems and dissatisfactions, must be understood in order to keep from falling behind social and technological changes. Problems and population changes are widespread. They are to be found in rural and suburban areas, where no ethnic groups may be visible, as well as in the inner cities and regional areas, where ethnic groups have concentrated residency.

Although it sometimes appears that libraries never change, or are the last to change, or *cannot* change from a rigid, institutional, establishment role, evidence strongly supports change among public libraries of all types when they are engaged in providing service to adult new readers. Changes *are* occurring in attitudes, policies, and practice.

In the last ten years, librarians' desire to serve segments of the population that were not being served has been highlighted. New studies and research have brought some information that is concrete and helpful for planning. The experience from the 1920s through the 1950s, in library adult education service, Americanization programs, and readers' advisory services, provides a foundation for new outreach services. In the 1960s and 1970s the development of the outreach programs, services to disadvantaged and advantaged, and independent learning programs have been emphasized in both large- and medium-size libraries.

Public library studies, from Berelson to Bundy, consistently show a limited service—limited to middle-class white users. Although the 1953 study on adult education activities in public libraries identified a variety of reading guidance services in group activities, the individual reader's advisory services were discontinued, were fragmented theoretically among all staff members or, regrettably, ignored.[2] Emphasis has focused on reference information and retrieval services. The gradual change is perceptible in library literature and reports of federal funds for outreach programs for disadvantaged. The focus in these programs has been on ethnic groups, ghetto areas, and neglected populations. Reading guidance techniques are being revised, and social responsibilities (stressed by some librarians) have resulted in new policies and social action programs.

Indicative of this changing focus are the many studies and programs that emphasize service to the major ethnic groups. Change has occurred —from the emphasis on homogeneity, which was so evident in the service to the white middle class during the 1950s, to the focus on ethnic and nationality groups during the 1960s and 1970s. Librarianship's regained awareness of groups is similar to that which was stressed in the 1920s. It has modified that awareness so as not to be concerned chiefly with the Americanization process. The 1974 publication, *Library and Information Services for Special Groups*, edited by Joshua Smith and published by Science Associates/International, illustrates this emphasis. Smith defines the special groups as a minority of the population that, for one reason or another, does not share equally in the social, economic, educational, and political opportunities offered by this nation. The collection of papers and bibliographies is concerned with blacks, Mexican Americans, American Indians, the Appalachian poor, and prisoners.

Changes, again, are occurring. Perceptive librarians are sensitive to the entire community and to the changes in society. Long ago they learned to conduct community surveys. The knowledge thereby gained has been used to support the improvement of existing library services. Recently, libraries have taken responsibility for service to adults who are not reached and frequently make up the ethnic segments of the community. Librarians recognize the individuality of each person's interests and differences, as well as common problems and needs. Reading development programs and carefully chosen reading collections, when set in the framework of individual and group guidance, present ideas and information that can have impact and meaning in the lives of men

[2]Helen Lyman Smith, *Adult Education Activities in Public Libraries* (Chicago: American Library Assn., 1954), p. xi–xii, 56–58.

and women. Adults can turn to librarians, as well as to teachers and reading specialists, to help them in becoming mature and independent readers.

During the last decade librarians, library trustees, adult educators, and publishers have become more aware of the problems of functional illiteracy. Librarians recognize the responsibilities which other educational agencies may have for ensuring that adults of all ages have opportunities to realize functional literacy and its consequent rewards and pleasures. Librarians are able, or should be able, to put readers in touch with teachers, reading specialists, adult educators, and others who are engaged in creating meaningful reading situations.

Libraries are providing varied types of extension services and new programs which often are coordinated with services of other community agencies and organizations. Services are taken outside the library to the streets, the correctional institutions, the homes, the apartment complexes, the churches. Libraries reach out to the residents of the urban ghetto, the mountain-hollow family, the isolated farm community, the native tribal reservation, the migrant and the immigrant populations with different languages and cultures. A few programs even reach into suburbia.

Outreach projects, learning and reading centers, store-front and neighborhood libraries, mobile and camper vans, more autonomous branch units, and innovative systems' projects testify to developments and changes. Opportunities for continuing education through staff development programs and library school workshops and institutes are provided for practitioners' learning more about services for adults who hitherto have been unserved. Library science curricula and experimental education programs include courses and field work for the education of librarians in these special areas. Basically, the problem is one of bringing together the adult and the library resources.

How can librarians promote and stimulate the use of reading materials with the information and ideas adults need and want? How can librarians demonstrate the values of reading? How can they identify the content that "means something" in the lives of people? How can all communication media be brought together to serve the interests and needs of the less affluent, less advantaged adults of all ages, and with varying educational backgrounds, who are not served, or only partially served, by the library? And, above all, why are libraries and librarians involved in service to those adults who are most likely to be deprived culturally and economically?

Obviously, answers to all these questions cannot be given here. Some solutions and procedures, however, are proposed for developing library services for adults. That education and accessibility are major correlates in reading and the use of libraries are well-known facts. An equally important consideration, and possibly more decisive factor, is "authentic" relevance. Life skills and daily needs of adults are served through library resources and communication media when, and only when, they have meaning and direct benefit to the adult.

For the purpose of serving adult new readers, emphasis will be on U.S. ethnic groups that are prominently characterized by economic and educational disadvantages. The hypothesis that ethnicity provides a way for reaching new readers can and will be supported. It in no way excludes service to individuals. Rather, it opens up and reasserts the importance of individual attention. Service to ethnic groups implies, in its methods of evaluation and selection of reading materials and in program planning, that individuals can be reached as members of groups. It will be assumed that this generality is true where discussion extends beyond the six separate groups which are differentiated in this discussion.

The general facts (which are presented in chapter 2) concerning these groups provide background information for the special reports (which are discussed in chapters 5 and 6) on each reader group: native peoples, blacks, Appalachian Scotch-Irish, Chicano or Mexican Americans, Puerto Rican Americans, and those for whom English is a second language.

WHOM IS THE BOOK FOR?

Interrelationships among adult new readers, adult reading materials, and library services for the adults are the theme of this book. The evaluation of materials is a central focus. The book is addressed primarily to those persons who, for one reason or another, are involved in service that provides reading materials and guidance for adults who are developing more mature reading habits and skills and are gaining knowledge of the range of ideas and resources to be found in the medium of print. The word *involved* is used advisedly, in the sense that the librarians, library specialists, and others in such service are absorbed and especially committed, emotionally and professionally, in their work with the adult clientele.

Librarian is used in this context as applicable to any staff member who provides library services to adult new readers. The specific or local personnel classifications of course will vary. Services originate in various types of libraries with developmental, educational, and reference functions which require reading collections that are selected with adult new readers in mind. Such libraries include the state library, central units of large public library systems, regional and branch units, small public libraries, mobile units, and academic libraries that serve students in education and library science. Librarians in these libraries serve adults whose literacy and reading needs and interests, as well as reading problems, represent various ages, geographic locations, educational backgrounds, places of origin, life styles, attitudes and values, and life-cycle responsibilities and interests. It is hoped that adult educators, teachers, reading specialists, and editors and publishers also will find the ideas and suggestions useful.

This book is intended to help its users identify and evaluate practical informational materials, works of literature, and writings that portray the experiences of different clientele and ethnic groups. Emphasis is placed on the need to select and interpret reading materials, while keeping in mind the necessity of identifying those authors and contents that are concerned with subjects and values that present facts and portray individuals and various groups in an honest, truthful way. Such literature will portray and represent men and women as human beings who share experiences of common humanity and yet are, in some ways, unique.

The selected materials should provide information that is useful to adults who are learning life skills and coping with daily problems. The ideas and concepts in the library's collection should serve as an intellectual stimulus and contribute to the individual's search for identity. The selection of authors and their writings, which present different life styles and ethnic heritages, can be of as much interest and importance to readers who are outside the cultures as to the members of these groups. Materials should be selected for use by adults who participate in literacy, adult basic education, and reading development programs, as well as self-study.

Library Materials in Service to the Adult New Reader, the result of a study conducted by the author from 1967 through 1974, is the foundation of much of this book.[3] That investigation included a survey of the reading habits and behavior of adult new readers and an analysis of existing materials that were suitable to their interests and needs. Criteria for the evaluation of reading materials for adult new readers—or, for

[3]Helen Huguenor Lyman, *Library Materials in Service to the Adult New Reader* (Chicago: American Library Assn., 1973). The investigation of library materials in service to the adult new reader was conducted over a period of five years, from 1967 to 1972. In a survey of readers, 479 adults in five metropolitan cities answered over sixty questions about their viewing, listening, and reading habits, including a limited number of questions about themselves—their age, education, place of origin, occupation, free-time activities. During the period of the study, reading materials were analyzed. Concurrently, administrators and teachers in adult education and job training programs were asked about the use of noninstructional reading materials in the context of the programs. On the bases of data collected in these studies, criteria for the evaluation of materials were developed.

that matter, for adult readers—were developed and tested as part of the research project. A product of the research, that is included in the published study, is the "MAC Checklist—Materials Analysis Criteria: Standards for Measurement." It provides a guide and procedure for aiding the librarian make a critical, objective analysis of reading materials for the adult. It will be discussed in some detail.

Attitudes, beliefs, and values, as presented in reading material, are decisive elements which influence comprehension, readability, impact, and use. They significantly affect acceptance or rejection of the contents by men and women readers. Because of the importance of this aspect in materials evaluation and library service, six major reader groups in the United States are focused on in some detail. These groups constitute large segments of the population. They are native peoples (American Indians), blacks, Appalachian Scotch-Irish, Chicanos or Mexican Americans, Puerto Rican Americans, and those for whom English is a second language. Whether as individuals or as members of a group, they are learners in search of culturally relevant materials. The genuinely held beliefs, attitudes, and values in the culture of each group to be served should be known and appreciated by librarians. Recognition and understanding of the cultural background and life styles of any reader group make the objective evaluation of such factors in the literature more possible.

WHAT THIS BOOK CONTAINS

Before consideration of the specific reader groups, criteria for the analysis of materials, and the implications for library service, a framework of reference—which may be mutual to the author and the user of this book—is necessary. This framework of reference for the subject, reading and the adult new reader, as set forth in this book, is found in the first four chapters. Chapter 1 relates to reasons for reading services, trends in society, the purpose of this book, and to whom it is addressed. Chapter 2 provides background and points of view on adults and adult reading, what is meant by adult literacy and the adult new reader, and ethnic groups. Chapter 3 looks at communication, literacy, and the mature reader; values and satisfaction in reading; and the meshing of readers' and library's objectives.

Beliefs, attitudes, and values that affect readers are the theme of chapter 4. Heritage, values, and reading interests are discussed in chapter 5 in relation to three reader groups: native peoples or American Indians, blacks, and Appalachian Scotch-Irish. Similarly, the focus in chapter 6 is on the heritage, values, and reading interests of Chicanos or Mexican Americans, Puerto Rican Americans, and those for whom English is a second language. The author incorporates into these two chapters the research reports of six experienced representatives of these groups. Each presents important facts and opinions which have significance for librarians and library service.

Chapter 7 deals with adulthood, adult information needs and reading interests in various areas, and kinds of reading materials which may have appeal for adult readers. The evaluation of reading materials is the subject of chapter 8. Criteria for the analysis of reading materials, for selection in developing library collections and use in reading guidance service and activities, are presented. The criteria developed in the Library Materials Research Project, in an instrument for the measurement of materials, are the central focus of this discussion.

Implications of the facts and principles set forth in the preceding chapters for planning and administering library service to particular reader groups and individual readers are discussed in the last chapter, chapter 9. Effective library service to adult new readers, as in any successful program, requires attention to various aspects: policy and principle, identification of reader groups, staff, material resources, budgeting and procedures, programs and activities, continuing educational opportunities for staff, and evaluation of the service.

The major limitation of this discussion is obvious. The entire emphasis is on the print medium and its corollary reading. In no way, however, should this limitation be thought to exclude other communication media. All mass media and forms of audiovisual materials in the technology of today are vital for communication: the various audio and visual forms, 16mm and super-8mm films, slides, videotapes, phonodiscs and phonotapes, and radio and television.

It is essential that all librarians support media-center concepts and create integrated resource collections. Nevertheless, for purposes of this discussion, no further attention will be given to multimedia resources. It is assumed that literate, up-to-date librarians recognize the values of all media and coordinate such resources as the situation warrants in active, creative service.

Personal and highly individual pleasures and satisfactions relate to psychological and social values of reading. Contact with the minds of others, the significant moment of insight, and flashes of understanding (stimulated by content which flows endlessly through the media of communication) add new dimensions and satisfactions to the life of the individual reader. To strengthen the library's efforts, the librarian will search out the enduring, the brilliant, and much that is less valuable— or that is unorthodox, controversial, and appeals to individuals and parts of the community less frequently served or served not at all. It may be true, as Gertrude Stein said, that being alone with reading is more intense than hearing; it can be more intense than anything.

Maya Angelou, the novelist and poet, found a friend in a small rural community who transmitted the "secret" to her. "I wouldn't miss Mrs. Flowers, for she had given me her secret word which called forth a djinn who was to serve me all my life: books."[4]

Today men and women of all ages can read for amusement, instruction, and, most of all, in order to live.

[4]Maya Angelou, *I Know Why the Caged Bird Sings* (New York: Bantam, 1971), p. 170.

2

Adult Reading: Dynamic or Static?

Who Is Adult?

An adult is one who has arrived at full development, especially in size, strength, or intellectual capacity. An adult is one who has reached maturity. Under civil law, it means a human male after the age of fourteen or a human female after the age of twelve. Under common law, it means a human male or female after a specific age, usually twenty-one or eighteen years. *Youth* has come to mean the stage between childhood and adulthood, and *adult* to mean the stage between youth and old age. In the context of this discussion, *adult* includes persons fourteen years of age and older. *Adulthood* includes all stages of development from youth to the end of life.

An adult, it is said, is one who knows how to love, to play, and to work. When looked at from the point of view of responsibilities and social relationships, a person may be considered adult when he or she assumes such responsibilities and social relations as earning a living, parenthood, serving in the armed services, participating (or not participating) in the aesthetic, intellectual, and political life of the community. Adults today generally have long life, continuing mental and physical health, and continuing lifetime learning and recreational opportunities.

Adult, in itself, implies maturity. The adult man or woman reaches some point of growth and development in life which is considered mature. Every individual arrives at maturity at a different period. The state or quality of full development, defined as maturity or mature, is in a sense a measure. It is difficult to have agreement on *what* constitutes maturity.

Who is mature? When is the adult mature? How do characteristics of maturity relate to library science and librarians who evaluate reading materials for adults? These questions are more than academic. The attitudes and behavior projected between adults are based to a great extent on the concept of what *adult* means. Although a child may be protected, with justifiable reason, the adult is considered to be capable of making decisions and choices. Library resources and reading materials need not be prescribed for the latter, and the adult's demand for relevance in a "live" collection can be depended on in selection.

Since Thorndike's studies nearly fifty years ago, the capabilities of adults have been seen as the foundation for new and continuing education. Libraries have been, and continue to be, an important social agency, contributing to lifetime learning and the pleasures of reading.

Gray and Rogers in 1956, after summarizing various studies, reached some tentative conclusions on the general aspects of maturity. Basically, maturity is seen as a "process rather than a level of achievement or a specific pattern of behavior."[1] Growth and change occur after maturity is attained. General maturity implies a "capacity for self-direction, a keen sense of social responsibility, and capacity to adjust to different groups and times."[2] They concluded that general maturity "is distinguished by an adequate development of each individual's attitudes, understandings, and abilities to enable him to participate fully and creatively in the all-round business of living." The mature person is one

whose contacts with life are constantly becoming broader and richer because his interests and attitudes are such as to encourage their development. . . . Maturity in reading as one aspect of total development is distinguished by the attainment of those interests, attitudes, and skills which enable young people and adults to participate eagerly, independently, and effectively in all the reading activities essential to a full, rich, and productive life.[3]

Several assumptions are made within the context of this book:

It is assumed that, in the satisfaction of interests and needs through reading, a mature reader will continue to grow in capacity to interpret broadly and deeply.

[1]William S. Gray and Bernice Rogers, *Maturity in Reading: Its Nature and Appraisal* (Chicago: Univ. of Chicago Pr., 1956), p. 50.
[2]Ibid., p. 51.
[3]Ibid., p. 55–56.

It is assumed that the progress of the adult new reader from minimal literacy to an increasingly mature use of print is aided by the relevance of materials to the adult's basic motivation, strong interests, value system, life style, and adult roles and tasks.

It is assumed that the continued reading of materials by the adult at any stage of reading literacy serves as a reinforcement in the development of basic reading skills and as a source of general information, enrichment, general understanding, aesthetic pleasure, and immediate goal satisfaction.

It is assumed that the discovery of useful content in reading resources requires that the adult reader and librarian share the selection and evaluation process and determine ways for active use, maximum accessibility, and interpretation of materials to users.

The adult learner has the capacity to continue to learn. Adults have more experience and different kinds of experience to bring to the continuing education process, whether in formal or informal learning situations. During the life cycle, adults are able to develop independence and self-realization where they have adequate information and aids to solving daily problems. Literacy is essential to this process. Communication media of all kinds contribute either positively or negatively to this development.

Understanding of the past and some "knowledge of the future" are as important as information to meet daily needs and interests. Nonspecialists and specialists alike require information and intellectual and aesthetic stimulation. Life styles and values, life-cycle responsibilities and interests merge in today's global village and space age.

Some of the myths about adult learning point librarians in the wrong direction. Adult educators have been aware for a long time that adults can learn effectively. The idea that you can't change human nature or teach an old dog new tricks is no longer held. Neither must learning be only fun or all pain. Adults have had more experience than the young and have learned much through merely living. Adults, though they may have limited vocabularies and reading skills, are neither unintelligent nor lacking in adult life experiences. Teachers who reported in the Library Materials Research Project on adult reading, generated by adult basic education studies, recommended that materials which contain moralizing lessons be replaced by materials which emphasize the worth of the individual and his or her contribution to society. Adults can draw their own moral conclusions. Adults are mature people with mature problems, and should have relevant material at their reading level.

The adults with whom the librarian is concerned must be defined within the immediate local situation. Who are the adults who make up the community? What are their problems? What are the experiences of the adults with whom the librarian works and serves? What reading materials are relevant to their lives? How can the library help adults know the choices they have among the library's resources?

Who Are the Adults?

Adult new readers make use of all communication media. Nearly everyone watches television and listens to radio broadcasts. They read newspapers more than magazines and magazines more than books. Their book reading spans a wide range of subjects; the titles they reported are as numerous as the individuals who reported. At the same time, dominant reading patterns are evident. Most popular are authors and subjects that are related to the adult's cultural background, best sellers of the current publishing scene, and materials for adult basic education classes.

Adult new readers live everywhere, in rural and suburban areas as well as small cities and large metropolises. The specific reader groups include various segments of the population: blacks, whites, Chicanos or Mexican Americans, Puerto Ricans, native Americans, Appalachian people, and recent immigrants from Europe, Central and Latin America, Mexico, and Asia. Several of these groups are emphasized in the discussions in chapters 5 and 6 of this book.

The general population figures indicate the extent and importance of the potential clientele for public libraries. These populations—native Americans, Appalachian Scotch-Irish, blacks, Chicanos, Puerto Ricans, and persons for whom English is a second language—although not always disadvantaged, frequently are "deprived" or at a disadvantage because of a lack of opportunities for quality education and library services and because of handicaps imposed by poor living conditions and inadequate incomes. In general, such groups have a large number of persons who are young, have little schooling and low incomes, and live in metropolitan areas. Although many have rich experiences in their distinctive cultures, they are "alienated" by strange forms of communication and by more dominant cultures that are foreign and antagonistic. The diversity of cultures creates barriers, and ignorance between cultures causes tensions. Although smaller groups are outside the dominant white culture, the values and attitudes, language, experience, and interests of these minority groups are influenced by the dominant culture as well as by the specific culture of each group.

The dominant minority groups are well known. The figures reported at various points in this book are primarily from 1970 and 1973 population reports. Revisions, based on the later, more accurate data, generally show population growth in each group. Differences among various statements result from variations of time and place in data collection.

Literacy and the Adult New Reader

The art of reading is a highly complex act, with various physical, psychological, and cognitive aspects. Adults who develop real reading skills and find both practical use and enjoyment in reading have experienced success with reading materials. They are able to read easily, to understand what is read, and thus to gain practical information and satisfy interests. For the adult who has developed a practical literacy skill or can read critically and independently, a collection of materials of depth and breadth is eminently desirable. For the beginning adult reader, a carefully selected collection of reading materials, within the individual's skills and needs, is essential. The complex demands which are placed upon individuals today require an understanding of literacy skills, their acquisition, and practical application of these skills in innumerable activities and at many levels. The measurement of the skill may be comprehension, a test, performance, achievement, meaningful application, a grade level, or a vague description of a perceived state. Regardless of level, it is evident that complex demands require practical literacy achievement beyond that required at any time or place in the past. Reading is an active process, an act of discovery, in which a person uses eyes, ears, and intelligence, thinks, and imagines.

Specifically, what is meant by literacy? And what is the relationship between literacy and the adult new reader? Over the years, definitions of literacy have varied. The earlier measurement, that a person is literate who is able to read and write at a mere beginning level, gave place to increasingly higher levels, as measured by grade-level attainments. Today it may be shown that twelfth to thirteenth grade proficiency is necessary to function adequately. A recent concept defines functional literacy as the ability to use the skills and knowledge needed for meeting the requirements of adult living. Literacy is measured by the degree of success the adult has in managing day-to-day affairs so that an adult man or woman is reasonably satisfied and finds some reward.

Five stages of literacy or reading levels have been identified in defining reading skills. The first stage, *reading readiness*, prepares the learner for success in reading. It relates to the aspects of physical, intellectual, and personal readiness and spoken-language ability which are desirable or prerequisite to learning to read. One must want to learn to read—that is, have motivation and desire. One must have the physical and mental ability: be able to hear and differentiate sounds in words; have a language base—a spoken language; and be able to give attention to the necessary learning and study. Usually this stage has been defined in relation to early childhood, from birth to six or seven years of age, but it is equally applicable to adult ages.

The second stage of literacy is an *introductory stage* and corresponds to the first grades in school, from one through three. At this level one gains word mastery; learns to recognize words by their shape or forms —that is, to acquire a sight vocabulary, or sight words, and learns the sounds of various letters and letter combinations that are represented in words; and is able to get some meaning from clues in the context. One is able to read simple material, do simple arithmetic, and write and spell at comparable levels. The adult learner may be at different levels in these areas.

The third stage of literacy, sometimes called the *elementary stage*, is comparable to fourth, fifth, and sixth grade school levels. It is a period of vocabulary building and increasing skill in the use of reading. In arithmetic, skill is attained in multiplication. One is able to spell, write, see purpose in reading, and use these skills to read and interpret essential information for daily life and work at beginning levels. Besides vocabulary growth, teachers define this stage of literacy to mean ability to read traffic signs, street names, deal with prices, and fill out simple forms. It can also mean the acquiring of "survival" literacy skills, such as ability to read somewhat critically and compute arithmetic problems needed in jobs.

The fourth stage is seen as *partial literacy* or an *intermediate stage*. It is comparable to eighth, ninth, or tenth grade school levels. One is able to read alone and improve the skills that were gained at the elementary stages. Understanding what is read is extended. It is at this period that many persons leave school and literacy programs.

The fifth stage of literacy is a *developmental* stage. It corresponds to levels of adult high school study, independent educational programs at high school and junior high school, or the first years of college. It is often neglected or missed. Instead of development, nonuse, concentration on other communication media, and disregard and disinterest are common.

Because the stages of learning are correlated with the school-grade system, each stage may be defined within the framework of grades. Although the chronological age of the adult differs from that of the child, these stages have been defined in the same terms as a child's progression in school.

Rather than try to correlate reading abilities with grade levels that are, at best, arbitrarily decided, some reading specialists have formulated other definitions. Kohl offers four stages that are useful: beginning, not bad, with ease, and complex. He defines each level and the corresponding skills:

1. Beginning—knowing print, known words, words that connect and words that place, alphabet, sounds and combinations of sounds, simple sentences;
2. Not bad—combination of sounds, complicated words, complex sentences, everyday reading, paragraphs and stories;
3. With ease—unfamiliar words, different forms of writing, voice, test taking;
4. Complex—knowing about language, special uses of words, special languages, critical analysis.[4]

Recent research suggests changes in the old practice. It has become quite evident that reading is not synonymous with years of schooling and education. According to the Adult Performance Level (APL) concept, functional literacy or competency is more complex than correlation with the ability to read or write at some arbitrarily chosen low-grade level.

Functional literacy, then, is defined as the ability of an adult to apply skills in several major knowledge areas which are important to success in adult life. These skills are classified, variously, as coping, survival, performance, and functional competencies. The important skills for the adult are communication (reading, writing, speaking, listening); computation; problem solving; and interpersonal relations. These skills are to be applied in general knowledge areas that are necessary to living, including occupational knowledge, consumer economics, government and law, health, and community resources. It is in these areas that library resources are so important.

Librarians, in order to serve the educational system—in this instance formal and informal literacy and continuing education for adults, either directly to the adult or indirectly through the educational program—must keep abreast of changes in literacy concepts, objectives, measurements, and teacher training. Libraries will need to find ways to respond to the demands and interests of adults and adult educators as the educa-

---

[4]Herbert Kohl, *Reading, How To* (New York: Bantam, 1973), p. 124.

tional system responds to the problems of millions of adults who strive to achieve functional competency or literacy in terms of this broadened concept. A high level of literacy competency is reached only if the adult gains the ability to understand, comprehend, analyze, and make comparisons of what is read. The skilled reader is able to evaluate and use what is gained, either at certain adult performance levels or in a mature interest which adds to life.

Adult new readers make up a large segment of those who are engaged in learning at each stage of literacy. They may be completely illiterate, beginning readers, college students, or mature adult learners. They are part of every library community.

Perhaps more important than any of the statistics on literacy or illiteracy, however optimistic or depressing they may be, is the fact that the United States has the highest level of educational attainment in the world; 86 percent of the population have had high school or some college-level education. At the same time, 54 percent are unable, or only marginally able, to cope with basic reading tasks, regardless of formal education. What is even more important is that 20 percent of Americans cannot understand what they can read.

Freire states:

Insofar as language is impossible without thought, and language and thought are impossible without the world to which they refer, the human word is more than mere vocabulary—it is word-and-action. . . . If learning to read and write is to constitute an act of knowing, the learners must assume from the beginning the role of creative subjects. It is not a matter of memorizing and repeating given syllables, words, and phrases, but rather of reflecting critically on the process of reading and writing itself, and on the profound significance of language.[5]

Adult new reader was defined originally in the context of the Library Materials Research Project study. In general, the adult new reader is progressing from beginning literacy to an increasingly mature use of print. Such development may be through formal or informal adult education and library programs, and consciously or unconsciously through self-education and reading activities. At the very minimum, functional literacy today requires reading competency comparable to an eighth grade reading-achievement level, or, measured in other terms, eleven grade-years of schooling. The adult new readers whose characteristics, reading behaviors, and interests are reported in the Library Materials Research Project were within the adult ages, from sixteen years to sixty-five years

---

[5]Paulo Freire, *Cultural Action for Freedom*, Monograph Series no. 1 (Cambridge, Mass.: Harvard Educational Review and Center for the Study of Development and Social Change, 1970), p. 12.

and over. They resided primarily in the inner city of five metropolitan areas.

The adult reader attains complete literacy when he or she is able to read critically, evaluate what is read, integrate facts and ideas, and use the concepts thus gained to help understand further reading. An adult who is functionally literate must be able to function in everyday situations that are dependent on reading and on interpreting into action the meaning of words. Many adults lapse into functional illiteracy because they failed to learn in school, are school dropouts or pushouts, had poor or very limited schooling, failed to find pleasure or satisfaction in reading, and because they have no reading materials suited to their needs and interests and no knowledge of or access to resources that constitute a rich and relevant reading collection.

Most adults have the intelligence and capacity to become mature readers. Many are nonliterate rather than illiterate. They are not "new" readers in the sense of "for the first time" or in developing reading skill from a point of complete illiteracy. They are "new" in the sense that they are beginning to resume or regenerate their previous acts of reading. They have come to a new recognition of reading as indispensable to their life. Having come only recently to this awareness, to constant use, and to increasing comprehension and competency in the medium of print, the adult new reader may be at any stage of literacy. Librarians are in a particularly advantageous position to recognize such change and development when they are in close contact and serve as advisers to such adults. The reading experience of the adult new reader is different from anything experienced before because it is more novel.

Adults who have achieved partial literacy with five to six years' schooling are able to read and to use information essential to daily living and work. At this time the right material and guidance by the librarian and teacher are crucial to their continuing improvement. It is at this point that readers who have achieved partial literacy may become active readers. Such readers are not only capable of making use of reading materials, but *do make use of them.*

At the stage of variable literacy, adults with between seven and nine years of schooling are more likely to become active readers. At this stage, guidance and access to effective materials that meet individual interests and needs, as well as develop further reading skill, have particular significance. At this point the quantity and wide range of reading resources can be most useful to the adult new reader.

The nature of disadvantaged adults, who make up the 57 million or more adults in the United States with less than a high school education,

has been identified in four major groups by the Appalachian Adult Education Center (AAEC) at Morehead State University (Kentucky).[6] In general, a relationship, it seems, exists between economic security and literacy level, and these two factors in turn influence attitudes toward learning.

Adults in groups 1 and 2 are partially secure economically and personally and believe in social and educational services. They are easier to reach, to teach, and to serve. They can profit from informal educational opportunities. They can be recruited through mass media. They have relatively high skill levels in reading and learning. They can use formal and informal services.

Adults in group 2 have less schooling than adults in group 1. Although they are part of the 37 percent in the 1970 census of the employed population who have less than a high school diploma, and account for 66 percent of those with an annual income of less than $3,000, they are more secure than persons who are unemployed. They learn quickly. They are "star performers"—showing large, quick achievement gains in economic levels and life styles. They have large families, do seasonal work, and work on shifts.

Adults in group 3 have had little employment, in "low-paying, dead-end, and short-term jobs." They have limited literacy skills but see advantages to public services. They can be reached only through direct and personal recruitment methods. They require carefully structured formal programs, and professionals and paraprofessionals trained in the instruction of learners with certain characteristics. The AAEC is convinced that adults in this group can be reached only through one-to-one recruitment and services. They tend to relate to human beings and to clearly articulated subgoals toward which they can work.

Adults in group 4 are caught in poverty and perpetuate the poverty cycle. They are unemployed and unemployable. They are fatalistic and without self-direction. They can be served only in their homes. They cannot profit from informal education in a group. Although they are the hardest to reach, they are the smallest group, which should be of some advantage to educational agencies. Intense and concentrated efforts are necessary. They seldom interpret their problems as information needs. They seldom seek answers or use mass media. They strive only to sur-

[6]Ann Hayes Drennan, "The Nature of Disadvantaged Adults and What Those Characteristics Imply about Service Needs" (paper delivered at Florida State Library Conference on Adult Basic Education and Public Library Service, 1974), p. 1–5. Mimeographed by Appalachian Adult Education Center. The quotations in this section are from Drennan's paper.

vive. Yet the AAEC studies show that this group can go from nonreaders through high school completion in four years when approached through the appropriate delivery system—home instruction.

The problem in providing library service to adults who make up these four groups is most acute and critical when it comes to the adult new reader. The librarian's understanding is a decisive factor. To a large extent, the characteristics of these four groups are found among the adult new readers in the Lyman study. A majority of the respondents who were interviewed in the Library Materials Research Project reader survey would be among adults in AAEC groups 1 and 2. Three-fourths of the adult new readers were from the black population of the inner-city ghettos, and two-thirds were women. All were developing literacy skills in adult basic education and job training and library reading development programs. They were sixteen years of age and over.

In terms of formal education (the last year completed in school), adult new readers had attended an average of 10.2 years. The majority, 62 percent, had completed between 7 and 11 years of school. Nearly 20 percent had less than sixth grade schooling, but an equal number had completed high school. For the majority, the native language was English; about one-fourth were learning English as a second language. The annual family income averaged $5,000, and individual income averaged $3,000. The range of income was from zero to over $10,000. The majority had the low income and limited schooling which are common to the more disadvantaged members of society. Occupations were divided fairly evenly among white-collar, blue-collar, clerical, and service jobs. Keeping house and going to school were also significant occupations. Many of these adults aspired to positions in professional and technical work. They wished to advance in their present work or enter new fields. Leisure-time interests, which many engaged in at relatively little or no cost, included visiting friends and relatives, going to church and movies, reading a book or magazine, walking or driving around town, watching sports, going to dances and taverns, and listening to records. The adults with the least schooling participated in adult basic education programs and those with more schooling in employment and high school equivalency programs.

The various communication media were used by many. Everyone watched television, particularly news, weather, adventure programs, and movies. Nearly everyone—95 percent—listened to the radio for news and various music programs. About 93 percent read newspapers, with half of these persons reading them daily. A lesser number, 88 percent, read magazines and 69 percent read books.

A reading activity index provided a measure of the adults' reading activity by their use of print materials. Each respondent was assigned a score between 0 and 10, based on the frequency of newspapers read, use and type of magazines, reading or not reading comic books, and the number of books read within the six months previous to the interview. The adult new reader with a score of zero was classified in the *least active* group, readers with a score from 1 to 4 in the *somewhat active* group, those with a score from 5 to 7 in the *active* reader group, and those with a score of 8 to 10 in the *very active* group. A majority of respondents was among the *active* reader group, a third was rated as *somewhat active*, and over 10 percent as *very active*.

Education is a correlate to reading activity. Most reading studies confirm the conclusion of a close relationship between the amount of reading done in a community and its educational status, the accessibility of libraries and reading materials, the extent of literacy, the ability of adults to read easily, and productivity of the citizens. It may well be that this conclusion is distorted by the "circular" nature of the dependent relationship between the current educational system and reading. The idea that learning and reading begin at infancy and conclude at adulthood is held no longer. The cycle can be broken at any stage, and it can be entered at any stage.

The direct relationship between the stages of literacy and the accessibility of relevant reading materials has definite implications for library service. Lyman concluded that the reading activity of adult new readers in the Library Materials Research Project investigation showed a similar relationship between the use of print materials and education. Adults with less than five years of schooling are at low level of literacy at the point when continuing use of the newly acquired skill is essential to prevent loss of literacy. Adults who had five to six years of schooling were at a stage of partial literacy. In comparison to adults of minimal literacy, who were the least active readers, many of those with partial literacy were active readers. They were not only capable of making use of print materials, but *did* make use of them.

Adults who achieved the next stage of variable literacy had between seven and nine years of schooling. They were close to functional literacy. They were active and very active readers, as were those with ten and eleven years of schooling. At these stages, guidance and access to effective materials that meet individual interests and needs, as well as develop further reading skills, have particular significance.

Adults who had completed twelve and thirteen years of schooling were mainly very active readers. It is at this stage that the adult reads with ease and critical understanding. An autonomy is achieved which permits the independent use of reading materials. As a mature reader, one can make productive use of a wide range and variety of materials.

Native Peoples

Today the estimated 800,000 or more "native peoples"—original Americans, American Indians, native Americans—live on reservations and in metropolitan areas of the United States. Census figures vary, and Indian sources challenge the U.S. Bureau of the Census figures as underestimations. The census of 1970 identified 340,367 persons as urban residents, 357,822 as rural nonfarm residents, and 47,405 as rural farm residents.[7] The Census Bureau reported 213,770 Indians on 115 reservations, and 549,824 not on reservations. One source claims that "long considered the 'Vanishing American,' the First Americans are now the fastest growing minority."[8]

The Bureau of Indian Affairs lists 482 official Indian tribes, bands, villages, pueblos, communities, and groups as eligible for its aid (216 of these in Alaska). They range from tiny settlements, scattered around the country, to eleven reservations that contain over a million acres apiece. One might contrast the Golden Hill Reservation in Connecticut, consisting of two persons on two-tenths of an acre, with the Navajo Reservation of 13,989,222 acres and a population of 131,379.

The ten states with the largest Indian populations in 1970 were:

Oklahoma	96,803	Washington	30,824
Arizona	94,310	South Dakota	31,043
California	88,263	New York	25,560
New Mexico	71,582	Montana	26,385
North Carolina	44,195	Minnesota	22,322

Standard metropolitan areas with an American Indian population of 5,000 or more identified in the 1970 census were:

Albuquerque	5,822	Phoenix	10,127
Buffalo	5,606	San Bernardino–	
Chicago	8,203	Riverside–	
Dallas	5,500	Ontario	5,941

[7]U.S. Census Bureau, *Final Report: American Indians*, Subject Reports, Pc2-1F (Washington, D.C.: Govt. Printing Office, 1973).

[8]*The First Americans* (San Jose, Calif.: Gousha Publs., 1973).

Detroit	5,203	San Diego	6,007
Los Angeles–		San Francisco–	
Long Beach	23,908	Oakland	12,041
Minneapolis–		Seattle-Everett	8,814
St. Paul	9,911	Tucson	8,704
New York	9,984	Tulsa	15,183
Oklahoma City	12,951		

Although many American Indians have moved to urban areas, only seven big cities, with populations over 50,000, have more than 5,000 Indians, according to the 1970 census. They are:

New York	9,930	Chicago	6,575
Los Angeles	9,172	Phoenix	5,893
Tulsa	8,510	Minneapolis	5,829
Oklahoma City	7,361		

Fifty-three percent of the native peoples are estimated to live in five states: California, Oklahoma, Arizona, New Mexico, and North Carolina. (The Navajo, Hopi, Papago, and several other tribes own 26 percent of Arizona's total land area.) Settlements of nonurban native Americans represent all sizes, terrains, climates, legal arrangements, populations, and histories. They span the full spectrum of prosperity, although it is so heavily weighted at the poor end that even the middle range is pointed to as evidence of extraordinary successes. Some reservations have natural resources, but because reservation lands on the whole are located in some of the poorest geographic and climatic areas of the United States, much of the land is relatively unproductive and sustains a low standard of living.

Native peoples in rural areas are the most disadvantaged of disadvantaged groups in the United States. New enterprises, however, are helping to change this low social and economic standard. Small tribal and private industries, arts and crafts products, lumbering, and tourism are being developed. Benefits go to the entire tribe. Gradually improved educational policies and practices are creating better schools, opportunities, and staffs.

Approximately 142 major tribes are listed according to self-identification in 1970 census records. Although they are distinct communities, they have cultural similarities and names that are familiar to many Americans. They frequently are considered part of the United States or as dependent (rather than independent) nations. The naming of only the major tribes indicates the variety of tribal groups.

They include Achomawi, Atsugewi, Chimariko, Pit River, and Shasta; Alaskan, Athapaskans; Apache; Arapaho; Arikara; Assiniboin; Blackfeet; Caddo; Cahuilla, Luiseno, Gabrielino, and Serrano; Canadian and Latin American; Catawba, Oto, Missouri, and Iowa; Chehalis; Cherokee; Cheyenne; Chickasaw; Chinook; Chippewa; Choctaw and Houma; Coeur d'Alene; Columbia-Wenatchee; Colville and Lakes; Comanche; Costanoan, Washo, Yana, and Yuki; Cree; Creek, Alabama, and Coushatta; Crow;

Delaware and Stockbridge; Flathead; Gros Ventre (Atsina); Hidatsa and Mandan; Hupa; Iroquois-Mohawk, Oneida, Seneca, Onondaga, Tuscarora, Cayuga, and Wyandotte; Kalapuya; Karok; Kato; Mattole, Tolowa, and Wailaki; Kaw, Omaha, Osage, Ponca, and Quapaw; Kickapoo; Kiowa; Klamath, Modoc, Cayuse, and Molala; Klikitat; Kootenay; Lumbee;

Maidu and Miwok; Makah; Menominee; Miami, Piankashaw, and Wea; Navajo; Nespelim, Okanagan, Sanpoil, and Spokane; New England and Long Island Algonquians; Nez Perce; Nooksak; Ottawa; Palouse and Topenish; Papago and Pima; Pawnee; Pomo; Potawatomi, Powhatan; Pueblo-Hopi, Keresan, Tanoan, and Zuni; Puget Sound Salish; Quileute and Chimakum; Sac and Fox, and Mesquakie; Salinan and Chumash; Seminole; Shawnee; Shoshone, Northern and Southern Paiute, and Chemehuevi; Sioux (Dakota); Southwest Oregon Penutians and Athapaskans; Straits Salish;

Tillamook; Tlingit and Haida; Twana; Umatilla; Ute; Walla Walla; Wappo and Yurok; Warm Springs; Wichita; Winnebago; Wintun; Wiyot; Yakima; Yokuts; Yuman; and many others.

The culture of these tribes

has contributed valuable elements to the dominant culture and could make an even greater contribution if the dominant culture were wise enough to adopt more from the Indian culture. Among these admirable traits is the extended family: the survival of the individual was possible because within the clan, food, clothing and material possessions were shared, and working together, sharing and cooperation were emphasized. Another is that religion was part of every aspect of Indian life. Indians believed in living in harmony with nature and that the earth was to be shared by all and owned by none. Another is the extension of generosity to strangers; still another is that there is a limit to the effectiveness of criminal punishment as a solution to law and order problems and that it is better to rely on group pressure and disapproval.[9]

Vine Deloria, Jr., who is a Standing Rock Sioux and an independent spokesman, says:

[9]June Smeck Smith, "Library Service to American Indians," *Library Trends*, 20, no. 2:224 (Oct. 1971).

It is difficult for most Americans to comprehend that there still exists a living community of nearly one million Indians in this country. For many people, Indians have become a species of movie actor periodically dispatched to the Happy Hunting Grounds by John Wayne on the "Late, Late Show." Yet there are some 315 tribal groups in 26 states still functioning as quasi-sovereign nations under treaty status; they range from the mammoth Navajo tribe of some 132,000 with 16 million acres of land to tiny Mission Creek of California with 15 people and a tiny parcel of property. There are over half a million Indians in the cities alone, with the largest concentrations in San Francisco, Los Angeles, Minneapolis, and Chicago.[10]

No description can be given of a typical native American today. The majority live on reservations which are controlled by the Bureau of Indian Affairs (BIA). Recently many young Indians have left the reservations to seek employment and a better life in metropolitan areas. Few find steady employment; and many of those who leave the reservations return broken and discouraged.

On the reservations, more than half of the employable Indians are unemployed. Today it is impossible for the Indian male to exercise his traditional role as hunter and warrior. He is forced to remain idle on the reservation or leave for the city to find employment. In this situation, the Indian woman has become the provider and key family figure.[11]

The United States' official Indian policy can be described as forced assimilation. (A futile attempt to make the Indian into a white man has been going on for over a century and a half.) Official Indian policy has gone through four major stages.

In the first stage, vast Indian lands were given to the United States government through treaties. These treaties were signed in good faith by the Indians in return for fishing rights and economic assistance. Reservations were set up and controlled by white BIA officials. Indian children were taken from their parents and sent to BIA boarding schools, where Indians were supposed to be taught the ways and values of the white man.

The second stage of Indian policy went into effect with the passage of the Allotment Act in 1887. Under this law, many Indian groups were forced to surrender their large reservations to white land speculators. In return the Indians received small family-size farms, consisting of 10 to 640 acres. (The politicians who passed this law justified their action on the rationale that the Allotment Act would break up the tribes and

[10]Vine Deloria, Jr., "This Country Was a Lot Better Off When the Indians Were Running It," in Alvin M. Josephy, Jr., ed., *Red Power* (New York: American Heritage Pr., 1971), p. 248.

[11]Edgar S. Cahn, *Our Brother's Keeper: The Indian in White America* (New York: World, 1969), p. 1–25.

instantly change all Indians into God-fearing and industrious small farmers, indistinguishable from anybody else.) Land-speculation interests were the greatest supporters of this bill. Through the Allotment Act the American Indian lost 90 million acres.

In 1934 the third phase of Indian policy was initiated with the passage of the Indian Reorganization Act. This act ended allotments. An attempt was made by the government to regain some of the lost Indian lands. Native religion, art, and traditions were encouraged.[12]

This policy was short lived. It came to an abrupt end in 1950 with the fourth stage: establishment of the policy of termination. The purpose of termination was to remove all federal obligations vis-à-vis the Indian. Only a few tribes have been terminated by specific acts of Congress (one such tribe is the Menominee of Wisconsin). When a tribe is terminated it falls under state jurisdiction. Many benefits, such as special hunting and fishing rights, health care, and federal support for education, are lost with termination.[13] The policy of termination was not changed until 1974.

On the whole, the official policy of Americanization has been a dismal failure. Assimilation has failed because Indian values are in direct opposition to white middle-class values. Most Indians cling to their traditional values because they believe their values are more humanistic and democratic than those of white society.[14]

Indian society is not oriented to the future, whereas the dominant society is very much oriented to the future. Indian society is based on consumption. However, only what is needed for survival is taken from the environment. Dominant society, on the other hand, is based on production economics and the profit motive. Everything the environment has to give is taken. The profit motive does not exist in Indian society.[15]

A tremendous amount of literature has been written about the American Indian, but much of it paints a very erroneous picture of Indian culture. Countless books have been written about blood-thirsty, savage Indians scalping pioneers and molesting children. Very little has been written about the severe treatment all Indians suffered at the command of the United States government.

Fortunately, a small body of literature is unbiased and presents an honest picture of Indian life, past and present. There are excellent col-

[12]William Brandon, *The American Heritage Book of Indians* (New York: American Heritage Pub. Co., 1961), p. 360–75.

[13]Joyce M. Erdman, *Handbook on Wisconsin Indians* (Madison: Univ. of Wisconsin Extension, 1966), p. 43–49.

[14]Robert L. Bennett, "American Indians," in *Differences That Make the Difference*, Roma K. McNickle, ed. (Washington, D. C.: Joint Commission on Correctional Manpower and Training, 1967), p. 28–29.

[15]Ibid., p. 29.

lections of folklore representing almost all U.S. Indian groups. Like any other group of people, Indians are interested in all types of literature and printed information. They have a special interest in their cultural heritage. A great need exists for thoughtful, carefully researched writing about the Indian. There is a need for Indians to write about themselves and their people.

The young adult Indian is an important part of this population whom librarians and publishers must try to reach. Fifty percent of the native-peoples population are seventeen years of age or less. (A significant percentage leave school, and reject white values, and yet do not completely accept traditional native-people values.) Native peoples are proud of their cultural heritage and do not want to lose it. This heritage has been maintained for centuries through an oral tradition.[16]

The approximately 315 distinct tribal groups in existence today (speaking 150 tribal languages) demand rights and recognition. In the Hirschfelder bibliography, *American Indian Authors*, more than 106 tribes are identified in the many authors who have contributed to the history and literature of their people: Abenaki, Acoma Pueblo, Apache, Arapaho, Assiniboin, Athapaskan, Bella Bella, Blackfeet, Cahuilla, Carrier, Catawba, Cherokee, Cheyenne, Chinook, Chippewa, Choctaw, Clackamas Chinook, Colville, Coos, Cree, Creek, Croatan, Crow, Delaware, Flathead, Fox, Gros Ventre, Haida, Hidatsa, Hopi, Isleta Pueblo, Jemez Pueblo,

Kalapuya, Kashaya, Kiowa, Kiowa-Apache, Klallam, Klikitat, Kwakiutl, Loucheaux, Luiseno, Maidu, Menominee, Micmac, Minsi, Modoc, Mohawk, Mohawk-Delaware, Mohegan, Narragansett-Wampanoag, Natchez, Navajo, Nevada, Nez Perce, Nootka, Odawa, Okanogan, Omaha, Oneida, Osage, Otomi, Ottawa,

Paiute, Papago, Passamaquoddy, Pawnee, Penobscot, Pequot, Picuris Pueblo, Pima, Pomo, Ponca, Potawatomi, Powhatan, San Juan Pueblo, Santa Clara Pueblo, Sauk, Sac and Fox, Seneca, Seneca-Cayuga, Shawnee, Shinnecock, Shoshone, Shuswap, Sioux, Slavey, Southern Diegueno, Spokane, Takelma, Taos Pueblo, Tewa, Tlingit, Tsimshian, Tuscarora, Ute, Wailaki, Walapai, Wawenook, Winnebago, Wintun, Wishram, Wyandotte, Yana, Yaqui, Zuni Pueblo (plus many anonymous authors).[17]

The authors from these tribes present an impressive literature about historical and contemporary Indian life and thought. The 1970 bibliog-

[16]I am indebted to Roye Werner and Mary Hickey Teloh for assistance on compilation of data for this discussion.

[17]Arlene B. Hirschfelder, comp., *American Indian Authors: A Representative Bibliography* (New York: Assn. on American Indian Affairs, 1970), and *American Indian and Eskimo Authors: A Comprehensive Bibliography* (New York: Assn. on Indian Affairs, 1973).

raphy also includes a selection of anthologies of American Indian oral and written literature and twenty-one periodicals published by American Indian tribes and organizations.

The oral tradition of native Americans can be transmitted and preserved through audiovisual media. Recent programs are developing new library programs with native Americans in charge. In various ways, native peoples are taking their affairs into their own hands. In spite of dissensions between traditionalists and modernists, native Americans are making decisions and directing their own lives.

Deloria has stated:

> The message of the traditionalists is simple. They demand a return to basic Indian philosophy, establishment of ancient methods of government by open council instead of elected officials, a revival of Indian religions and replacement of white laws with Indian customs; in short, a complete return to the ways of the old people.[18]

He feels that the modernist upholds an opposing view, as demonstrated by the National Congress of American Indians, which represents officially elected tribal governments that are organized under the Indian Reorganization Act as federal corporations. He defines a tribe as "a modern corporate structure attempting to compromise at least in part with modern white culture."[19]

No library should neglect resources about and for the native peoples of this country. No librarian should be ignorant of the culture, traditions, and needs and problems of the tribes in the local community, the region, the state, and the nation as a whole. Local and national decisions are being made which require an informed population, outside as well as within individual tribes. Direct service must be defined on the bases of facts about each area, each tribe, each community, and the residents' views and opinions regarding their information and literary needs.

Blacks

The population of blacks was approximately 24 million in 1974. They constitute over 11 percent of the total population of over 213 million. The majority of blacks are metropolitan central-city dwellers; slightly more than half (52 percent) live in the South, about 40 percent in the North, and 10 percent in the West. Six out of ten blacks live in the central cities of the major metropolitan areas, where three-fourths

[18]Deloria, "This Country Was a Lot Better Off . . . ," p. 256.
[19]Ibid.

of all black families live. Blacks make up more than half the population in four large cities: Washington, D.C., Newark, Gary (Ind.), and Atlanta.

Between 1965 and 1970 about a quarter of a million blacks moved from the South to central cities in the North and West, of whom about half were from the nonmetropolitan areas of the South. The majority of black persons who moved to the South between 1960 and 1970 were returning to their region of birth.[20] This trend of reverse migration appears to continue.

During the 1960s blacks made substantial gains in income, employment, education, housing, and health. In recent years progress has continued in education. But in 1973 blacks still remained behind whites in most social and economic areas, although some families were able to increase their income, particularly where both husband and wife were earners.

About one-third or one-fourth of the black population are estimated to have the incomes and status of the middle-class population. (In attempting to define the middle-class status of blacks, one may "only succeed in showing that when defined it is not the same definition which applies to middle-class white.")[21] They are successful in professional and technical positions as doctors, lawyers, engineers, teachers, writers, entertainers. They are employed as managers, officials, and officers in industry, business, universities, and the military.[22] The rising educational attainment of young black men and women is evidenced by larger numbers of high school and college graduates.[23] Notable gains have also been made in the number of blacks elected to public office.

However encouraging these facts are, the discouraging fact remains that one-third of the black population are on the lower edges of the middle class and one-third are in the poverty group. Many are without work, or hold unskilled or semiskilled jobs, or are on welfare. (Educational attainment, however, continues to rise.) It may continue to be true that black Americans on all levels are confined by overt and subtle prejudice. A considerable segment has inadequate educational, economic, and other types of opportunities. Although the black "revolu-

---

[20]U.S. Bureau of the Census, "The Social and Economic Status of the Black Population in the United States, 1973," *Current Population Reports*, Series P-23, no. 48 (Washington, D.C.: Govt. Printing Office, 1974).

[21]*Ebony*, special issue, "The Black Middle Class," 28, no. 10 (Aug. 1973).

[22]"America's Rising Black Middle Class," *Time*, June 17, 1974.

[23]U.S. Bureau of the Census, "Social and Economic Status of the Black Population."

tion" of the 1960s achieved greater equality, the challenge to make sure sure that results follow has implications for libraries.

Jordan states that "three centuries of injustice have brought about deep-seated structural distortions in the life of the Black American. . . . Library service of a relevant nature may be one means of setting these distortions straight and assisting in untangling the social pathology."[24]

Blacks in America, whether in the central-city black ghetto or rural communities, desperately need the learning skills, professional knowledge, and various kinds of social and cultural experience that come from higher education. They need skilled teachers, lawyers, businessmen, public officials, and scientists, who emerge from the community and are prepared to link their knowledge with action.[25]

This insight is urged upon librarians by Josey, who envisions the place the library can take in reaching disadvantaged students with action-oriented programs. He states: "The academic library can provide disadvantaged students with many new kinds of learning experiences by providing high quality staff, a wide range of resources and facilities, and meaningful programs that will involve students in the critical analysis of the social values and interactions that underlie the foundations of education."[26]

One of the most important changes in education and library development has been the black studies movement. Although the movement can be traced back several centuries, most black studies programs have developed since the late 1960s. They have spread throughout the educational system. Jessie Carney Smith, in her detailed review of the development, stresses that a natural relationship exists between black studies and libraries: "In a sense, they created each other, and their natural dependency upon each other for survival is obvious."[27] It is equally obvious that libraries of all types must continue to meet the needs of black studies and a clientele of all ages. Libraries have an essential role at every level of education. "Their interdependencies are immeasurable, while the contributions that each has made toward the development of the other are unparalleled elsewhere."[28]

[24]Casper Leroy Jordan, "Library Service to Black Americans," *Library Trends*, 20, no. 2:275 (Oct. 1971).

[25]E. J. Josey, "The Role of the Academic Library in Serving the Disadvantaged Student," *Library Trends*, 20, no. 2:432–44 (Oct. 1971).

[26]Ibid., p. 443.

[27]Jessie Carney Smith, "Librarianship and Black Studies . . . a Natural Relationship," in Joshua I. Smith, ed., *Library and Information Services for Special Groups* (New York: Science Associates/International, 1974), p. 233.

[28]Ibid., p. 219.

Appalachian Scotch-Irish

Appalachia encompasses 397 counties in thirteen states—Alabama, Georgia, Kentucky, Maryland, Mississippi, New York, North Carolina, Ohio, Pennsylvania, South Carolina, Tennessee, Virginia, and West Virginia. In the 1970 census, out of a population of 76,069,000 who lived in the "Appalachian" states, 18,212,913 lived in the Appalachian region. At that time the per capita personal income in the Appalachian region was $3,199, while the per capita income for the non-Appalachian portion of these states was $4,025, and for the entire United States, $3,920.

Not all Appalachians are white, nor are all Appalachian migrants whites, but the overwhelming majority are. They have had a profound effect on the history, language, and culture of the region. They are an important part of the population that constitutes three-fourths of the poor-white Americans.

Because the thirteen states in the Appalachian region are not homogeneous, the Appalachian Regional Commission (ARC) in 1975 reclassified the area, according to distinctive differences and needs, into new subregions. Three subregions—Northern Appalachia, Central Appalachia, and Southern Appalachia, along with the Highlands area—were identified as having distinctive income, population, and employment characteristics and distinctive development needs.

Northern Appalachia is composed of the Appalachian portions of New York, Pennsylvania, Ohio, Maryland, and all but nine southern counties of West Virginia, which are in Central Appalachia. The Northern Appalachia subregion is the most populous and most urbanized—54 percent in 1970—and the largest geographically, with 42.9 percent of the region's land area. It has two distinct divisions—the valley and ridge section, with steep slopes and cliffs, valleys, and streams, and the Appalachian Plateau, which runs adjacent to (and west of) the valley and ridge section. The plateau section extends the length of the subregion and runs across the subregion in New York.

The population is primarily urban. Programs in vocational and technical education to upgrade labor resources have been initiated. The area is extensively modernizing an old and outmoded industrial-base economy in order to respond to a growing, diversified economy. The area is much in need of public services to support a better quality of life.

Central Appalachia extends diagonally across almost the entire width of the middle portion of the Appalachian region and includes all of Appalachian Kentucky, the northwestern counties of Appalachian Tennessee, seven counties in the southwestern tip of Virginia, and the nine southern counties of West Virginia. The smallest of the three subregions, its population in 1970 was 1,744,712, or 9.6 percent of the region's population. Population density is relatively low: fifty-five persons per square mile. The entire area is predominantly rural, with 71 percent of the population living in rural counties (in contrast to a national average of only 12 percent). The nonrural population lives in small towns. No city of more than 100,000 population is in this subregion.

The heart of Central Appalachia, which consists of most of Kentucky and the southern counties of West Virginia, is the mountainous or hilly Cumberland Plateau. It lies entirely on the western slope of the mountain core and thus does not adjoin the populous lowlands of the Atlantic Coast and the Piedmont. It is rich in coal and forests. Residents live in densely settled pockets along river valleys and up mountain hollows. The area has many socioeconomic deficiencies, but emphasis is being placed on community development.

Southern Appalachia is an elongated subregion, extending from the Highlands of Virginia to the Mississippi coastal plains. It includes the Appalachian portions of Alabama, Georgia, Mississippi, North Carolina, South Carolina, the eastern counties of Appalachian Tennessee, and fourteen counties in southwestern Virginia. In 1970 Southern Appalachia, with 40.7 percent of the region's land area, accounted for 37 percent of the regional population. The outstanding characteristic of this subregion is rapid population growth. The 1970 per capita income was $3,019.

Southern Appalachia has changed from an agrarian-based economy to a new, modern industrial economy, with problems of urban growth. Many disparities exist between rural areas and urban growth centers. Health, education, and community development are major topics of concern (see table 1).

The Highlands constitute a fourth subregion. It is an overlay area, made up of high topography, that is, 1,000 feet or more. It constitutes the best potential recreation portions of the three subregions. The major concern here is the development of recreation and conservation projects.[29]

Not all Appalachians live in Appalachia. A total of 3.3 million moved out of Appalachia between 1950 and 1970. These Americans, who are compelled to move by the lack of economic opportunity at home, tear up their roots and move to the city, where they constitute an "invisible

[29]Data from "The Appalachian Subregions," *Appalachia*, 8, no. 1:1–27 (Aug.–Sept. 1974).

Table 1. POPULATION, INCOME, AND LAND AREA OF THE THREE APPALACHIAN SUBREGIONS

SUBREGION	1970 POPULATION[1]	METRO-POLITAN	URBAN	RURAL	PER CAPITA PERSONAL INCOME[2]	SQUARE MILES	PERCENT OF REGION
Northern	9,733,298	5,353,882	2,769,349	1,610,067	$3,483	83,581	42.9
Central	1,744,712	194,334	309,378	1,241,000	2,306	31,906	16.4
Southern	6,734,903	3,432,249	1,703,107	1,559,547	3,019	79,384	40.7
Appalachian Region	18,212,913	8,980,465	4,781,834	4,450,614	$3,199	194,871	100.0%

[1]Tabulation by ARC staff of final 1970 Census of the Population data from Bureau of Census.
[2]Department of Commerce, Bureau of Economic Analysis, Regional Economic Measurement Division, computer printouts.
Source: *Appalachia*, 8, no. 1: 26 (Aug.–Sept. 1974).

constituency." They remain closely knit family groups. They create no political presence, as many other groups do, and rarely join organizations.

Where do they go when they leave Appalachia? Until recently the majority moved to the industrial cities of Ohio, such as Cleveland, Cincinnati, Columbus, Dayton, Akron. In 1970 the largest number of Appalachian families moved to Atlanta, Washington, D.C., Detroit, Birmingham, and Knoxville. Although black immigrants into Detroit, Chicago, and Cleveland outnumbered immigrants from Appalachia during the periods 1955 to 1960 and 1965 to 1970, Appalachian migrants into Cincinnati, Dayton, and Columbus exceeded the number of black immigrants into these cities.

Appalachians in the far southern areas of the region, in Alabama and Georgia, tend to move toward Atlanta and other Southern economic capitals. Residents of Central Appalachia—those who live in the Cumberland Plateau and surrounding areas of West Virginia, Kentucky, Tennessee, and Virginia—generally move into the industrial heartland of the Midwest, primarily Ohio. Persons who move from the coal fields of eastern Kentucky and Tennessee generally head for Cincinnati and Dayton; persons from the southern coal fields of West Virginia move to Columbus, Cleveland, and other cities in Ohio. Indianapolis, Detroit, and Chicago draw more equally from all of these areas.

Appalachians depend on kinfolk for help. They become a stable, productive part of the labor force. They avoid public service agencies. Those who leave are apt to be young, with more education and a higher family-earned income than those who stay. They live in Appalachian ghettos, which cities downgrade. High percentages of the young people leave school—as high as 40 to 62 percent. From 1965 to 1970, the typical migrant had approximately twelve years of education and an income of $4,000. The Appalachian group has little or no political control. They are made to feel ashamed of their heritage. Their contributions are unknown and ignored.

Cultural isolation, long a characteristic of many parts of Appalachia, is diminishing daily. One reason may be that in recent years a change in migration has been evident. Between 1970 and 1975 population trends show that, for the first time in decades, the region received more migrants than it exported.[30] In 1975 population of the Appalachian region was estimated to be 19 million. If the trend continues, a population of 19.7 million by 1980 is estimated. To date, the greatest growth has been in Southern Appalachia and in nonmetropolitan areas. Major factors in population change have been: decentralization of manufacturing, growth of retirement and recreation facilities, increase in the number of higher education centers, resurgence of employment in the coal mines, effects of Appalachian development programs, increase in social welfare, return of military service personnel, and unemployment and housing costs in other metropolitan areas, especially in the North.

Television is a major influence. Television brings the outside world to Appalachia and develops an intraregional communication network. "The Medium and the Message in the Region," in an issue of the journal *Appalachia*,[31] reports the influence of the communication media in the region. Telecasts of documentaries on topics of prime interest in the Appalachian region are health care, aging, criminal justice, land use, housing, and transportation. Local videotape and cable TV provide a video network. Communication media and service programs testify to active developments. Currently these activities include videotape programs by Broadside TV; the Instant Library at Buffalo Creek, West Virginia; publications of Appalachian researchers; the highly popular national television program "The Waltons"; the Library-Adult Basic Education Project; and the Appalachian Adult Education Center at Morehead State University.

No librarian should miss the Newman study, which looks at library/media services in Appalachia.[32] The author defines the Appalachian area and the characteristics and value orientations of its people. She

[30]Data on migration from Appalachia are based on "The Invisible Urban Appalachian," *Appalachia*, 7, no. 5:24–31 (Apr.–May 1974) and Jerome Pickard, "Appalachian Population Estimated at 19 Million," *Appalachia* 9, no. 1:1–9 (Aug.–Sept. 1975).

[31]"The Medium and the Message in the Region," *Appalachia*, 7, no. 5:2–23 (Apr.–May 1974).

[32]Mayrelee Newman, "Library/Media Services in Appalachia: An Overview," in Smith, ed., *Library and Information Services for Special Groups*.

describes the library/media services which have been developed in the area and extends the overview of the Southern Appalachian subregion described by Coskey in her article.[33]

A phenomenon in the United States is the mobility of individuals and families, and mass migration—such as has taken place in Appalachia since 1914. Throughout its history, immigrant groups have entered the United States and migrant movements have occurred within the country. The mass movement of rural people to urban industrial and metropolitan areas of the country has been continuous within the twentieth century. In a society in which such mobility and transience are facts of life, the movements of people—whether Appalachian residents, native Americans, blacks, or suburban residents—are an important concern for the public library as well as school and college libraries. A library with advance study and wise planning would be in a position to respond rapidly and efficiently. Such a response requires sensitivity to the slightest change in the population of residents in the library service area, as well as immediate response in changes within library resources and programs.

Latinos

Latinos, persons of Spanish origin, number 10.8 million, or constitute 5 percent of the total population. This group, the second largest outside the dominant culture, has a distinctive culture and language of its own. At the same time, distinctive subcultures exist in the heritages and interests of the various Latino groups. The terms and definitions mean different things to different people—Chicano, Mexican American, Hispano, Spanish, Spanish speaking, La Raza, Latino, Puerto Rican, Cuban. The U.S. Bureau of the Census identifies this group as Spanish speaking, or of Spanish origin or descent, or with Spanish surname. In March 1974 the census identified five major groups in this population. Of these, 6.5 million, or about 60 percent, were of Mexican origin and over 1.5 million, or 14.6 percent, were of Puerto Rican origin. Persons of Cuban origin totaled about 700,000, as did persons of Central or South American origin, and about 1.4 million persons reported themselves as of other than Spanish origin.[34]

[33]Evelyn Coskey, "Public Library Service in the Southern Appalachian Region," *Library Trends*, 20, no. 2 (Oct. 1971).

[34]U.S. Bureau of the Census, "Persons of Spanish Origin in the United States: March 1974," *Current Population Reports*, Series P-20, no. 280 (Washington, D.C.: Govt. Printing Office, 1975).

The Mexican ethnic origin group includes persons variously designated Chicano, Mexican American, Mexican, and Mexicano. The preferred name depends to a great extent on age, geography, ethnic heritage, and political beliefs. They make up the largest group of the 6.3 million Chicanos or Mexican Americans, of whom 5.4 million or 86 percent live in the five Southwestern states of Arizona, California, Colorado, New Mexico, and Texas. In San Antonio (Texas) alone, half a million Spanish-speaking residents constitute half the population. Before World War II, Chicanos lived primarily in rural areas of the five Southwestern states. Through the 1940s to the 1960s, they moved from rural to urban areas. In Los Angeles the Chicano population numbers more than a million. About one family in four of Mexican origin lives in a non-metropolitan area.

Latinos include an indigenous population with the longest cultural heritage of any people in the United States—other than the native peoples or native Americans. Their history within the geographical boundaries of the United States extends over four centuries. It was from southeast Texas to southern California that their North American history began, among the established cultures of the Indian tribes of Mexico and the Southwest—the Pueblos, Apaches, Pecos, and many others —and the first Spanish and Old Mexican populations. Until 1848 the Southwest region, within areas of New Mexico, Texas, Colorado, California, and Arizona, was among the northern provinces of Mexico.

The Spanish first settled in New Mexico in 1598, in Texas after 1700, and in California in 1769. The oldest capital in the nation, Santa Fe, was founded in 1610. Here began the merger and incorporation of the Indian, Spanish, and Mexican cultures, before Anglo Americans immigrated into Texas and California. Between 1810 and 1848 the cultural and ethnic relationships between Mexicans and Anglos developed. In 1846 about 10,000 Mexicans of Spanish stock and over 20,000 Indians made up the population of the California coast—where about 500 settlers from the United States had begun colonization. By the Treaty of Guadalupe Hidalgo (Feb. 2, 1848), Mexico gave up its claims to Texas and sold the rest of the Southwest (Arizona, California, New Mexico, Utah, Nevada, and part of Colorado) to the United States. Then began the long period of unrelenting discrimination—against their cultural heritage, language, and customs—and the economic exploitation of Mexican Americans, of disregard and failure to protect their rights, as guaranteed by the treaty. Mexican Americans today represent various heritages and populations—Indian, Spanish American, Anglo, Mexican, mestizo, and the Mexican immigrant.

Puerto Rican Americans, who in 1973 numbered over a million and a half, are concentrated in the Northeast United States. Seventy-five percent of Puerto Ricans on the United States mainland live in New York and New Jersey.[35] About one family in twenty lives in a non-metropolitan area. The numbers and diversity of this population are shown for "Nueva York" in figures estimated by Eliu Schoen.

Table 2. LATINO POPULATION, NEW YORK, 1970

	GREATER NEW YORK
Puerto Ricans	1,300,000
Cubans	300,000
Dominicans	200,000 to 300,000
Colombians	150,000
Ecuadorians	40,000 to 60,000
Peruvians	30,000
Spaniards	30,000
Panamanians	15,000 to 20,000
Argentineans	2,500
Bolivians	2,000

Sources: New York—Eliu Schoen, *New York*, 5, no. 32 (Aug. 7, 1972).

Ninety-seven percent of Puerto Rican families lived in metropolitan areas, as did 76 percent of Mexican origin families. Within metropolitan areas, residence in central cities was markedly different between families of Mexican origin and Puerto Rican origin. Among the Puerto Rican population, about 81 percent lived in central cities, compared with 43 percent of Mexican origin families. It is estimated that 500,000 Cubans live in all fifty states and Puerto Rico. Dade County, Florida, has the largest concentration of Cubans, with 318,000 out of a total population of 626,000. The number of Spanish-speaking persons living in the United States is three times the population of Madrid. It was estimated that there were 15 million Spanish-speaking peoples in the United States in 1975.

A recent survey, based on statistics from 1972 and 1973, showed wide differences within the various Spanish origin groups and with the larger ethnic group of blacks identified by the Bureau of the Census. Both the Spanish and the blacks had lower incomes than whites, but blacks had higher educational achievement than the Spanish. The Span-

[35]Samuel Betances, "The Latin Diaspora," *New York*, Aug. 7, 1972, p. 27–31.

ish population was considerably younger than the rest of the population, with 13 percent of persons under five years of age and 4 percent who were sixty-five and over. The median age in March 1973 was 20.1 years, compared with 28.4 years for the non-Spanish population. The Cuban American population had a median age of 35.3 years, while that of Mexican American and Puerto Rican populations was 18.8 years. Most families live in metropolitan areas—1.9 million of 2.4 million total, or 83 percent.

In education among the Spanish-speaking population, 35 percent had completed four years of high school or more, compared with 65 percent of blacks and 90 percent of white Americans. In the national groups, 27.3 percent of Mexican Americans finished high school; 26 percent of Puerto Ricans; 52.4 percent of Cubans; and, among all other "Spanish," 53.8 percent.[36]

Although the Spanish origin population significantly lags behind the total population in educational attainment, in recent years this attainment has changed; about 53 percent of persons twenty-five to twenty-nine years old had completed four years of high school. Fewer are in professional jobs; about 56 percent of employed men were working in blue-collar jobs. Of all employed men of Spanish origin, men of Mexican origin had the greatest proportion, 11 percent, working as farm laborers.

In employment, Spanish-speaking Americans were in lower-paying occupations, with 27 percent in such jobs as service station attendants, clothing ironers and cleaners, dressmaking, garage workers. Many (18 percent) were employed as craftsmen—machinists, carpenters, automobile mechanics. Another 13.6 percent held professional and technical positions; 13.6 percent were managers; 6.2 percent were sales workers; and 6.8 percent were clerical workers.[37]

Spanish is spoken in the homes of an estimated half of the population designated as of Spanish origin; but few would question that bilingualism is a vital fact. This multinational group is culturally rich and diverse. The common linguistic and similar cultural characteristics must be recognized and considered. Cultural ties and economic stability vary, but the language is the same. As television broadcasters and advertisers have recognized for a long time, large parts of the country are bilingual.

[36]U.S. Bureau of the Census, "Consumer Income: Characteristics of the Low-Income Population, 1972," *Current Population Reports*, Series P-60, no. 91 (Washington, D.C.: Govt. Printing Office, 1973).

[37]Paul Delaney, "Spanish-Americans Far Behind in Report on Income and Status," *New York Times*, May 11, 1974, p. 34C.

Spanish-speaking groups are not abandoning their language through assimilation. Although many younger members know only English, they too are becoming bilingual.

Significant differences make it necessary not to be misled by these similarities; the cultural and social differences among Latinos must be understood. Each library community will have individual characteristics and intergroup relations that must be taken into account. The educational, occupational, economic, and social characteristics, values and attitudes, and political opinions held by different groups within Latino populations are essential facts, to be established as the foundation for developing library collections and services. Public libraries, particularly in metropolitan areas of Los Angeles and Oakland, Albuquerque, New York City, and Miami, as well as smaller communities, strive to provide suitable bilingual collections and services.

English-as-a-Second-Language Group

Readers in the English-as-a-second-language group represent diverse backgrounds, different languages, and a greater variety of cultural and social traditions than any other group. Nationalities from every country where the native language is not English may be represented. The common characteristic is the need to learn English. At the same time, basic education in various customs, habits, naturalization, and living in a new country is necessary.

In 1970 the census showed that for about 30 million Americans, or approximately 15 percent of the population, the English language was not the mother tongue. About 9.6 million Americans were foreign born. Census figures on immigration reveal the effects of the 1965 Immigration and Nationality Act.[38] The changes of the 1965 act increased the volume of net alien immigration. The 1972 immigration figure of 385,000 was 30 percent higher than the 297,000 immigrants admitted in 1965.

The 1965 act also affected the distribution by country of origin. Previously, almost 25 percent of the immigrant population came from northern and western Europe and another 14 percent from southern and eastern Europe. The former has been reduced to less than 7 percent for northern and western Europe, and the latter has risen slightly, to 17 percent, for southern and eastern Europe.

[38]U.S. Bureau of the Census, "Population of the United States, Trends and Prospects: 1950–1990," *Current Population Reports*, Series P-23, no. 49 (Washington, D.C.: Govt. Printing Office, 1974). The bureau defines an immigrant as an alien admitted for permanent residence.

The source for major increase has been Asia. In 1965 Asians contributed 7 percent of the immigration, but in 1972, 31.5 percent of the immigrants into the United States came from Asia. Over 70 percent of the increase in Asian immigration was accounted for by China, Taiwan, India, Korea, and the Philippines.

Immigration from North America dropped from 42.7 percent to 37.5 percent of the total immigrant population. Mexico contributed 16.6 percent of the North American immigrants; Canada 2.8 percent (compared to 12.9 percent in 1965); Cuba 5.2 percent; Jamaica 3.5 percent, and the Dominican Republic and other parts of the West Indies 7.3 percent of the immigrants. South America's influx to the United States dropped from 10.4 to 5 percent of the total.

The figures for persons who are reported as immigrants in 1973 are revealing. Some of the largest numbers are indicative of groups otherwise overlooked or merged into the larger population (table 3).

The intended permanent residences for about 45 percent of all immigrants were New York and California. New York was favored by a large number of Italian, Polish, Chinese, Cuban, and British immigrants. California was chosen as residence for many immigrants from Mexico, Canada, the Philippines, Taiwan, mainland China, and other Asian countries. Over 70 percent planned permanent residence in New York, California, Illinois, New Jersey, Texas, Florida, and Massachusetts. In general, persons coming to the United States tend to settle near family members and employment opportunities.

Library communities require continuing study to be alert to these changing populations, and the Italian American population is an example of these changes. The Italian Americans are one of the largest ethnic groups to have migrated voluntarily to this country. They number approximately 20 million, roughly 11 percent of the population. Theirs has been a bittersweet heritage, mainly because America has seen Italy as a backward country or museum for years.[39] Prejudice, discrimination, and bigotry helped convince Italian Americans that they were an inferior people. But, through it all, Italians retained a few unique ethnic qualities, aside from Old World names. These qualities make Italian Americans a unique ethnic group.

Italians formed ethnic groups in communities across the country, both in large cities and small rural areas: New York, Philadelphia, Buffalo, Cleveland, Milwaukee, Chicago, Omaha, San Francisco—and in

---

[39]Alexander DeConde, *Half Bitter, Half Sweet* (New York: Scribner, 1971), is a definitive study of the relationship between Italy and the United States. DeConde outlines the effects on both countries of emigration to America from Italy.

Table 3. IMMIGRANTS (1973) BY COUNTRY OF LAST PERMANENT RESIDENCE (ALL COUNTRIES: 400,063)

Europe	(91,183)	
Largest numbers from		
Great Britain		11,860
Greece		10,348
Italy		22,264
Portugal		10,019
Spain		5,538
Asia		10,283
Hong Kong		11,975
India		22,313
Korea		30,248
Philippines	(119,984)	
America		
Canada		14,800
Cuba		22,537
Dominican Republic		14,011
Mexico		70,411
West Indies		21,641
Africa		5,537

Note: Only the countries from which the largest number of immigrants came are listed here.

Sources: U.S. Immigration and Naturalization Service, *Annual Report*, no. 156, "Immigrants by Country of Last Permanent Residence: 1820 to 1973," (Washington, D.C.: Government Printing Office, 1974), p. 99; U.S. Bureau of the Census, *Statistical Abstract of the United States: 1975* (96th ed.; Washington, D.C.: Government Printing Office, 1975), p. 101.

Wisconsin, Missouri, and Indiana. At least 85 percent of the Italians who came to the United States are estimated to have emigrated from the Mezzogiorno, the area south of Rome. (Gambino calls it "the land that time forgot." In *Blood of My Blood* he details the southern Italian and Sicilian attitudes of the Mezzogiorno and how these old-country viewpoints blended or clashed with the culture in America.[40])

The New York City Board of Education's excellent series "Call Them Heroes," a collection of brief biographies which is used in schools and adult basic education programs, does not represent Italian Americans among the outstanding members of various ethnic groups. This illustrates the need for careful analysis of even widely used material to identify what is missing and to provide complementary material.

[40]Richard Gambino, *Blood of My Blood: The Dilemma of the Italian-Americans* (New York: Doubleday, 1974).

Italian Americans are only one of the numerous ethnic groups—Irish, Polish, Slavic, Greek, Chinese, Japanese, Latin American, Mexican, Puerto Rican. Their history and culture, attitudes and beliefs, and their place in and contributions to American society offer fascinating areas of study. Wherever they are, their attitudes and values underlie community attitudes and values, even when, after several generations of living in the United States, they are no longer "visible" or found in "little Italys," or Irish or Polish neighborhoods, or "Chinatowns." Later generations are avid searchers for knowledge about their heritage.

The library has a central role in finding and supplying those resources which speak to each national group. Such materials serve the double purpose of providing materials for the particular group and of promoting understanding of that group by "outsiders."

3

Reading: What It Is

Reading is an essential element in the intellectual and cultural life of the adult, and printed materials continue to increase in rate of growth. The increases are evident not only in U.S. production and use but also in worldwide figures. There are some 450,000 titles in print. Every year 30,000 to 40,000 new titles appear in the United States and 35,000 or more in Britain. In 1975 39,372 new titles and new editions were published in the United States. Not counted in that figure are U.S. government publications or those of any governmental unit, and university theses. Underreported are textbooks and mass market paperbacks, which are estimated to be over 16,000. Such figures demonstrate the problem of selection and evaluation and the immensity of the task for the identification of the types of reading materials with appeal, interest, and value to the potential users.

Reading is essential to daily living in an increasingly complex world. The highly developed postindustrial society, the global village, requires use of all media for communication. Thus reading is used concurrently with other media. It is in competition with film, radio, television. It continues to be a foundation of education. It is essential to continuing education, whether formal, informal, or self-directed. Although other media in many instances supersede it as a means of communication, it continues to be the medium that the reader most directly controls. It is an individual and private method. It is eminently mobile, unrestricted in time and place. Above all, it is the communication medium in which information and ideas may be developed in depth. It continues to be a successful method for transmission of the cultural heritage, as well as current and immediate knowledge. Any change in form, whether microform, photocopying, or electronic, does not change the message. It provides unparalleled freedom of expression and user control.

Not *all* control rests with the reader or user. Various elements restrict this reading power and many factors influence ease or lack of ease of communication: availability, accessibility, literacy level, readability, accuracy, and integrity. Obstacles to communication include censorship, ignorance, interferences and distortions, vocabulary, and incompatible values.

Reading is an act of communication. Lasswell's relatively simple description of the act of communication continues to provide a model of the communication process which librarians can apply to advantage:

Who
Says what
In which channel
To whom
With what effect?[1]

Librarians have a special interest in each aspect of the question. They are directly or indirectly concerned with the separate questions as well as the whole process. The factors for librarians' analysis center on the who, the communicator, the suppliers of information, the content communicated, and the channel which, in the medium of print, has numerous forms, from a single page or posters or broadsides to literature of science and art as presented in a book or scientific treatise. Librarians must analyze and know "to whom" the communicator of the work speaks and the content and style appeal. Nor can the librarian neglect the question of what impact or effect the message may have. It is this latter area that information and research fail.

The librarian may be the communicator, either as a source of the messages, as interpreter, or as individual transmitter in the interconnected network of communication. Librarians may be influential opinion leaders as they deliver reading materials. They are part of the two-step flow of communication. As interpreters, librarians are a channel for the message. As selectors of materials, they control the availability of materials and, consequently and inevitably, the accessibility of ideas and

---

[1]Harold D. Lasswell, "The Structure and Function of Communication in Society," in Lyman Bryson ed., *The Communication of Ideas*, Religion and Civilization Series (New York: Institute for Religious and Social Studies, Jewish Theological Seminary, 1948), p. 37.

information to the audience of readers. Their social and intellectual place in the community and their interpersonal relations are vital aspects in the flow of communications which they help to create in the network of communications.

Whether influential or not, they perform what Lasswell has termed a relay function, as an "agent who is a vortex of interacting environmental and predispositional factors."[2] It is as legitimate to ask the same questions of the librarian's relation to input and output as are asked of reporters, government, editors, and publishers. What materials are included in library collections? What are excluded? What are withdrawn? What are republished? How do differences in input and output correlate with cultural attitudes, and with whose values and attitudes?

Other models developed by researchers extend Lasswell's concept. The Shannon and Weaver model comprises five major components in which the place of the librarian can be seen. The components of this model are the information source; the transmitter, which transforms the message into a signal for transmission; a channel, which carries the signal from the transmitter to the receiver; the receiver, which constructs the signal with a message; and, finally, the receiver of the message.

Wilbur Schramm, in *The Process and Effects of Mass Communication*, points out that "the essence of communication is getting the receiver and the sender 'tuned' together for a particular message."[3] The sender and the receiver establish the "commonness" that is necessary to sharing information, ideas, and attitudes. Schramm pictures this process as one in which the source encodes the message and transmits it in coded form through a signal—spoken or written words, telegraph, telephone, radio, cable. The message, thus encoded, must be decoded by the receiver to complete the act of communication and have it reach a destination (figure 1a). Similarly, in an electronic communication (for example) the microphone is substituted for the encoder and earphones for the decoder.

The capacities of each part of the system influence the accuracy, clarity, distortions, interferences, and amount of redundancy. The amount of redundancy is the percentage of the message which is *not* open to free choice. Both language redundancy and communicators' redundancy influence the choice which must be made between transmitting more information in a given time or transmitting less and repeating—giving more examples and analogies in the hope of being better understood.

To be "in tune," the sender and the receiver must have some common

[2]Ibid., p. 48.
[3]Wilbur Schramm, ed., *The Process and Effects of Mass Communication* (Urbana: Univ. of Illinois Pr., 1954), p. 3.

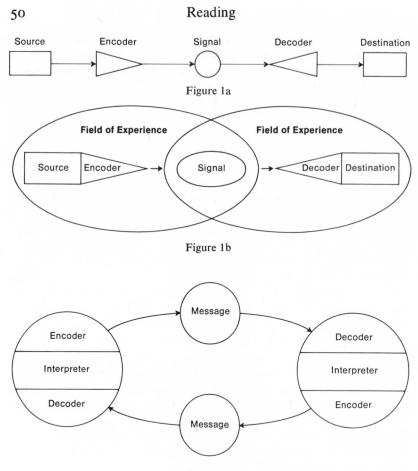

Figure 1a

Figure 1b

Figure 1c

Figure 1a-c. Schramm's models. (Reprinted, by permission, from Wilbur Schramm, ed., *The Process and Effects of Mass Communication.* © 1954 University of Illinois Press.)

knowledge and experience. The source must take into account common language and experience that will make it possible for the decoder-destination to take meaning from the signal (figure 1b). Both sender and receiver decode, interpret, and encode the message. Messages flow back and forth through various channels—words, voices, headlines, type, electronic signals, film, and cable (figure 1c).

Although it is not possible easily to predict the effect of message content, it is recognized that the receiver re-creates the message, as well as that the sender creates the message. Schramm suggests that certain conditions must be fulfilled in order to achieve the intended response, that is, success in communication.

1. The message must be so designed and delivered as to gain the attention of the intended destination.
2. The message must employ signs which refer to experience common to source and destination, so as to "get the meaning across."
3. The message must arouse personality needs in the destination and suggest some ways to meet those needs.
4. The message must suggest a way to meet those needs which is appropriate to the group situation in which the destination finds himself at the time when he is moved to make the desired response.

It can thus be seen why the expert communicator, and in the context of this work the librarian (who is a communicator, mediator, or transmitter of messages in a multitude of forms), must know all that is possible about intended destinations and why "know your audience" is a practical first rule for librarians (as for mass communicators).

Messages must be designed and selected so that the timing, placing, and cues will appeal to the receiver's interest. Messages must be designed in a language and at a level that cause minimal conflict between experiences the receiver will accept. An effective message must satisfy a need and also satisfy action. It must relate in some way to the receiver's needs of security, status, belongingness, understanding, and freedom. The message must also relate to standards, values, and experiences of the group of culture and institutions with which one is involved.

What determines which message will be selected by any individual or group? The individual or group is more likely to select the communication if it promises them more reward or requires less effort than comparable communications. Schramm defines this choice as determined by the "fraction of selection":

$$\frac{\text{Expectation of reward}}{\text{Effort required}}$$

Schramm later modified this fraction of selection to "likelihood of selection":

$$\frac{\text{(perceived reward strength)} - \text{(perceived punishment strength)}}{\text{perceived expenditure of effort}}$$

In either case the fraction is made larger by either increasing reward or decreasing effort.[4]

One is more likely to read, listen, or look at what is easily available, most accessible, and understood with the least effort. For that matter, one is more likely to attend to and use messages with which one agrees.

The communication process and the conditions for effective communication of information, ideas, and attitudes are the same, whether between individuals, communication in a group, or mass communication.

The SMCR model for the communication process, developed by David Berlo, has particular relevance in the context of reading materials service for adult new readers. The four major components of SMCR are source, message, channel, and receiver. The elements which make up each component further extend the concept to specific aspects and the interrelationship between source and receiver (see figure 2).

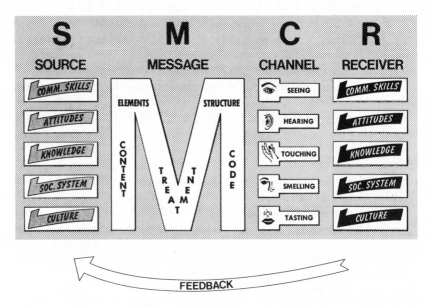

Figure 2. Berlo's SMCR model of communication. (Reprinted, by permission. from D. K. Berlo, *The Process of Communication.* © 1960 Holt, Rinehart and Winston, Inc.)

---

[4]Wilbur Schramm, "Why Adults Read," in Nelson B. Henry, ed., *Adult Reading* (55th yearbook of National Society for the Study of Education, part 2) (Chicago: National Society for the Study of Education and Univ. of Chicago Pr., 1956), p. 64; Wilbur Schramm and Donald F. Roberts, eds., *The Process and Effects of Mass Communication*, rev. ed. (Urbana: Univ. of Illinois Pr., 1972), p. 32.

Berlo's SMCR model is particularly applicable to the theme of this book. It is simple and direct (deceptively so) insofar as it can be used at various levels. The more knowledge and background the librarian has in human behavior, literacy skills, and research, the more meaningful it will be.

The source (author-editor) of the message is analyzed in terms of literacy (that is, skills of communication), attitudes toward the subject (the receiver or reader) and toward oneself, and the author's knowledge about the subject. How authoritative and accurate is it? At what level is it? What is one's knowledge of the receiver or reader to whom it is addressed or intended for? What beliefs and values are held by the source? What roles and norms influence the content and manner of communication? What beliefs and attitudes are revealed in the subject matter? What is the cultural background? Is the author from the group about which the subject matter is concerned?

Second, what is the message? The content is conveyed in symbols— letters combined into words, words continued into sentences, sentences combined into paragraphs, illustrations combined with words. The level of writing is of particular importance. The readability and level of understanding of source and receiver are affected.

Third, the channel through which the message is conveyed is considered. It may be any format of print, from hardcover book to broadside. The format may make a great deal of difference. The popular appeal of paperbound work versus that of hardcover demonstrates the effectiveness of its format. The senses of seeing, hearing, touching, smelling, and tasting are channels for the communication. By extension, the channels may be telephone, radio, television, film, newspaper, print.

The social system and background, the life style and experience of the source, influence and set the tone and authority of the message. The cultural background is similarly influential, and colors the message.

At the other end of the communication is the receiver, within whom the same elements combine to influence the reception of the message. What are the receiver's communication skills? Literacy abilities? Comprehension and understanding? What are the attitudes and values, knowledge and experience, life style, social context, and cultural background of the receiver? Is there a common experience? How will these elements affect the message? The receiver re-creates the message. Is it understood?

The feedback from the receiver to the source is an essential component for accurate understanding between speaker and receiver. Librarians and teachers may play an important role here. They can serve as liaison and interpreter for receiver and source, that is, for the reader and author or publisher. On the basis of the analysis of the major components of communication, they can predict to whom the message or work will be of interest or use. They can point out changes or kinds of works needed.

The librarian and teacher attempt to determine the nature and characteristics of each component in the communication process, to evaluate the level of the communication skills in the presentation, to identify the treatment in style, content, and cultural background, and to predict the receivers among the library or student clientele. Finally, an overall evaluation or judgment is made.

The elements which inhibit effective communication in the communication process are many. Among the many variables which affect the learning process and communication (such as lack of interest, physical discomfort, literacy skills, failure to understand, too many words), the most difficult to identify and take into account are prejudice, experience, and cognitive knowledge.

Rarely does the writer or the communicator speak directly or the receiver receive directly. The multiple channels through which the message passes both separate and bring together source and receiver. The original source—pen, pencil, type on paper, book, paperback—may pass through the human mediator channel and interpreter's mind and voice—the librarian, reporter, editor, or other media: the paper, cassette, reel, phonodisc, film.

Common components make up the source and the receiver. Communication skills and a sufficient level of literacy are necessary for creating and re-creating the message. Attitudes will determine how the speaker and the reader feel. The level of knowledge, the social group and environment, and the cultural context in beliefs and values are influential in what is said and in how the message is interpreted or understood. The message tells what the content is about. The source or transmitter selects content for communication and weaves it together in structural framework, treatment, and style. The natural channels through which the message is transmitted are bodily senses—eye, ear, finger, mouth, tongue—which are extended by artificial channels—television, radio, newspaper.

Marshall McLuhan views the extension of the human being through technological developments in which the bow and arrow extends a person's reach, the automobile extends the legs, the telephone extends the voice, writing extends the voice and memory, the computer extends the nervous system.

Osgood constructed a model with three levels of responses to explain the meaning process. The word *stimuli* is decoded, interpreted, and involves responses when encoded by the receiver. Habitual responses which occur at the sensory motor-skill level include learned integrations, attitudes, and values; expectations are at the dispositional level; and internal mediational responses are at the representational level. Varieties of meanings are classified as denotative, connotative, and structural. At the denotative stage, words have a direct and specific meaning, which denotes objects, events, conditions. At the connotative level the meaning carries implications. Strong connotative associations convey and suggest meaning, along with or apart from the thing it explicitly names; a quality or feeling is implied. At the structural level the meaning may be determined by its placement in the organization of the sentence. Here again clues are significant.

As valid as these assumptions are, consideration must be given to the paradoxical fact that difficulties of understanding and agreement as to meaning frequently exist between the source of the message and the receiver. Even the simplest message may be received and interpreted differently. The parlor game of Rumor, in which a statement that is repeated around a circle comes out garbled, is an example of misstatements and misunderstandings. As in all human transactions, simplicity is achieved only through a combination of many factors. They can be identified in various ways and in diverse models—channel, speech, writing, transmitter, interpreter, values, attitudes, beliefs, dissonance, meanings connotative and denotative, feedback, social environment.

At other times, surprisingly or not, messages come through loud and clear. All the pieces fall into place. Across centuries or in today's news, "that marvelous collaboration between the writer's artful vision and the reader's sense of life" takes place, as Ellison so accurately states. One becomes "acquainted with other possible selves—freer, more courageous and ingenuous and, during the course of the narrative, even wise."[5] In the search for the practical, the immediately and eminently useful, the librarian keeps in mind this broader, deeper vision.

Literacy training programs, like most educational programs, are an expansion of the theories and principles, beliefs and values of individuals and groups, and ultimately of the society. The resources supporting such programs in the main reflect, and are derived from, the theories and beliefs held by individuals and society.

Paulo Freire, the Brazilian educator, has conceived an educational theory, within the context of revolutionary social change, that is carried out through a literacy training program. The central concept of his theory is "conscientization," which means to make aware or awake

[5]Ralph Ellison, *Shadow and Act* (New York: New American Library, 1966), p. xvii–xviii.

consciousness. It is the social process in which human beings achieve a deepening awareness of the reality which shapes their lives and of their capacity to transform that reality.

The illiterate is not a marginal man, existing on the edge of society in hunger, pain, crime, and despair, who has chosen such a life. The assumption of the marginality of the illiterate as men and women on the edge of society results in the "digestive" concept of knowledge. The illiterate is not recognized as able to know and to create texts. He is viewed as a "sick man," as some would assume, for whom literacy would be medicine for the cure and enable him to return to health. Educators become benevolent counselors who restore the poor, the illiterate, to happiness. In Freire's views, these concepts of seeing human beings as outsiders result in oppression and dependency. They are "beings for another."

His interpretation of man within the world places "thought language," the process by which man transforms reality, at the center. The adult literacy process "is an act of knowing in which the learner assumes the role of knowing subject in dialogue with the educator."[6] Speaking the word is not a true act unless it is "associated with the right of self-expression and world-expression, of creating and recreating, of deciding and choosing and ultimately participating in society's historical process."[7]

Illiteracy is the mark of men robbed of their words, who exist not for themselves but for another. Through the literacy process they free themselves and transform their culture.

When illiterate human beings are interpreted as marginal to society, the literacy process reinforces the original view of dependency, the myth of reality, and words and phrases serve to alienate. Once illiterate human beings are interpreted as oppressed within the system, the literary process becomes a cultural act for freedom. The learner is creative. The experience and perception of the learner and the educator are joined. "Learning to read and write ought to be an opportunity for men to know what *speaking the word* really means: a human act implying reflection and action."[8]

The adult literacy process becomes an authentic dialogue between equally knowing subjects—learners and educators. In the theoretical context of the dialogue, the concrete context of facts and social reality of existence are critically analyzed. His problem-posing theory of educa-

---

[6]Paulo Freire, "The Adult Literacy Process as Cultural Action for Freedom," *Harvard Educational Review*, 40, no. 2:212 (May 1970) (a special issue, "Illiteracy in America").

[7]Ibid.

[8]Freire, *Cultural Action for Freedom*, p. 12.

tion sees individuals living for themselves, committed to personal and social liberation, rather than domesticated and indoctrinated and controlled by teachers and society. Education is cultural action for freedom; it is an act of knowing and not of memorization. The act of knowing, of learning to read and write, presupposes the theory and process Freire has applied in Third World programs in Brazil and Chile.

The Freire adult literacy method includes the use of discussion groups, with specialists as resource persons. Materials are drawn from the direct experience of the people and move from the simple to the more complex. The problem-centered, experience-centered approach goes beyond self-improvement or individual self-fulfillment to societal change or reevaluation.

The problems posed by Freire for adult educators who are committed to education that supports the values of middle-class society are the same problems faced by librarians in public library service. They have to do with neutrality. From whose perspective are problems to be viewed, and whose interests does education serve? Whose interests are dominant? What social responsibilities do librarians have? Conscientization is a means to liberation, self-liberation, whether among oppressed, disadvantaged, deprived, or discriminated-against persons. In the present case, the largest number who make up this group are among the populations of blacks, native Americans, Latinos, students, and women. With the extension of literacy programs and the use of materials concerned directly with rights of people, new demands come from those persons who are most directly affected. For example, information on consumer buying, tenants' rights, miners' safety laws, or women's rights give rise to movements and legal protective organizations which gradually challenge existing situations. Puerto Ricans in New York have organized food markets and tenants' organizations, and miners in West Virginia have demanded safety regulations.

Freire saw, implicit in literacy materials, the assumption that man has spatialized consciousness, to be filled by teachers who select words reflecting the teachers' values. Similarly, librarians would be seen as selecting materials reflecting personal or society's values. Some librarians and teachers are quite aware of need for materials at an adult level and reflecting other cultural backgrounds, life styles, languages, and experiences.

Media change is part of human development and of the communication process. The changes within each medium, as technological processes develop, deserve equal consideration. Literacy in the languages of the motion picture, television, recordings, tapes, and computers is essential in the twentieth century. The medium of print—newspapers, magazines, books—cannot be an exclusive concern. Libraries are or must become involved in assembling, organizing, and interpreting all media. To some persons it seems that concern with the written word is illogical and antiquated, but print will continue to have a place and to influence man's perception of reality. The paperback phenomenon, the popularity of comics, the rise and fall of magazines are influential, and have been influential in the increasing use of books.

LITERACY

What is literacy? What is illiteracy? These simple questions occur and recur. The answers vary, depending primarily on the framework within which the definition is established, the geographic location, the period in history, the census definition used by the U.S. Bureau of the Census, the literacy requirements for achievement goals, and the stage of research knowledge.[9]

The simplicity of dictionary definitions provides a useful starting point. *Literacy*, according to Webster's *Third New International Dictionary*, means the quality or state of being literate—ability to read a short, simple passage and answer questions about it. *Literate* means being able to read and write, as opposed to *illiterate*. At an advanced level, *literate* means possessed of learning, that is, educated and cultured. *Illiterate* is used most commonly in reference to the inability to read and write, or to gross unfamiliarity with the written language—that is, uneducated, uncultured. It would be far more accurate and fair to say *unlettered*, because the stress then rests on the fact of unfamiliarity with reading and writing, or with written learning, and often without any implication of condemnation. To call a society literate implies that most of the adults are able to read and write. If *literacy* is used in a historical or modern comparative context, the implied contrast is with *illiteracy*.

Illiterate, it would seem, means most simply the lack of ability to read and write. By extension it has come to mean the lack of education, because today education is so highly dependent on the opposite ability to read and write. Complete illiteracy means that one is unable to read English or any language at all. Definitions, however, become arbitrary. Many persons use the terms without attempting to define them. Minimum literacy is of little value unless it is practical, that is, a skill of some effective use in the culture or group in which one lives.

The usual grade school equivalent for judging literacy has been the completion of the fourth or fifth grade level. UNESCO, the U.S. Bureau

[9]Lyman, *Library Materials in Service to the Adult New Reader*, p. 1–45.

of the Census, and the U.S. Army use this standard. A broader concept recognizes the complexity of literacy function which sees conceptualization of literacy as a tool, the learning of reading and writing skills, and the practical application of those skills. Grade levels of measure are not accurate indicators of reading achievement levels. On the whole, they overestimate, or in their very nature are meaningless as measures. Current estimates show that millions of adult men and women are functionally illiterate. In spite of efforts to eradicate illiteracy and a steady decline in the number of persons unable to read and write any language, the problem persists.

If literacy level is to be measured by grade level, it appears that an individual must have attained, at the very minimum, a tenth grade literacy achievement level, regardless of years of schooling measured by grades, and at least a thirteenth grade reading achievement level to be able to read at the practical level which is required in daily life. The demands of modern society necessitate this amplified definition of literacy.

For over a century the various aspects of reading have been under investigation. However, mass literacy is a recent phenomenon. Its achievement is a goal now striven for in most countries in the world. Adult literacy has become an index of educational development and a characteristic of postindustrial societies.

The major areas of reading studies relate to explanations of the process of reading, the skills and abilities of reading, and the purpose and values of reading. There are as many definitions and models as communication processes. Simply defined, reading is an act of communication, or, more complexly, it is the act of knowing.

A vast literature has been produced within the past fifty years in which scholars, researchers, educators, political scientists, journalists, and reading specialists define, classify, and debate the questions of concepts, values, process, and skills. The various ideas provide the eclectic foundation for librarians who find them useful in the development of a library's adult services.

Literacy has been defined as traditional and functional. It is traditional as it is limited to simple transmission of reading and writing skills and the first elements of arithmetic. Literacy is defined as practical or functional when it becomes part of an integrated educational process and helps people see themselves in perspective, qualify for work, and play a conscious and creative part in public life. This conception of functional literacy covers the areas of fundamental education, technical and professional education, and training for taking part in local and national life.

Illiteracy and literacy are being equated with nonsurvival and survival, with oppression and freedom. It is true, of course, that throughout history human beings have survived and countries and cultures have managed without most of its members being literate, and with a small minority in control of the spoken and written word. Today, literacy is accepted throughout the world as essential to civilization. The great achievements of speaking, reading, and writing are recognized as rights which belong to everyone. They are skills needed by everyone.

Attempts are being made to define illiteracy and to identify the illiterate population by performance measurements. One such survey, *Survival Literacy Study*, was conducted for the National Reading Council in 1970 by Louis Harris Associates and is made available through the Education Research Information Center. It measured the extent of reading deficiencies in the United States and the percentage of Americans who lacked the functional and practical reading skills that are considered necessary to survive in this country. Americans were tested by their performance in reading and by correct and incorrect answers in filling out five "survival" forms, measured according to a simple percentile scoring system. The forms covered an increasing range of difficulty, from an application for public assistance, an identification record, an application for a driver's license, and an application for a personal loan to an application for Medicaid. In consequence, the survey was considered fundamentally a study of functional rather than by-rote literacy, and reached a civilian noninstitutional population.

The test answers were used to classify respondents in four types of literacy groups, defined as low, questionable, marginal, and likely survival thresholds of literacy. These groups reflect "the range of illiteracy"; that is, the range between the "low survival" and the "marginal survival" group. The first three groups would be considered functionally illiterate, insofar as they are unable to perform literacy tasks which may be considered requisite to their survival in the United States. Performance on these tests indicated that from 4.3 to 18.5 million Americans are functionally illiterate.

The low-survival respondents averaged more than 30 percent incorrect answers, that is, less than 70 percent correct answers on all the forms.

The questionable-survival respondents averaged more than 20 percent incorrect answers, that is, less than 80 percent correct answers (it includes members of the low-survival group). They filled out the forms with considerable difficulty.

The marginal-survival respondents answered more than 10 percent of the questions incorrectly, that is, correct answers were less than 90 percent. They include members of the low- and questionable-survival groups, and lack total-survival reading ability.

The likely-survival threshold literacy group was respondents who answered less than 10 percent of the questions incorrectly; that is, they gave 90 to 100 percent correct answers. This group is considered functionally literate.

The average range of illiteracy, that is, between low- and marginal-survival groups, was 3 to 13 percent. Three percent of all Americans had difficulty filling out an application form for public assistance. Seven percent had difficulty filling out a simple identification form (similar to a Social Security form). Eight percent had difficulty filling out a driver's license application. Of the people with some college education, 26 percent missed more than 10 percent of Medicaid questions.

Women surpassed men slightly in reading ability. The range of illiteracy among immigrants to the United States was 7 to 16 percent, compared with the 3 to 13 percent range among the total population.

The average range between low- and marginal-survival functional illiteracy was slightly greater among rural than suburban residents. Fewer persons who lived in small towns and cities had difficulty reading forms, and suburban residents filled them out most easily.

The South had the highest functional illiteracy; the East was slightly higher than the Midwest. People in the West tended to have fewer reading deficiencies than those in the other areas.

Practical illiteracy seems to decrease in direct proportion to income. The age group sixteen to twenty-four proved the most literate, and those fifty and over were the most deficient in reading ability. Older persons, fifty years and over, and the poor, with under $5,000 annual income, have serious reading problems; but the elderly poor must struggle most for "survival."

Reading ability increased in direct relation to education, the final dimension. The illiteracy range of people who completed eighth grade or less was 7 to 23 percent, 2 to 12 percent for high school, and 1 to 8 percent for those who had some college education.

The researchers concluded that the practical reading ability needed to complete the forms essential for "survival" may differ somewhat from the achievement-oriented or theoretical reading skills stressed in many of our schools and colleges.

As is apparent, the ability to use skills and knowledge with the functional competency needed for meeting the requirements of adult living has these various meanings: "functional literacy," "survival literacy," "coping skills" and, most recently, "adult functional competency." Why is reading important? was the fundamental question addressed in the recent Adult Performance Level (APL) project. This four-year research, carried out at the University of Texas, was summarized in the 1975 report, *Adult Functional Competency*. Researchers replaced the term *literacy* (with its limited connotation, mere ability to read and write one's name) with *functional competency*, which relates to the application of a set of five skills to a set of five knowledge areas. These sets are meaningful in a specific culture and period of time.

The APL model identified adult literacy as to meeting the adult needs of general knowledge areas: consumer economics, occupational knowledge, health, community resources, and government and law. Four primary skills seemed to account for the vast majority of requirements placed on adults: communication (reading, writing, speaking and listening), computation, problem solving, and interpersonal relations.

The APL project developed a general index of literacy which classifies adults into one of three categories: APL-1, adults who function with difficulty because of unsatisfactory mastery of competency objectives; APL-2, adults whose mastery of competency objectives is functional; and APL-3, adults who are proficient in mastery of competency objectives. Competency was defined by different levels of adult success, as measured by income, job status, and education. The study shows adults to be "not as competent as we thought." Nearly 20 percent of Americans cannot cope—not because they cannot read but because they cannot understand what they read. A substantial number of people lack those basic skills that are necessary in day-to-day life.

Attainment of literacy skills is only a beginning. What are the purposes and values of reading? Will the attainment of reading skills and abilities lead to improved understanding of issues and problems? Does reading power lead to political control, create obedient citizens, docile consumers? Does reading extend the individual's control of his life and environment and assist him in making rational decisions? Does it help the oppressed become free of oppressors or powerful enough to control their own destiny and life? Is reading far more than a skill? Is it a process by which a human being knows and thinks and achieves freedom?

The society in which we live is a symbol-using society. Reading and writing skills mean mastery and understanding of highly abstract communication symbols. The communication source and the receiver of the communication, regardless of the channel through which the message comes, must have mutual understanding of the meaning. For an individual in a symbol-using society the lack of literacy, that is, functional literacy at various levels, has social consequences. Psychologists, adult educators, and philosophers increasingly recognize that symbolic activity is among the most characteristic features of human existence and that the whole development of human culture is based upon man's capacity for transforming simple sensory material into symbolic vehicles—carriers of the finest intellectual and emotional distinctions.[10]

As is noted frequently, without this capacity for symbol manipulation the illiterate becomes an outsider and adapts for survival by forming a subculture of his own, one that further isolates and alienates him from the mainstream. Common sense would add "and vice versa." The dominant culture and the highly literate word-symbol-oriented person may become isolated from what, for lack of a better term, may be designated "real life." The dominant culture, secure in a facade of symbolic activity, fails to know and appreciate the subculture. Literacy is functional when it can be integrated into the life of the adult, when men and women can interpret written and printed symbols so that they are meaningful in their education and work, in their personal and interpersonal relations, in taking part as a citizen in local and national affairs. They will find reading and literacy achievement interesting, useful, creative, and enjoyable.

The reading abilities of the adult reader are linked closely with the intellectual capacities and the intentions of the reader and the readability of the materials. The librarian, in order to "match" these various links —that is, find the material suitable to the adult's purposes and abilities—needs to have as much information in each area as it is possible to have to ascertain these links between the reader and the material.

Let us reconsider what is known about measuring literacy and readability. What do the scientists and reading specialists contribute to the solution of the problems?

Literacy means being able to take meaning from written language and place it in one's mind. If men and women are to know what is contained in the communication resources (in this context in written documents collected and stored in libraries), they must be able to read by responding to written language and have access to the facts and knowledge accumulated in library collections. In modern culture a literate population is held in high esteem. Yet, in spite of numerous theories and studies, little agreement exists as to what it means to be literate and how literacy can be achieved and measured.

When has the adult achieved literacy, or can be said to be functionally literate? When does one read well enough to understand what one wishes

[10]Bernard Kaplan, "An Approach to the Problem of Symbolic Representation: Nonverbal and Verbal," in Leon A. Jakobovits and M. S. Miron, eds., *Readings in the Psychology of Language* (New York: Prentice-Hall, 1967), p. 363.

to learn or "take" from what is read? The unsatisfactory measure by number of years of schooling, as shown in grade level, is evident. The incommeasurability between grade level and reading achievement levels has been shown again and again. What is known is based primarily on reading research related to the education of children. The more that is known about defining and assessing literacy, the less surety that definition and measurement can be made. Reading specialists and scientists do not agree. Neither do they provide concrete, constructive aid to librarians who are faced with evaluating and interpreting materials suitable to the range of adult reading interests and abilities. They are, nevertheless, the major source of help to librarians. To this central question of "how well a person should learn to read, . . . only preliminary and partial answers exist."[11]

Scientists in linguistics and psychology focus on decoding skills in word recognition while specialists in reading instruction center their attention on the higher-level skills of comprehension, critical reading, literary and aesthetic appreciation, reading flexibility in terms of comprehension, and study skills. Librarians must take into account these same behavioral factors when they analyze materials and judge their use. All too often the evaluation must be made without knowledge and techniques that enable the evaluator to judge the value of the material to the reader who is developing word recognition or comprehension skills.

In teaching literacy, certain literacy behaviors are selected and "placed in the curricula because they are valued for the tangible and intangible things that those behaviors enable individuals and society to attain."[12] Bormuth further states that if literacy is to be defined realistically, several questions must be answered. What reading behaviors are to be valued? How are performances to be tested and effects identified? What effects and results are to be valued? What kind of language is needed with regard to which people? Different areas of discourse and different purposes to be achieved require different languages. In this respect language used will vary in vocabulary structure, sentence structure, and discourse structure. Different structures require different literacy skills. Perhaps the identification of various reading behaviors, achievement levels, testing of performances, and effects of literacy can be left to the reading specialists and teachers. Yet librarians cannot ignore any aspect of literacy. Their awareness and knowledge of certain characteristics of

---

[11]John R. Bormuth, "Reading Literacy: Its Definition and Assessment," *Reading Research Quarterly*, 9, no. 1 (1973–74).
[12]Ibid., p. 44.

individuals and populations can result in extended and more successful programs. Literacy factors regarding the library user, such as one's natural capacities, literacy abilities, reasons for use of resources, and (insofar as possible) aspirations and expectations related to use of the reading resources, will influence evaluation and selection of those resources and permit more accurate interpretation for analysis of the material and advisory situations.

Many adults have no knowledge of the sources of information and understanding of how to use such sources. Adults who are deprived of education and lack literacy skills are unable to use sources of information which are written or printed. Adults who are deprived of libraries and reading collections that are suitable to their daily problems have no conception of all that has been published and no access to reading materials. Many adults suffer from physical, economic, and cultural deprivations. They have minimal incomes; are poor, unemployed, unwell. Poverty and discrimination give rise to corollary problems of undereducation, unhappiness, alienation, dependence, and further discrimination. Many such adults experience discrimination because of age, sex, ethnic background, societal attitudes, and continuing punishment for mistakes or crimes. These problems, and psychological damages, are added to the daily problems of existence.

In no way, however, should it be construed or assumed that all minority group members are undereducated, deprived, poor, alienated. In fact, a large proportion of blacks, Latinos, and immigrants are educated, employed, and among the middle class of the population. Many never think of themselves as having been deprived or disadvantaged, or consider their lives as very different from other middle-class members— except for ethnic discrimination. (Similar discriminatory practices operate against women, youth, elderly, handicapped, and imprisoned.)

Many adults have literacy problems—*how* many is many? Estimates vary with time and circumstances. Different estimates and projections result from different classifications. Education is one indicator, ethnic background another. Figures for literacy are misleading because it appears that they overestimate the number of persons functionally literate.

By the most conservative estimates, 21 million Americans cannot read or write. The oldest group, who are sixty-five years of age and over, makes up 45 percent of this population. This proportion will increase as more younger persons are educated. Partial literacy exists among a large part of the population. One out of seven Americans is functionally illiterate which means that thousands are unable to read and comprehend help-wanted advertisements, job applications, credit forms, leases, and driver tests. In 1963 Laubach estimated that 8.3

million people, twenty-five years of age and over, had less than a fifth grade education. Over 57 million adults have less than a high school education. Within the minority groups and immigrant populations, many have literacy and language problems, and are disadvantaged because of poverty and lack of the skills needed to function in a highly technological society. Language barriers and distrust separate the English-speaking population from those who use English as a second language. Native peoples and Appalachian residents are separated by distance and environment, as well as by culture and distrust.

This human dilemma of the adult, to understand language, is illustrated graphically by Peter Hutchinson, an artist who welcomes rather than rejects a story element in art, either visual or verbal. In his "Alphabet" series, Hutchinson irreverently mixes objects, photographs, and stories. The stories provide a lot of reading and make the photographs more meaningful. In the story "Struggling with Language"—under a silver *S* and a color photograph that shows Hutchinson stripped to the waist, doing battle with three-dimensional letters that are coiled about him in a sunlit field—he confesses about his lifelong problems with language.[13] Who has not encountered, if not lifelong problems, at least recurring problems?

WHY READ?

Has the electronic media supplanted print medium? Are readers of today the illiterates of tomorrow? New technology brings change, whether it is mass paperback production or cable television. The dimensions and validity of the debate on electronic media versus print medium are not questions for discussion here.

Certain assumptions are made in relation to written or printed communications. Reading is an essential and dynamic means of communication. It is important to awareness, knowledge, and information. Print materials are transferred into other media—audio, phonodisc, tape, and film. Print is a mass communication medium, particularly in formats of paperbacks or softcovers, newspapers, comic books, and magazines. Reading increasingly is integrated with seeing, listening, and even feeling channels of communication. It is a major means of learning in the educational process, and is vital to learning. As changes in education have occurred, less and less emphasis is placed on textbooks and lectures. The formal and informal adult education programs use various and more diverse reading materials and coordinated audiovisual resources.

[13]James Collins, "Story Art," *New York*, Oct. 28, 1974, p. 101–2.

Yet literacy, that is, the ability to read and comprehend what is read, becomes necessary to survival in a society dependent on literary skills and comprehension. From the simplest aspects of daily needs to the most complex subject matter, reading is required. To survive on city streets, or rural highways, adults must be able to read street signs, directions, and maps. To acquire knowledge and skill for vocational and professional work, reading is a major ingredient.

Purposes for reading may be defined as motivation which causes a person to read. Frequently purposes may mean the results or effects of reading, that is, social effects for security or information. Purposes may be stated in relation to the objectives of readings, such as problem solving, recreation, and pleasure. Three types of problem-solving areas are: the immediate environment, in relation to a job or household task; a large group, in relation to the civil rights or welfare of the group; and the moral, ethical level. Five kinds of recreational reading may be identified: enjoyment or habit reading (the addictive); enjoyment through escape (emotional release); enjoyment in contact with the familiar (reinforcement of attitudes); enjoyment through critical and intellectual appreciation; and aesthetic.

Ten major purposes have been identified by Gray and Rogers' research (which omits reading that is habit, killing time, and from a sense of duty):

1. Know and understand current happenings
2. Gain immediate personal satisfaction or value
3. Meet practical demands of daily living
4. Further a vocational interest
5. Carry on and promote professional or vocational interests
6. Meet personal-social demands
7. Meet socio-civic needs and demands
8. Obtain self-improvement and extend cultural background
9. Satisfy intellectual and aesthetic needs and interests
10. Satisfy spiritual needs.[14]

The effects of reading are various. Empirical studies and subjective testimony show evidence that reading has effects on persons of all ages. *What* the effects are and the *degree* of impact are not so clear. In the early 1940 study, *What Reading Does to People*, Waples, Berelson, and Bradshaw identified five effects or causes:

1. Instrumental—that is, gaining greater competence in solving practical problems and discovering information for a definite purpose
2. Prestige—relieving feelings of inferiority and increasing self-respect

[14]Gray and Rogers, *Maturity in Reading*, p. 92–93.

3. Reinforcement—strengthening one's attitudes and beliefs or developing new related attitudes
4. Aesthetic—appreciation and satisfaction, escape and relaxation from tension
5. Respite—escape from anxiety, respond to art, literature.[15]

In a first study, *What People Want to Read About,* Waples and Tyler reported that "reading motives may be ranged from 'reading to learn' to 'reading to forget.' "[16] Between these two extremes, many motives exist. Waples and Tyler attempted to find what subjects adults would like to read when they are grouped together by ways in which they are alike: sex, amount of schooling, type of occupation. For individuals, it should be pointed out, reading interests are what people would like to read and not actual reading (they may or may not be the same). The facts indicate certain tendencies among readers. All groups of adults express genuine interest in reading about significant matters. People like to read about themselves. Groups that are alike have similar reading interests.

The major conclusions from the Library Materials Research Project study and two related studies have been that the recognition and evaluation of values and attitudes through the analysis of content are essential to the selection of materials and to informed reading guidance. Cultural factors are strong determinants of the cognitive and affective learning responses among adult readers of ethnic groups. Six reader groups were clearly identified in the population being served or to be served by libraries. Consequently, the librarian's awareness and knowledge of beliefs, attitudes, and values among various cultures, and portrayed in the content of reading materials, appear to be a vital part of evaluation.

Personal ideas, beliefs, and values greatly influence what is read. When the reader's attitudes and experiences are supported and confirmed, the author's appeal to the reader increases. Readers find pleasure in rereading "old friends" and in moving from one title to another of the author whom they like. The ideas and opinions of such an author are stimulating. The "conversation" between writer and reader extends horizons and offers escape from problems and sorrows of life. The natural curiosity and desire to learn about the unknown, the sense of adventure that human beings have, exert an influence of particular importance. Adult new readers, responding to questions in Library Materials Research Project interviews, demonstrated keen interest in lives of other

[15]Douglas Waples, Bernard Berelson, and Franklyn R. Bradshaw, *What Reading Does to People* (Chicago: Univ. of Chicago Pr., 1940), p. 9.
[16]Douglas Waples and Ralph W. Tyler, *What People Want to Read About* (Chicago: American Library Assn. and Univ. of Chicago Pr., 1931), p. 4.

persons, in poetry, in news and current events. A wide range of titles and authors was read: Baldwin, Bennett, Hemingway, Malcolm X, Parks, Shakespeare, Spillane, Steinbeck, Susann, Wright. Black literature and best sellers were popular. Magazine stories about lives of other people, adventure, crime and mystery, travel, love, sports, war, and space and science fiction were popular.

The uses of books, as classified by Ennis, serve as guidelines to librarians and are obviously not too unlike previous researchers' conclusions. Readers use books to

1. Escape
2. Gain information in a pragmatic instrumental way
3. Search for cognitive order, that is, an intelligent informed guidance, clear standards, and knowledge of proper values
4. Search for personal meaning, that is, "a map to the moral landscape"
5. Save face or celebrate beliefs or support in a personal crisis
6. Learn for one's job or community position, through vocational and professional as well as leisure time reading where the line between work and play blurs
7. Keep up with the book talk of friends and neighbors that exists in social contacts and pleasures.[17]

Regardless of the importance of these uses and values, a minority of adults pursue them. The barriers and obstacles are many. Obviously, the difficulties in acquiring sufficient reading skill which can permit pleasurable, efficient use of that skill are a foremost consideration. Tasks and responsibilities of adults during the life cycle, which has different patterns for different persons, interfere with or accelerate use of information and content found in the medium of print. Examples of such periods in life are school, family responsibilities, earning a living, job situation, age. Pressures of daily living are great, both from the environment of urban life and from demands and actions of others. Pressures of job and school compete for time and energy. The attitudes toward reading for immediate reward, for delayed reward, and for pleasure exert strong influences. Availability of the right kind of material is an influential factor. Accessibility of the right information, together with the appealing author, determines use. An atmosphere conducive to reading, both in physical and human environment, makes a great difference. When family and friends have the same interests, when space and time (as well as peace and quiet) are available, and when reading materials are easily accessible, the adult reader's use increases. Television

[17] Philip H. Ennis, *Adult Reading in the United States*, Report no. 105 (Chicago: National Opinion Research Center, Univ. of Chicago, 1965), p. 24–26.

and radio, sports and motion pictures, all offer competition to the book. At the same time, they frequently stimulate desire for further information and understanding.

Adult new readers, interviewed during the Library Materials Research Project, reported use of reading materials for school and job, as well as for pleasure reading, as a help in understanding oneself and others, to relax, to sharpen vocabulary and spelling, and to read street signs. Reasons for reading generally included helping educate oneself, for enjoyment, to help with school work, to learn to do something, and (less frequently) for employment. The readers perceived other benefits from reading, such as a better job, self-confidence, ability to communicate better with others. Readers viewed learning as something that gives them confidence and more personal and social security. They read for self-improvement, for advancement on a job or career, and in preparation for new jobs and work.

Nevertheless, the motivations and rewards in other areas are not to be underestimated. The reader, introduced to men and women who speak out of similar life experiences, who relate events from the history and culture of the ethnic group, and who describe life styles that are known, is more than likely to be "hooked." Fader demonstrates how this can happen in his accounts of young men in the Michigan correctional institution and younger children in the Washington, D.C., school. Lyman identifies the individual appeal of cultural content which supports personal and social security, whether portrayed in Malcolm X's autobiography or the current best seller. Strang's conclusion (in 1942) that "a central core or radix" determines the person's reading appears to contradict the conclusions of Ennis and Lyman, who found the infinite variety of interests and needs is almost as great as the variety of books. Reading patterns reflect a wide range of life interests. At the same time, many adults perceive a core and pattern over the years.

Reading with a purpose (the old slogan in the library adult education series) is as vital an idea as when it was conceived in the 1930s. Equally important is reading for fun—that pleasurable, stimulating, eminently private, personal, intimate, and challenging experience between reader and author. It is the reader who benefits.

Reading habits and preferences vary considerably. Most adults give considerable time to talking, listening, and televiewing. In 1969 in San Diego, four hundred adults, who were selected randomly, reported on the time they spent daily in various communication activities. Among various occupational groups, it was found that retired people, students, and engineers logged the highest reading time. Among the various groups, 50 percent logged reading as their lowest communication activity, while only engineers ranked reading highest.[18] The time that is spent in reading throughout an adult's daily life is rarely considered. Percentages of time engaged in reading rise perceptibly, and often surprisingly to the individual, when logs are kept of every reading activity, such as cereal boxes, recipes, signposts, street signs, store guides, travel schedules, billboards, bulletins, floor numbers, driver's tests, school work, and job-related reading.

A consistency in adults' perceptions and expectations appears to exist, whether in basic or advanced training in reading. Among 479 respondents in the Library Materials Research Project investigation, 78 percent had less than twelve years of schooling, 21 percent had twelve years or more. Nearly 49 percent read for both information and pleasure, 18 percent for pleasure, and 31 percent for information. The main reasons or purposes for reading were education, enjoyment, help with school work, learning to do something, and employment.

Dulin and Otto assessed the attitudes and expectations of sixty-four adults enrolled in advanced training in reading. Half the respondents had more than twelve years of schooling, and a fourth had graduate degrees. Their reasons for wanting to improve their reading skills were to enjoy leisure reading, 46.9 percent; to perform their jobs better, 32.8 percent; to meet the needs of future schooling, 29.7 percent; and to keep pace with associates, 17.2 percent. The primary goal of two-thirds of the class was to increase reading rates. They also were able to evaluate their skills as heavy, moderate, or poorly skilled readers.[19]

Why people read what they do is influenced by what Schramm suggests as expectation of reward in relation to the effort required. In his terms, expectation of reward is a broader way of saying motivation. Effort required is a broader way of talking about availability. Availability is dependent, to a large extent, on the reader's skill in reading—the length of a book, vocabulary, complexity, time considerations, space, and other environmental factors, such as travel distances, bookstores, economic considerations of cost, and the individual's nature and characteristics. If motivation is strong enough, these obstacles will be overcome. Generally one reads what is most easily accessible, easiest to

[18]Larry A. Samovar, Robert D. Brooks, and Richard E. Porter, "A Survey of Adult Communication Activities," *Journal of Communication*, 19:301–7 (Dec. 1969).

[19]Kenneth L. Dulin and Wayne Otto, "Backgrounds, Felt Educational Needs, and Expectations of Adults Seeking Advanced Training in Reading," in G. B. Schick and M. M. May, eds., *Reading: Process and Pedagogy* v. 1 (19th yearbook of the National Reading Conference, 1970; Milwaukee: National Reading Conference, Inc., 1971), p. 116–21.

read, and requires the least effort, and offers some reward, either immediate or delayed.[20]

Schramm's typology of reading motivations is arranged from the most immediate to the most delayed rewards. They offer a broad framework which permits more specific identification of motivations. Assuredly, no one motivation is apt to appear alone; motivations seldom occur separately. Schramm observes—rightly—that "a grouping of motives, usually with one motive dominating the combination, lies behind almost every act of reading."[21] The catalogue is placed on a continuum.

1. Compulsive ritualistic reading—reading that is habitual like reading the newspaper every morning, the cereal box label, the billboards, and posters. Almost unconscious and easily forgotten
2. Reading for respite—reading as a tool for relaxing, for escape, for submerging problems, to gain refreshment. The student reading light novels or comics, the librarian reading mystery novels
3. Reading for a sense of personal security—reading for identification with characters, either in biography, fiction, or news—vicarious pleasure in life of others, bolsters ego, gains confidence, self-identity
4. Reading for a sense of social security in a changing world—reading for reinforcement of attitudes and values and for information about major social problems—survival in economic, political, environmental, social climate of destruction
5. Reading for vicarious experience—reading to travel in unknown and strange countries, for adventure
6. Reading for social contact—reading which replaces mediated contact, and gives vicarious experience with personalities, political figures, sports. To find out roles one must take in stages of adulthood
7. Reading for aesthetic experience—reading at various levels, from escape, vicarious pleasure, to understanding and heightened appreciation of arts, literature, science
8. Reading as a value in society—for prestige value that society puts on reading, for intellectual aura. (Reading as a value gains wider natural acceptance than formerly. Has less prestige, possibly because of pervasive media of television and film, to lesser extent radio)
9. Reading as a tool of daily living—reading for life skills or coping skills information such as legal information, consumer buying, job information
10. Reading as a tool of self-improvement—to learn how to do it, how to advance or get better job, how to live with family and neighbors
11. Reading as a device for scanning the horizon—news reading to know what is happening, what may happen, events
12. Reading for interpretation—reading as an aid to understanding

[20]Schramm, "Why Adults Read," p. 57–88.
[21]Ibid., p. 81.

points of view on social, economic, and political issues and problems.[22]

To Schramm's twelve points might be added:

13. Reading for sheer delight and pleasure, combined with gaining new insights and ideas and rereading favorite literary authors, philosophers
14. Reading for the sake of reading—for itself. Reading need not always be for the sake of something else—it is closely allied to reading for delight
15. Reading to satisfy curiosity—reading to explore the environment
16. Reading for sake of learning for its own sake—reading in problem solving, intellectual challenge, to think, for stimulation outside everyday happenings—adventure, danger, mystery, occult, space, science fiction.

Reading for excitement and adventure may overlap with reading for interpretation. Reading for learning may combine reading for self-improvement, and personal and social security. Rarely are several motives not combined. Motivations or intentions vary at different stages in the life cycle and with different adult roles.

THE LIBRARY AND THE ADULT READER

Why is the library concerned, or why does it seek involvement? Obviously the public library has a legal responsibility to serve, with all the communication resources at its disposal, the residents of its community. The adults who live in that community—and frequently beyond the geographic or legal boundaries in a designated, extended area—have a right to service.

The library has a wealth of educational and recreational resources in reading and audiovisual materials for adult men and women. Its goals, to assist and participate in the lives of adults and the life of the community, can be achieved only when adults find satisfaction and pleasure in the use of those library resources.

Libraries have a major responsibility to help adults acquire literacy skills, become independent and mature readers.

Librarians have knowledge and skills which serve adults in selection and guidance in the use of the communication resources—which interpret those materials, which instruct people in the use of the library and specific resource guides and aids, which promote and stimulate use of resources. They provide, through library service and programs, oppor-

[22]Ibid., p. 80–81.

tunities for intellectual development, reading development, pleasurable learning, and recreational experiences.

All of this means, in the final analysis, that librarians must identify the interests and needs of adults and adult groups, evaluate and find suitable materials for use by adults, cooperate with other agencies and organizations, and respect the rights of adults to the service and to a part in making decisions about the nature of the service. Libraries have a responsibility to help adults become functionally literate, acquire the reading habit, feel at ease with all communication resources (not merely print), and integrate information and ideas (transmitted through the various communication channels) into their life tasks and adult roles.

The types of materials and the range of subjects will include the various print formats: book (hardcover and paperback), booklet, broadside, leaflet, magazine, map, newspaper, pamphlet, poster, reader, textbook, and workbook; and various types of literature, autobiography and biography; personal essay and essay of information; folklore; historical and scientific accounts; how-to-do-it materials; humor; novel, play, poetry, and short story; political, social, and religious tracts; travel; and reference and anthologies.

The objectives of the reader and the library will mesh. The common interrelationships will be identified. An active library program will become an integral and meaningful part of the life of the adult and the community. The resources of the library will be intelligible to the adult at whatever reading level he or she requires. The content of those resources will relate directly to his or her informational and life-cycle needs and interests. The staff will know, and in their selection of resources, take into account the beliefs, attitudes, and life styles of various groups in the community.

Libraries should have a dynamic part in helping communicators and receivers of communications attain mutual understanding and respect.

4

Beliefs, Attitudes, and Values
Affecting Readers

IMPORTANCE OF THESE CULTURAL FACTORS

Beliefs, attitudes, and values that affect readers raise complex matters in the evaluation of reading materials for adults. Although librarians have taken such factors into account either consciously or unconsciously, almost no concrete information is found in the literature. Librarians concerned with materials for children and youth have looked more carefully at the beliefs and attitudes expressed by authors. Recently more careful analyses of textbooks and other material in relation to ethnic reader groups has pointed out limitations and inaccuracies of content and prejudiced, derogatory attitudes of the sources. On the whole, it is necessary to go to the anthropologists, psychologists, and social scientists for pertinent information.

On the basis of findings in the Library Materials Research Project, Lyman concluded that the recognition and identification of values and attitudes, as indicated in the analysis of the content, are essential to the selection of materials and to informed reader guidance. In related studies Deligdisch[1] and Sherrill[2] found that cultural factors are strong determi-

---

[1] Yekutiel Deligdisch, "The Reading Comprehension of Adult New Readers in Relation to their Ethnic Background" (Ph.D. dissertation, Univ. of Wisconsin–Madison, 1972).

[2] Laurence L. Sherrill, "The Affective Response of Ethnic Minority Readers to Indigenous Ghetto Literature: A Measurement" (Ph.D. dissertation, Univ. of Wisconsin–Madison, 1972).

nants of the cognitive and affective reading response of adult readers among blacks, Mexican Americans, and Puerto Ricans.

The emphasis on the identification and classification of beliefs and values presented in the reading material is a result of the findings in the Library Materials Research Project study. The beliefs and attitudes communicated in the reading material may be more influential or important, in the reader's view, than format, type and style of writing, authority, legibility, readability, or even the subject itself. For the reader group being described, positive, honest, recognizable roles and life styles stimulate and maintain interest. Prejudiced, dishonest, derogatory, and discriminative opinions repel. The latter type of material misleads and reinforces stereotypes for any reader.

The identification and classification of beliefs and values are one of the most complex aspects of materials analysis and critical evaluation. Although in many instances the feelings and values are obvious, frequently they are implicit, obscure, unobserved, or subtly concealed. Identification and classification require knowledge and understanding of variations and different value systems within society, as well as professional objectivity.

The many definitions and theories, disagreements, and opinions which surround the subject of values would seem to stop consideration by other than experts—or one can be accused of rushing in where angels fear to tread. In defense, it must be said that the seriousness of the problem and the conviction that the consideration of beliefs and values is a sensible approach to the evaluation of materials support this tentative exploration. Library science must go to anthropology, sociology, and psychology to clarify the scientific and philosophical issues. Comparative research in verbal behavior, linguistics, semantics, and content analysis, as well as the other social sciences, would develop new directions and guides. Perhaps the matter can be defined further.

A value system represents what is expected or hoped for, required, or forbidden. It is a system of criteria by which conduct is judged and sanctions are applied. It is not conduct itself. Value premises may be defined in various ways—as desirable or undesirable, prescribed or prohibited, approved or disapproved, encouraged or rejected, valued or disvalued.

Beliefs and values are learned at home, at school, in religious faiths, in written tradition, in the mass media, and in society at large. The mass media are one of the institutions, the one for social communication, that meet certain social needs. Through this pattern of communication, human beings create a symbolic environment that in many ways influences what is thought and done. Such an environment is a major force which influences attitudes and actions. The media are carriers of beliefs and values; they perpetuate and reflect the social, economic, and political forces in society. As a part of society, they have similar characteristics—mass production, mass distribution, mass promotion, standardization, and technological progress. In many ways (in programs of entertainment, enlightenment, and advertising) they reflect the values and beliefs, opinions, and tastes of the majority. The media transmit and reflect both virtues and prejudices.

At the same time, mass media are a force for change. They affect the behavior and influence the attitudes held by individuals and groups. Media themselves are changing. A new sense of social responsibility on the part of publishers and broadcasters is emerging. For that matter, librarians demonstrate this same awareness. Libraries, as part of the communication and educational systems of this country, see that transmission of a culture and philosophy of intellectual freedom may not be wholly objective and open to all. A new sense of social responsibility in relation to communication resources, technological developments, and multiethnic cultures is apparent.

Verbal and visual communications continue to be a major means of learning. Books and other print materials are made up of words, phrases, illustrations, and pictures that continue to be a powerful force in transmitting and helping to formulate everyone's ideas and beliefs. Reading continues to be a most effective way of transmitting information, directions, and individual control.

A major belief or faith is that which is described as the American dream. Achievement of this dream and the democratic ethic, which supports it, undergoes a continuous process of change. During the last decades the melting-pot concept has given place to an intense consciousness of the needs and interests of both a multicultural, pluralistic society within the United States and a global society of the world. Insistent demands by ethnic groups, nationalities, women, homosexuals, and other oppressed groups have forced a rethinking of the contributions, responsibilities, and rights of such groups.

(It should be noted that *ethnic* is defined, in this discussion, as pertaining to a group of people who have a common and distinctive origin, background, and cultural tradition. It refers to racial and national groups who may have a common life style, experience, language, or other distinctive patterns of life. The ethnocentric concept that fosters belief in the inherent *superiority* of one's group and culture, accompanied by contempt for other groups and cultures, is rejected. Diversity and distinctive patterns of life are looked upon as advantages and contributions to be respected and fostered if they are neither destructive nor purposeless.)

Insistent demands by ethnic groups and women have forced a rethinking of the ethnic and sexist contributions of all groups. Recognition of a wide range of variations which are respected and respectable among these groups has led to new action. Recognition of unfair, distorted, stereotyped images, projected in the medium of print, and of subtle influences, exerted either consciously or unconsciously by authors, organized groups, illustrators, and publishers, has occurred. The development and application of new criteria for analysis of reading materials have resulted.

Ethnic groups, members of these groups, teachers, parents, librarians, and publishers have a new awareness of what constitutes a positive image and its opposite (a derogatory, racist, or sexist image) as projected in books. The search has been for material that presents individuals and groups fairly, honestly, and realistically. Criteria for judging content result in the identification of stereotypes, of unfair representation of ethnic groups or individuals, romanticized ghetto life, distorted history, the sexist stereotype, and didactic and moral hypocrisy. On the positive side, many formerly unrecognized authors and works are identified and become useful in active programs. Surely only such material need be recommended and selected for use in service activities.

Many popular books, such as *Dr. Doolittle, Mary Poppins*, and *Laughing Boy*, are recognized as perpetuating disrespect and false attitudes. A survey of six hundred new children's books about native Americans rejected four hundred as conspicuously offensive. Illustrations frequently confuse the dress and symbolic features of native American tribal customs. Similarly, the features and color of blacks are unrealistic or exaggerated in many books.

On the positive side also is emphasis on literature that promotes pride and respect, truthfully depicts the heritages and cultures of ethnic groups, and identifies and creates materials that show achievements and contributions of a group rather than failures and problems. Publishers' councils, committees within the library and teaching professions, citizens' groups, and bibliographies with critical annotations help to develop criteria for evaluation of this aspect of communication.

Of major importance are writings and publications of ethnic-group authors, illustrators, and publishing houses. The indigenous literature that is made available in this way is valuable in education, reading improvement, and the self-directed reading of adult readers. Such literature stimulates interest, motivates learning, and has powerful identity appeal.

In the Indigenous Literature Study, which was a part of the Library Materials Research Project, this special literature was examined. Indigenous literature is simply the creative product of special individuals and groups—in this instance the literature of particular ethnic or minority groups. It originates in, and characterizes, a particular group or member of the group. It bears organic relationship to the culture from which it comes. The author's origin is in the group. The content focuses on and speaks directly to the group. It carries special appeal, and its primary audience is the group. The close connection between the material and the environmental influence is clear. The authority of the source and the reliability of the publisher are part of this characteristic.

Generally, indigenous publications are found outside the regular trade and commercial channels. Some ethnic publishers are becoming well known and have fairly extensive lists, such as the Broadside Press in Detroit. Some publications, however, reach best-seller status through the usual channels, such as the *Autobiography of Malcolm X, Soul on Ice, From the Ashes, The Learning Tree,* and *House of Dawn.* Some of the local, lesser-known literature gradually reaches broader attention. The poem "I Am Joaquin" gradually gained such recognition, along with the film.

The content of indigenous literature is crucial. The major part of the content, or the theme of the work, has its origins in the group and is reflective of the individual and group experience, regardless of the mode of treatment. Autobiography, biography, poetry, and essays are major sources. The communication has direct connection to experience, life style, values, and beliefs, both for the communicator and for the receiver of the message. To the reader outside the group, the appeal may be not only because of the subject and content but also because of the obvious reality and authenticity of the tone. The ethnic component, while local or limited in origin and with ethnic appeal, attains a universal quality. The desire for identification, knowledge about the lives of others, and curiosity and interest in what is new and different may be strong factors in the appeal of the indigenous literature.

Several assumptions are made in this discussion. A complex value system exists within the culture, and, at the same time, variations and different values and beliefs permeate the culture. The basic data about cultural values may be found in verbal behavior. Verbal statements indicate value judgments, goals, approval and disapproval, respect and contempt, praise or blame. Consistent use of words, phrases, and ideas may be traced in printed literature. This completely verbal medium lends itself to analysis. It is supplemented by visual aids such as illustrations.

It is assumed, also, that quantitative and qualitative analyses reveal values, attitudes, and opinions.

Librarians who are responsible for selection and interpretation of materials and for the investment of public monies are in a position to use criteria for analysis of reading materials most effectively. The complexity of the problem, however, may intimidate and discourage the librarian who would assume this responsibility. To carry out a systematic, continuing evaluation of resources in developing reading collections requires the sanction and belief in the value of the activity. It is not an area of evaluation to omit because of ignorance, insensitivity, lack of knowledge, or evasion. (Unfamiliar and different meanings create semantic problems for communicator and receiver.) Neither should this evaluation result in censorship that arbitrarily rejects material without consideration of the complete work, its place in history, and its overall strengths and weaknesses.

Inherent in and irrevocably tied to the evaluation of any reading material, in whatever form and for whatever purpose, is the question of value judgment and ideological issues. The attitudes, beliefs, and values held by readers and writers, by the community as a whole, and by specific groups within the community are potent forces in the lives of individuals and in society. The importance of these cultural factors is ultimately demonstrated in the readers' responses to and uses of the material and library service.

Identification by the librarian of the attitudes, beliefs, and values held in these interrelated areas is essential to the dynamics of adult reading service. It is necessary to know the dominant beliefs, values, and attitudes:

1. Those held in a community as well as those in a mosaic of communities to be served by the library
2. Those held by a library staff as a whole and by a staff directly engaged in serving adults
3. Those held by individual clientele and by the organizations and groups of which they are members
4. Beliefs and attitudes of other educational and community agencies —church, government, hospital, welfare, school
5. Those beliefs, attitudes, and values treated in the reading materials and authors' points of view if they are indicated.

Several other assumptions are made in the context of this general theme. Every existing culture—the way of life followed by a people— is a valid human creation, entitled to recognition and respect. Librarians would join anthropologists in this conviction. Materials collected and organized in libraries contain the expression of human culture. These expressions may reflect or influence human knowledge, feeling, thought, and human effort. Directly and indirectly, they influence the beliefs, attitudes, and values held by individuals. The selection and subsequent use of these materials carry the implications of value judgments and ideological issues. Finally, the tendency to stereotype individuals and groups is thwarted by the process of understanding as well as by understanding itself.

Librarians, as describers and analyzers of these expressions of culture and its society, distinguish the characteristics and nature of the materials, that is, communications or messages in relation to cultural patterns and to those patterns and conditions of the particular segment of society that is represented. In analyzing the content of reading materials the librarian will use extreme caution in making judgments about the superiority or inferiority of any cultural system in comparison with others; be hesitant to ascribe cultural values because they are seen easily on the surface or are deduced from a reading; judge hastily on the word of a critic or reviewer; and refrain from comparisons with a way of life other than one's own culture and the standards it represents and reflects in terms of its own external logic. Concomitant with such behavior will be the definition of criteria that incorporate these aspects with the well-established criteria of demand, quality, and literary values.

The criteria for analysis will gain dimension and be enhanced by the broader view, this wider scope, the more diverse standards that are admitted as valuable in the development of any library collection. The tendency to reject the strange, different, unfamiliar, controversial, distrusting, repulsive, and unorthodox is overcome by the process of analysis.

Such philosophy and assumptions, combined with a humane concept of human beings, indicate an urgent necessity for knowing and understanding the cultural system and human conditions of various groups that the library serves and that make up society as a whole. What are the values and attitudes of readers or potential readers? What are their ideals, aims, ethical and aesthetic standards? What are their attitudes toward books and reading? What cultural patterns indicate attitudes, beliefs, style of living? Librarians need such information about potential readers, as well as external social characteristics about sex, age, education, occupation, income, and living conditions which are statistically available through the census or a community study. They also need to know and understand the internal, less visible life and culture of the individual in various adult roles.

Corollary with this knowledge, the librarian needs to have knowledge of expressions from an adult's own culture and self and published writings by representatives from and observers of the adult's beliefs and values, interests and needs, problems and confusions, loves and hates— life experiences. The popularity of the autobiographies, biographic novels, and poetry of black writers such as Nikki Giovanni, Sonia Sanchez, Maya Angelou, Malcolm X, and Don Lee among both black and white readers provides evidence of this corollary.

In spite of and because of the variety of conflicting and contradictory descriptions and interpretations of the human condition, concepts of "human being," and descriptions of minority groups, librarians learn a great deal from psychological, sociological, and anthropological studies about American culture, poverty, minority group cultures, literacy, and library service to the disadvantaged. The values, beliefs, and attitudes found in these cultures are as fascinating as they are instructive. Librarians can interpret this knowledge in relation to library service.

What are the meanings of these terms: *attitudes, beliefs, values*? Some common agreement is necessary to understand more fully the reasons for emphasizing these factors in relation to judgments and interpretations about written and published materials for adult readers. Beliefs and attitudes have their foundations in four human activities: thinking, feeling, behaving, and interacting with others. The psychological foundations of beliefs and attitudes are cognitive, emotional, behavioral, and social.[3]

Attitude is defined, according to *Webster's Third New International Dictionary*, as behavior representative of feeling or conviction, a disposition that is primarily grounded in affect and emotion and is expressive of opinions rather than belief. It may also be defined as the degree to which a person is for or against a person, group, object, situation, or value; that is, will the person react positively or negatively? It describes the prevailing tendency or inclination to react to life around one. Attitudes are likes and dislikes. They are rooted in emotions and social influences. They may have cognitive foundations, and they are influenced by beliefs.

Belief and *opinion* describe a more or less formulated idea or judgment which one holds as true. *Belief* means a state or habit of mind in which trust, confidence, or reliance is placed in some person or thing. It signifies mental acceptance of or assent to something offered as true, with or without certainty. *Opinion* implies a conclusion concerning something on which ideas may differ—not, however, excluding a careful consideration, weighing of evidence, or pros and cons, and usually

[3]Daryl J. Bem, *Beliefs, Attitudes, and Human Affairs*, Basic Concepts in Psychology Series (Belmont, Calif.: Brooks/Cole Publishing Co., 1970).

stressing the subjectivity and disputability of the conclusion. Emotional factors are involved. (In this respect the judgment or appraisal about adult reading is mentally acceptable because of evidence and is considered "true" to a greater degree than "not true," in spite of uncertainty. Nor should these beliefs be extended and thought to be universally true, and thus stereotype all adults and reading.)

A *belief* is held when one perceives a relationship between two things or between a thing and a characteristic of it. Beliefs relate to the choices and decisions made in a profession regarding behavior, practice, and service. Beliefs are products of direct experience, as seen and heard through one's own senses—and also are based on the authority of others, who may provide the basis for beliefs or strengthen one's belief.

The high-order belief is highly elaborated on differentiations based on a chain of syllogistic reasoning. Major factors contributing to a cognitive belief system rest on a differentiated vertical structure of beliefs, a broadly based horizontal structure, and, in their underlying importance to other beliefs, maintain a coherent system which is internally consistent. The belief system may be consistent without being logical or rational. Faulty logic, faulty premises, and inconsistencies between beliefs and attitudes may distort the system.

Value may be defined as relative worth, utility, or importance—that is, the degree of excellence of something, its status in the scale of preferences. Philosophical and social psychological theories are not and cannot be handled competently here. Whether all values are only relative to a given culture—are derived from the culture or known from past memories—or are absolute are philosophical and scientific matters of importance, not to be discussed in this context. A value is a "primitive" preference for or a positive attitude toward a certain end. One also attributes value to a thing. Certain end states of existence, such as equality, freedom, good, beautiful, desirable, are valued. (Librarians value intellectual freedom, freedom to read; they strive to create a climate of freedom of choice.) Values may also derive from external authority. Attitudes, beliefs, and opinions may result from values and in turn influence the value system.

Values that are central to one's belief system underlie one's professional acts. The values held by men and women in the community, by all involved in providing and interpreting reading materials' content, and embedded in the content of communication are critical elements in the dynamics of adult reading. Whether seen dimly or clearly, they are crucial considerations in the evaluation of reading materials. The identification and understanding of values, portrayed as worthwhile or not worthwhile, add immeasurably to objective and accurate selection and interpretation of materials. Specifically, in the analysis of library materials, attitudes and values may be defined as the feeling or position found in the material with regard to any norm, object, situation, ideal, or principle in the material analyzed. It may or may not be the author's position or feeling.

Beliefs, attitudes, and values may be created, transmitted, modified, or changed by social influences. The influence may come from the mass media, family, friends, authors, teachers, colleagues, peers, librarians. All may exert strong influences, along with environmental, cultural, and ethnic influences. A consistency usually exists between what is believed to be true and what is thought to be desirable. A centrality of beliefs and consistency in belief systems is customary and can be identified.

Beliefs and prejudices are interrelated. Generalizations are abstractions based on a set of experiences. They provide a thinking device by development of categories. When generalizations are extended beyond a set of experiences on which they are based and thought to be universally true, or are extended on too limited a set of experiences, the stereotype results. The stereotype is based on hearsay, not valid experience, and is a way to rationalize one's prejudices. For example: Poor people are illiterate. Illiterates are ignorant. They cannot understand complex situations; therefore poor people are ignorant. The unschooled are illiterate. The unschooled cannot read. The unschooled cannot use libraries. Four-letter words are pornographic. Dialects are not to be printed in acceptable novels.

Prejudices may reflect the insecurities of a person. They constitute irrational attitudes of hostility, directed against an individual, a group, a race, or their supposed characteristics. The prejudgment results in hurt and harm. Prejudices against all "out groups" or particular groups result in ethnocentric behavior that is inimical to the group excluded (and to the library and librarians). Such prejudices center upon race and exhibit an incapacity for viewing foreign cultures dispassionately. One's own race or social group is regarded as the center of culture.

Librarians are more and more aware of the dangers and unfairness inherent in an ethnocentrism that judges foreign or "different" groups by the standards of one's own culture or ethnic group. A tendency toward viewing alien cultures with disfavor and a resultant sense of inherent superiority can result in emasculated, limited library collections and discriminatory, exclusive, and excluding library services.

Ironical indeed is the definition of discrimination which is most applicable to and popular in modern society. Discrimination, more often than not, means to make a difference in treatment or to favor a class on a categorical basis in disregard of individual merit, rather than to distinguish, differentiate, discern, that is, to perceive differences and peculiar features, objects, ideas, qualities.

Active positive discernment results in judgment and critical evaluation because of differences as well as similarities. The act of discrimination, then, requires the making or perceiving of distinctions and differences —such distinctions leading to affirmative action in recognition of positive virtues.

Librarians broaden their experiences and provide variety in collections through their range of contacts and their knowledge about diverse materials. Librarians, like teachers, have an authoritarian, unequal status with readers. They have a power of censorship as well as selection—for example, in regard to deceptively simple aspects of words. When the words offend the librarian-evaluator, it may be assumed the words offend others; consequently, that material is to be eliminated or rejected. On such foundations of experience generalizations develop and stereotypes occur. These patterns may be broadened by multiplying experiences which are new, and not merely those which reinforce the stereotype. Librarians' decisions in selection of library materials are influenced by the sociological and psychological assumptions they hold.

LEARNERS IN SEARCH OF CULTURALLY RELEVANT MATERIALS

These basic concepts regarding beliefs, attitudes, and values and the effect or lack of effect on development of reading collections and reading services for adults raise many questions.

Do librarians place high value on diversity in society? On differences as well as similarities?

Do librarians select books, pictures, films, recordings that reflect the personal beliefs and values of librarians or the potential users?

Do librarians know the beliefs and values held by others?

Do librarians distinguish language and cultural differences?

Do librarians strive for similarities and common aspects in appeal to users of libraries?

Do librarians recognize the pros and cons in the feelings presented in written and published materials—books, paperbacks, audiovisual materials?

How do librarians feel about suppression and censorship versus freedom to read, to look, and to listen?

How do librarians feel about reading?

What do librarians know about literacy?

The more precisely the librarian can distinguish the foundations, the interrelatedness of beliefs, attitudes, and values and their influences on components evaluated in reading materials, the more accurate can be the evaluative judgments. Faulty logic, distortion, inconsistencies, and faulty conclusions presented in published materials will be identified. More ways will be found to help potential and even hostile users modify their attitudes toward the library and its resources, see the values of ideas and information, and find rewards and satisfactions in the use of resources meaningful to their lives.

The six reports which follow in chapters 5 and 6 reveal the attitudes, beliefs, and values of each reader group and of the speakers representing the groups. They are included because they represent experiences and facts (whether new or old) to librarians and contribute important ideas for change and growth.

Values and attitudes change. The question remains: Can the human being, always involved in an aging process, resist stagnation and recognize and understand change? The behavioral foundations of beliefs and values may be very critical and controversial areas. The idea that, to change behavior, one must first change hearts and minds has become almost a truism. It may very well be more accurate that change in behavior will change hearts and minds (as Bem points out).

The importance of the points of view expressed by each speaker— Rarihokwats, Dudley Randall, Cratis Williams, Elizabeth Martinez Smith, Samuel Betances, and Gladys Alesi—can be known only to the librarian who judges them. It is this writer's belief that their points of view are pertinent to what librarians are doing. Librarians will interpret them in relation to local or individual situations and commitments. Individual points of view reflect what is important to each speaker. They reveal librarians' attitudes as well as those of the reader group.

Jean-Paul Sartre's idea of literature suggests imaginative and practical goals for librarians. "A literary work—that is, the written product of the mind—only exists as such where it is read. Always a writer for a reader and a reader for a writer."[4] This exchange between a writer and a reader through the medium of print—in whatever instrument: book, broadside, pamphlet; whether a literary work or the simplest of factual statements—is a transaction worthy of the public library and the adults it serves. Surely only human values are worthy of human beings.

---

[4]Jean-Paul Sartre, *What Is Literature?* Hazel E. Barnes, tr. (New York: Vintage, 1968).

5

Heritage, Values, Reading Interests: Native Peoples, Blacks, Appalachian Scotch-Irish Mountaineer Readers

The reader-learner's ability to read and to understand what is read is influenced by cultural backgrounds and culturally relevant factors. The individual's environment, educational background, language, personal problems, social relationships, work experience, ethnic heritage, and institutional contacts combine to form attitudes and beliefs. The heritage, beliefs, and values held by the reader and persons influencing the individual's experiences and life style may be more decisive factors in the understanding and use of material (whether in literature of fact or imagination) than such factors as content, readability, or format.

Current situations—personal and public life style—and daily problems, as well as adult education courses, generate the use of reading materials. No one author or source, no single collection of facts, can be all things to all persons. Because one young man struggles through *Manchild in the Promised Land* or *The Scarlet Letter* does not mean others with similar reading skills will do so. The material must pass rigid (although unexpressed) tests of interest and reward that are worth the effort involved.

Individuals and the groups they make up require individual attention in reading guidance and the resource collections selected for them. The

The contents of this chapter were generated under a grant from the U.S. Office of Education, Department of Health, Education, and Welfare, and is therefore in the public domain. However, the opinions expressed do not necessarily represent the position or policy of that Agency and no U.S. Government endorsement should be inferred.

87

persons who speak for the six groups on which this book focuses support the importance of identifying attitudes and values as well as interests and needs within the library community. The facts and ideas put forth in each statement, and in this entire discussion, are presented to librarians to assist them in assessing their community of readers and in evaluating the reading resources of libraries in the context of what beliefs and attitudes, life styles, and daily problems can be identified. Such an evaluation is difficult, frequently "intangible," and not always possible, but it is absolutely necessary.

The following discussion concerns heritages, values, beliefs, and language factors of six major groups: native peoples, blacks, Appalachian Scotch-Irish, Chicanos, Puerto Rican Americans, and persons with English as a second language. As has been shown in every general survey of demographic statistical factors, most communities—urban and rural —have residents who have the right to and need for library services.

The persons who speak for the groups they represent express opinions and facts that are based on experience and research. They have responded to the author's invitation to discuss the beliefs, attitudes, and values of the culture they represent. Each was known to have an interest in and direct contact with the developments of library service to the specific reader group he or she represents. Each contributor has taken into consideration that the information presented will be useful to librarians, teachers, reading specialists, and others who provide reading materials for the adult new reader.

Their statements differ in content, style, and depth. Each has its own unity. Each is provocative, original, and meaningful. Each is separate and different. Each refers to one segment of the United States population. The diversity of views is valuable. The insights have significance for librarians who are working directly with individuals and groups within the particular ethnic groups. Some of the ideas and insights also are applicable in working with other groups. Although each discussion stands alone, together they form an integrated whole.

NATIVE PEOPLES, OR THE AMERICAN INDIAN, READER

Rarihokwats, the speaker, is a member of the Bear clan of the Mohawk Nation at Akwesasne. He is editor of *Akwesasne Notes*, a major international newspaper for native peoples on native affairs, published by the Mohawk Nation at Rooseveltown, New York. As editor and news gatherer, he travels widely, visiting native peoples and tribes in all parts of the United States.

Akwesasne Notes reports events and developments, issues and problems. Prose and poetry intermingle. Drawings and critical reviews of books, poetry, films, and attitudes and values of all concerned, are set forth in aggressive, positive fashion.

Akwesasne Notes is assembled at Akwesasne (also known as the St. Regis Mohawk Reserve) by White Roots of Peace, an Indian communications unit. It covers varied aspects of contemporary Indian affairs: news events, poetry, critical reviews of books, records, and other publications.

Rarihokwats reviews the harm done to native peoples by white "invaders" and the ways in which educators should approach native people. *Native people* is the term he prefers, not the traditional terms: Indians ("the catch-all phrase"), American Indians, or native Americans. The more accurate description, native peoples, is used because the people are native to the country. He perceives an ambivalence and split that are difficult to bridge, however good the intention. He comments as much upon librarians' and educators' values and attitudes as upon the native peoples'. He describes an almost insuperable barrier, built by the white self-image of superiority, but goes on to suggest some realistic ways to remove that barrier.

It is not an easy task [Rarihokwats says] for librarians and educators to serve native communities. The cultural and cross-cultural obstacles are enough to cause all but the most dedicated to give up in frustration and disgust—and yet there is a vital need for information in native communities which is almost totally unmet. However, many professionals interpret these difficulties as a challenge, and dig in with great vigor to apply their skills. The purpose of this brief essay is to caution against this, and to demand a close examination about the meaning of "reading" and "education" and "knowledge."

One problem which most professional people working in native communities must face—and it doesn't matter if they are native people themselves or from Euro/American backgrounds—is that they have been raised with the implicit and unconscious arrogance that European white peoples have. That arrogance might have been more evident in the days of colonizing and when imperial majesties reigned supreme, but the same roots continue to flower and poison even today in ways less obvious but equally as deadly. While most educators consider themselves to be liberal in their views, and liberated from the constraints of their culture, this does not necessarily provide the world view and social skills to survive in a native culture. Thus many educators who come to

KVCC

KALAMAZOO VALLEY
COMMUNITY COLLEGE
LIBRARY

"work with the Indians" have a double arrogance which native people must bear with quiet discomfort.

Educators must purify themselves of the notion that they know what is best for native peoples. They must unload the jargon of "learning to beat the white man at his own game" or "learning the skills to survive in the modern world," which justifies their imposing their life styles on their students in the best of well-meant intentions. Educators must be comfortable with accepting the advice of people much less educated than themselves (in Western ways), and even aid people to obtain information and skills which seem totally contrary to all reason and sense. There must be a total faith that native people—given access to all available information and the freedom to act—will choose ways which are best for them. Anything less will be one more colonial personage carrying out tasks and roles which have been historically disastrous. Even if their students act out the usual Indian/white inferior/superior scripts (as is generally expected of them), teachers should respectfully decline the opportunity to play the wise and all-powerful paternal god-figure.

There is a great diversity of attitude among the many native peoples. Historically, the many native nations were categorized in the catch-all title of "Indians," and even today there is the expectation that "Indians" will become united. "If the Indians would just get together and make up their minds, we would go along with that," administrators tell the native people across the nation. But because of the divisive forces of educators, missionaries, government agents, and others, there is in every community widespread factionalism and diversity of life style. Some families have become totally assimilated into mainstream America, and will pursue reading styles of that middle-class group. Other families have either maintained, or are seeking, the ways of their people, and will want information on that life style—herbal remedies, tribal history, or even political theory—so that they can change the situation in which they find themselves. Many other families are in that nether land where they are not accepted or do not accept European ways, and yet have been deculturized in the ways of their own people by generations of oppressive and destructive treatment.

Unfortunately, most educational projects and libraries are under the auspices of persons who believe that the Original Ways should become one's "heritage" and the American dream is everyman's birthright. That might be true, or it might not—but that is not the point. Native people have the right to determine their own destinies, independent of whatever destiny Americans have chosen for themselves—and they cannot do this if their education is limited to freedom only within a predetermined framework. It is not safe, even, to assume that "Indian controlled" programs will offer a greater freedom. Proposal writers and tribal governments often represent "progressive" interests, and initially, at least, most usage of libraries and schools will come from the "progressive" factions. Unless there is a concerted effort to keep a free flow of information available, unless all factions of the community are made welcome in the premises, libraries and educational programs will become political tools serving vested interests and entrenching the same established forces which have created the very situation in which native peoples collectively now find themselves.

It is the traditional peoples who will be most poorly served by available material—there is little available to answer their needs. The current outpouring of materials is often by non-native writers, which misses the mark. Equally useless are materials by native writers who have been led to believe that the patterns set by their white instructors are best—we still get Dick and Jane, but in brownface. Educators who do become open and aware of what they need to have will often find it just isn't there.

Thus librarians and educators have a primary responsibility to collect and produce information as well as to distribute it. That could mean that portions of libraries and schools will have to resemble research centers—older people taping stories, sketches of maps with native place names, short pamphlets describing skills necessary to survive in that community, reproductions of family portraits and photos of past events.

Native people have had good reason to view libraries and schools as foreign institutions which have obtained a monopoly franchise and which therefore must be tolerated. Vast amounts of money and resources and energy are expended on programs with little result—and then the personnel employed in the programs explain that the community is "apathetic" and "lacks motivation." Often such programs have a great turnover in staff as employees determine that the people "don't appreciate" their efforts. As a result, much of the real education in the community must try to survive on an undermanned, nonfinanced hardship basis.

To alter this situation, professional people must develop representative community control, and must see that the facilities are available to community use in ways which are meaningful to the community, but which are not traditional in Western society. For instance, in the Mohawk Nation a social dance is an educational event. That is the way songs are passed down—not by music classes. That is the way in which history and beliefs and moral teachings are dispersed—not by books and bibles. Sometimes a feast is prepared and the people eat in silence while sacred instructions are intoned by an elder—a librarian might not even be permitted to attend. And yet this is an educational experience within the context of the community's culture. Interestingly enough, this latter role, performed by an elder, may be referred to as a "reading"—bringing a whole new thought to the title of this book.

Many native people also have a well-grounded suspiciousness of books and reading. They have seen "educated people" who are heartless and cruel in their ways. They have seen the distortions of their beliefs in history books, and have seen treaties and agreements—written in black and white—tossed aside as meaningless documents. They have seen people who have obtained knowledge from books become disabled and handicapped as social beings—they lose the skills necessary for survival, physically and socially, in that community, and they take on new ways which cause the community itself to fall apart. Often those who read—in English—cease to be able to converse in their own language, one of the first steps to the identity crises which lead many people to alcohol and suicide.

One of the things which is trusted more than books is the Creation. The Creation is its own best teacher, and offers vast knowledge to those who would study and experience. It cannot lie, as a book can. Science books may say that the Earth is a planet in a solar system, made up of certain elements and in certain dimensions—but native peoples know the Earth is their mother, and that fact must be understood before any others. Reading which does not strike the hearts of the people—as well as their minds—will be spurned. It is no wonder that so many native peoples are seen to have "reading difficulties" and have been awarded so much distinction as America's "number one dropouts."

Educators may assume that all people can learn in the same way—but this is not necessarily true. The American pattern is one of competitiveness—see who can do the best the fastest. The native pattern is one of cooperation. The American pattern is often to teach a portion of each task—"learning by doing." Native people, on the other hand, will often watch something being done until they feel competent to try it—and may then complete the entire task successfully. When this is applied to reading, it could be that students will report for long periods of time that they are unable to read. They will, perhaps, not be able to repeat even the simplest lines. Then, after a long period of time, a student may report that reading isn't so difficult after all—he was able to "learn in one weekend." And it is true—he can now read.

All of this is not meant to be an overgeneralization, or a complete guide, to native communities for educators and librarians interested in reading skills. It is intended rather to be a caveat, or warning, so that the assurance of educators will be shattered, and that they will approach native communities humbly, in almost complete ignorance, ready to learn a great deal before there is any attempt to exercise "technical skills."

Educators must also understand that while this book deals with a number of "minority groups," native peoples are in a category quite different from the rest. They come from a non-Western culture which still is in existence. While some of its people may be a part of American society, others are just as separate from the United States as the people of the Himalayas. Blacks, Puerto Ricans, Mexican Americans—granted, each have cultures of their own, but their Original Instructions, which they were given in the Beginning, have been destroyed in the advance of Western imperialism. That same advance has destroyed certain native cultures, and has caused serious disruption of others. Educators who do not understand this history will not "separate" their own activities, or prevent them from contributing to this destruction.

People who wish to help native adult new readers are faced with a choice—either they will be agents of cultural destruction (with the best of intentions, of course), or they can be agents of change and hope and a new future of renaissance for native nations. While professional educators may plead neutrality and objectiveness, or hide behind the skirts of academic freedom, what they do will have determined which choice they have made.

Ironic, isn't it, that when the Spanish conquistidores reached the Mayan people, they spent days and weeks burning books, the bonfires lighting the skies all night? Finally, the libraries were emptied and only a few choice volumes were sent back to Europe. After all, what possible knowledge could these superstitious pagans put in their texts the Spanish reasoned. Want to bet that there are now educators concerned with illiteracy among the Mayans?

The example is more graphic, perhaps, than most. But this irony will taint educational programs for many centuries to come. It is a burden which cannot be escaped. Those who have the humanity and stamina to survive with it—educators and students alike—may be the builders of a reconstructed native people.

BLACKS AS READERS

Dudley Randall, the speaker, is a distinguished poet, editor, publisher, and librarian. He was born in Washington, D.C., attended public schools in East St. Louis and Detroit, and graduated in 1949 from Wayne State University, where he was a member of the Miles Modern Poetry Group. He received his master's degree in library science from the University of Michigan in 1951. He has been a foundry worker in an automobile factory, a letter carrier, a post office clerk, and a librarian at Lincoln University of Missouri and Morgan State College. Since 1969 he has been reference librarian and poet in residence at the University of Detroit. He is known to librarians for his poetry, poetry readings, and articles.

Through his Broadside Press, founded in 1965, he has supported the talents of significant black writers. He publishes new writers and established writers such as Gwendolyn Brooks, Don L. Lee, Sonia Sanchez, Nikki Giovanni, Margaret Walker, Ethridge Knight, Audre Lorde, and James Randall. He publishes anthologies, broadsides, posters, records, tapes, short stories, and short books. The short books are a special pleasure for adult new readers; they are able to read a whole book without being intimidated or put off completely by the numerous pages in long books.

Dudley Randall's own poetry includes *Cities Burning, More to Remember: Poems of Four Decades, Poem Counterpoem* (with Margaret Danner), and *After the Killing*, which is his recent fifth book.

He focuses here on reading and the young blacks who search for identity and meaning.

It is evident [Dudley Randall says] that the number of black readers has increased. Signs of this increase are the emergence of black bookstores, black publishers, and black publications. Obviously, there would be no need for these institutions unless there were a demand for them. It is my belief that this interest in black writing grew out of the civil rights movement of the 1950s. Negroes saw and heard the confrontations on television and radio, and read about them in newspapers and magazines. Their curiosity about themselves was aroused, and they turned to books about the black experience. Their reading led to an increase in black consciousness. Black consciousness—a heightened sense of self, a quest for identity, a sense of belonging to a distinct group and not to an inchoate mass in the American melting pot—led to reading about Martin Luther King, Jr., Daisy Bates, and other leaders of the movement. Curiosity about self led to reading books about the movement and about social problems, as well as about leaders of the movement. In addition to reading about the leaders, they read books about ordinary people, like Piri Thomas's *Down These Mean Streets*[1] or Claude Brown's *Manchild in the Promised Land*.[2]

---

[1]Piri Thomas, *Down These Mean Streets* (New York: Signet Books, 1967).
[2]Claude Brown, *Manchild in the Promised Land* (New York: New American Library, 1971).

Interest in self led to the questions Who am I? Where did I come from? Where am I going? Answers were sought in histories like Lerone Bennett's *Before the Mayflower*.[3] Out-of-print books were reprinted and blacks read classics like W. E. B. DuBois's *The Souls of Black Folk*.[4] In the search for meaning in the black experience they did not stop at factual, nonfiction books, but read poetry and fiction, like the poets of the Harlem Renaissance and Jean Toomer's *Cane*,[5] for the insights which imagination can give.

In the 1960s many new writers appeared, interpreting the black experience. Many readers, in those changing and confusing times, sought direction from the writers. Don L. Lee, who reads to college students and many young people all over the country, states that young people are looking for direction. A couple of personal experiences show the truth in Lee's statement. A student, commenting on a love poem in an examination, said it was a pretty poem, but it didn't tell her what she as a black woman should do. A young factory worker found that poetry about past leaders, such as Booker T. Washington and W. E. B. DuBois, is all right, but how did it help him solve the problems of drinking and drugs on the assembly line? These are indications that many people, especially younger ones, are looking to literature for guidance and direction in a time of change and uncertainty.

Many younger readers—and their parents—are rejecting books which hold them up to the derision of their classmates. Children's books with characters they can respect and relate to are being sought.

The quest for self-knowledge and the black experience do not end with our experience in this country. Many people are looking back further, to their African origins. Travel to Africa has superseded travel to Europe among many blacks. They refer to Africa as the Motherland, and when they say "the Continent," they are not referring to Europe. Nor is travel to Africa limited to the affluent.

In addition to interest in Africa there is sympathy for the new and underdeveloped countries in the Third World. Latin America, and especially the black countries of the Caribbean, attract a growing number of black tourists. Guyana, in South America, is becoming better known to blacks. Blacks read Mao's *Red Book*, and sympathize with China, Cuba, North Korea, North Vietnam, and the Arab states.

The surge of the Third World countries to self-determination has its counterpart among blacks in America. There is an increasing drive

[3]Lerone Bennett, Jr., *Before the Mayflower* (Baltimore: Penguin, 1966).
[4]W. E. B. DuBois, *The Souls of Black Folk* (New York: New American Library, 1969).
[5]Jean Toomer, *Cane* (New York: Harper & Row, 1923, 1969).

toward self-determination, toward control of one's local community in the government, the police, the schools, the environment.

Don L. Lee's Third World Press has the motto "We Do It Ourselves." This may be a development from the widely misunderstood and feared Black Power movement, which was no more than the claim of a people to the right to control its own destiny, which every group should have. Such control is easier to espouse than to achieve. However, in some areas blacks have made their own definitions and have chosen their own terms. They have substituted "black" for "negro," have taken Arabian and African names, have adopted African holidays (like Kwanza at the end of the year), and many have African, not Christian, weddings and christenings.

For these latter, there are reference books describing African weddings and holidays, and books of African names. Other reference books are black yearbooks, handbooks, and biographical directories. One writer is compiling a book of black quotations.

Other helpful books that interest blacks are how-to-do-it books. Because most blacks have nowhere to go but up, books on how to pass civil service examinations and high school equivalency examinations are popular. Other how-to-do-it books are sought according to the individual's personal interests.

Many of the new readers do not have reading skills, and may be intimidated by long, fat books. Some of the small black publishers have put out books of sixteen, twenty-four, or thirty-two pages so the new or young reader can quickly finish them and move on to another book.

Reading for relaxation may be found in black periodicals. These may range from *Black Stars* and *Black Sports* to *The Black Scholar*. During the 1960s and the early 1970s many black periodicals were published, and many perished. *Ebony* and *Sepia* are among the few surviving picture magazines. *Jet* is a handy-sized newsmagazine, while *Encore* includes documents and world news of import to blacks. *Essence* is a magazine appealing to the interests of black women. *Black World and Black Creation* keep abreast of the arts.

There are still those blacks who would rather go to Europe than to Africa, and would prefer to read a book on Monet than on African art, but they are of the establishment, and are the more affluent, and have probably been reading for a long time. They are not the new readers. One must recognize, moreover, that black readers, like any large group of people, cannot be stereotyped under one label. There are as many different interests as there are individuals. Enlightened black youth, for instance, unlike the white youth of the counterculture, do not regard drugs as "expansion of experience." They regard drugs as a device of the white establishment to turn potential black activists into zombies.

At the same time, however—even though there are the more conservative folk who read for relaxation and entertainment—the experience of the last twenty years, with the civil rights movement, the assassinations, the flight of whites from the cities, and the Northern opposition to busing, has made even the conservatives more skeptical, less simply trusting, more conscious of the need for self-reliance and self-determination, and more conscious of black pride, black heritage, and black achievement; and they look to find these qualities in their reading.

The new readers have a heightened black consciousness. They read books about people and characters they can relate to; they seek their identity, a meaning to their lives, direction for their questing, solutions to their problems, control over their lives and surroundings, and practical knowledge to enable them to survive and advance in their everyday living.

THE APPALACHIAN SCOTCH-IRISH MOUNTAINEER READER

Cratis Williams, the speaker, is vice chancellor in academic affairs at Appalachian State University, Boone, North Carolina, where he has been a professor of English and dean of the graduate school. He is a distinguished scholar and teacher.

He loves and knows firsthand the Appalachian Mountains and the mountain people. He was born in Kentucky and has taught in the schools of his home state, West Virginia, and North Carolina. His personal knowledge of the life style and language of the mountain people strengthens his scholarly knowledge. He delights audiences with mountain stories and songs. He is author of *Mountain Speech* and a contributor to many educational journals. In the following essay he reviews the heritage of a strong people with an oral culture and fierce pride.

Poverty and deprivation make education all the more important to the lives of mountain folk, whether they remain in their native mountains or are transplanted to the city. Library programs in all thirteen Appalachian states, from New York and Ohio to Alabama and Georgia, are providing effective service and initiating new activities for Appalachian residents.

The natives of Appalachia [Cratis Williams says] are descendants of the borderers, frontiersmen, hunters, and herdsmen who began to penetrate the wilderness of the Southern Highlands a generation or two before the American Revolution. Mostly of British stock, but including a considerable number of religious dissenters from Germany, the early settlers in Appalachia were dominated culturally and ideologically by the Scotch-Irish. They were a group of people who had lived along the English and Scottish border before removing, in the early years of the seventeenth century, to Northern Ireland, where they prospered as linen makers, small farmers, distillers, and craftsmen. About the middle of the eighteenth century, their linen industries were crippled by taxation and they were reduced to poverty by famines. By 1775, approximately 600,000, or one-fifth of the total population of colonial America, were Scotch-Irish, a designation that was given to them after they arrived in the Colonies.

Most of the Scotch-Irish folk lived along the border just east of the Appalachian Highland, extending from Pennsylvania to central Georgia; but in a few places they had dared to penetrate the mountain region even before the American Revolution began. Following the Revolution, during which the Scotch-Irish had fought in the Colonial armies, they were able to claim lands as their bounties for military service and they occupied the mountain region.

They brought to this region their own kind of old-fashioned English, which had been a hundred years out of style when they left the English and Scottish border in the early 1600s. They transmitted a great body of oral tradition, including ancient songs, ballads, riddles, and folk tales. Their customs, attitudes, and beliefs encompassed medical and weather lore, superstitions and remnants of witchcraft. Their family structure and the political attitudes they held were those that had been current during Revolutionary War times. Deeply ingrained within their culture were religious convictions deriving from the teachings of John Calvin, for the Scotch-Irish mountain folk were staunch Presbyterians until religious revivals occurred along the Appalachian border in the early years of the nineteenth century. At that time their emphasis upon the assurance of "election" by the emotional experience of "conversion," following self-conviction of sin, led them in overwhelming numbers into Baptist and Methodist congregations.

Appalachian mountain folk, few of whom owned slaves, held little in common with the slave culture of the Old South. With origins, traditions, customs, and speech idioms different from other Southerners, they were, in effect, marooned in their highlands and parceled out among nine Southern states and commonwealths. They prospered as subsistence farmers, adapted their crafts and skills to the requirements of life in isolated valleys and mountain coves, multiplied their numbers (their families were large), and kept learning alive for their children until the

Civil War came. During the Civil War most able-bodied mountain men served in Union armies, for their pride in the American nation, their spirit of independence, and their conservative political convictions remained close to the concepts that were current at the time of the Revolution.

Following the Civil War, mountain folk, considered "traitors" by the antebellum political leaders who were restored to power after the Reconstruction period, shared little of the progress of the South and few of its benefits for several generations. State funds for roads, education, and care of the indigent and ill were spent mainly for those who lived outside the mountain regions.

By 1885 the culture of the Appalachian mountain people had become almost completely oral. Public schools were closed in some mountain counties for up to twenty years after the beginning of the Civil War, or were in session as few as two weeks a year in many counties. Overpopulation and exploitative agricultural practices had spread poverty, ignorance, and disease among the coves, hollows, and ridges of Appalachia. The darkness of isolation and neglect covered the land. By 1885, the nadir of despair and hopelessness for Appalachia, hundreds of violent blood feuds, resulting mostly from antagonisms engendered by local conflicts during the Civil War and subsequent animosities aroused by politically motivated leaders and aspirants to public office, plagued the entire region, but reached the heights of violence and bloodshed in eastern Kentucky, where fifteen major feuds raged during the decade of the 1880s.

Federal laws taxing whiskey distilleries, imposed during the Civil War but not really enforced until the 1870s, added to the woes of the mountain farmers, who resisted the taxes as infringements upon their personal rights. Strangers to mountain communities were suspected of being "revenoors." Neighbors, lest they be suspected as "informers," found it necessary to cultivate allegiance to a tenet of the mountain code, expressed in the commandment "Tend to yer own business and keep yer nose out'en the other feller's." Thus strife at home, suspicion of the outsider, fear of implication in raids on moonshine stills, and the natural independence of the mountain man weakened social organization and discouraged cooperation for community betterment as the population grew, the soil became depleted, and poverty became more widespread.

From 1885 to about 1910, Appalachia, occupying somewhat the status of a colony hidden away in the heart of a rapidly industrializing nation, was considered a "mission" field by churches and religious organizations of the North. By 1900 as many as two hundred church-related academies and collegiate institutes had been established throughout the mountain region to bring "enlightenment" to benighted and disinherited mountain youth. Staffed by generally capable teachers from outside the region, these schools made educational opportunity available to thousands of young people. Most of those who advanced through the programs, instead of remaining in Appalachia, left the region because their education had prepared them for middle-class living in the cities and towns of mainstream America rather than life among the grudging hills of their homeland.

Another adverse effect of the mission schools was the breakdown of pride in the origins and heritage of the people of Appalachia, for the teachers zealously set about to "shame" the youth out of their background and make them sensitive and uncomfortable about the old-fashioned English they and their relatives spoke. The result was that perhaps no other group of English-speaking people, numbering currently 9 or 10 million who live in the region and 4 or 5 million who were born there but now live elsewhere, ever became so intensely ashamed of their speech, manners, and customs as have Appalachians. Only since the relatively recent abandonment by teachers of prescriptive English, accompanied by a growing emphasis upon pluralism in educational philosophy, have teachers and scholars accepted with positive appreciation the diction and speech patterns, oral traditions, and cultural heritage of the Appalachian people.

The exploitation of the rich natural resources of the mountain region began during the latter years of the nineteenth century, with the ruthless destruction of the finest hardwood forests in the world, and continued with extractive mining operations. These industries, supported by capitalists from outside the region, have in general flourished at a disadvantage to the mountain people, who, because of weak local leadership, their disinclination to cooperate with one another for the common good, and their helplessness in wielding political power in states in which they have constituted a minority, became more poverty stricken as their timber, coal, and mineral resources were exploited by corporations which paid minimal taxes, or none at all, for the support of local schools, social programs, and government.

As public schools in the mountains were improved and native-born teachers were employed to staff them, most of the mission schools closed, but the native teachers for a long time followed the examples of the teachers in the mission schools in rejecting the cultural traditions and speech of the mountain folk. They, too, prepared their students for life outside the region. The migration of the best-educated mountain youth continued. During and following World War II, hundreds of thousands of unskilled and relatively uneducated mountain people left their crooked shacks in the hollows of Appalachia for the "hillbilly" ghettos in the cities of the North. In the unfamiliar urban environment their family structure broke down, their dignity and pride were trampled upon, their self-esteem and independence were destroyed, and they suffered a loss of their identity under conditions of poverty and degradation more terrible than they had ever known in the hills.

During the 1950s, the implementation of new techniques in extracting coal in the Cumberland Plateau threw thousands of miners out of work. Because they were relatively uneducated, unprepared for other types of work, overcome by despair, and often suffering from "black lung," their spirits were broken. Those who are past the prime of life remain in all-too-often inadequate company houses in the coal camps, strung along railroad tracks and up the steep hillsides of the narrow valleys of southern West Virginia, southeastern Kentucky, southwestern Virginia, and eastern Tennessee. There they subsist, hand to mouth on relief programs, and wait out the rest of their lives on the front porches of their depressing and shabby little houses.

The literacy level of adults over twenty-five years of age in the mountain region is perhaps the lowest in the nation for native-born Americans—and 95 percent of the people of Appalachia are not only native born but are descended from pioneers who came to the region when it was opened up for settlement. Those who continue to live on the land still possess most of the characteristics of their ancestors, but those who moved to the mining towns, "mill hills," and lumber camps have lost much of the traditional lore and most of the craft skills which are associated with the self-subsistent agricultural life of the region.

Mountain folk possess characteristics similar to those assigned to the borderers and pioneers who moved westward, ultimately to occupy the Midwest and the region between the Mississippi River and the Pacific Ocean. They are proud, sensitive, independent, strongly individualistic, courageous, and hardy. They are hospitable and friendly, but often appear shy and retiring in the presence of strangers because of self-consciousness about their speech, manners, and customs. They are conservative politically, fundamentalist in their religious views, patriarchal in family structure, and capable of blind loyalty to blood kin in times of stress. Hence they are brave soldiers, loyal allies, formidable and sometimes treacherous antagonists, and tend to be brittle and unbending in their judgments and harsh in their strictures of those whose points of view differ from their own. They have a high level of native intelligence and still possess the shrewdness and ingenuity which enabled their ancestors to survive in the wilderness.

Mountain people are generally handsome. As children, up to 85 percent of them have blond hair, which grows darker with age. About the same percentage have blue, hazel, or gray eyes. Men are taller than the national average for males. Women, small boned, with dainty hands and feet, mature rapidly and marry early. As mountain folk mature, they develop "balanced" faces, with straight, slender noses, bold expressions, and character lines which bespeak their openness, congeniality, and sociability—but also the struggle and hardship of life in the fields, the sawmill towns, and the mines.

Oriented toward the physical aspects of life, they pass along their cultural heritage orally. Their wisdom and traditional values are bodied forth in songs, ballads, rhymes, proverbs, adages, saws, and tales. A folk theology, derived ultimately from John Calvin's teachings and explicated by scriptural quotations which even unlettered mountain folk often know, is part of the oral tradition. The religious influence makes them fatalistic in their belief. Their struggle with hardship and their native shrewdness taught them long ago that "hit pays fer a body to keep his powder dry whilest a waitin' fer the will-be-that-will-be."

The language of mountain people is close to basic English. Among the relatively uneducated, few polysyllabic words of Greek or Latin origin are used. For "perpendicular" the mountaineer says "stickin' right straight out"; for "diagonally," "slaunchways" (with the eighteenth-century pronunciation "slanchways"); for "tangentially," "sigodlin' " ("sideoggling"). One is "financially rurnt" rather than "financially ruined." Shoes are "fixed" instead of "mended." A woman refers to her husband as her "old man" and a husband to his wife as his "old woman." Both single and married women are given the title "miss."

Such pleonasms as "tooth dentist," "widow woman," "riflegun," "ham of meat," and "rock clift" are heard from time to time. Prepositional clusters convey exact and precise relationships, as "a bold spring was a-gufflin' up out from away back down in under a ledge of rock." Generally folk speech is filled with "strong" past tenses, many of which are heard but rarely outside the Southern Highlands: "het" for "heated," "holp" for "helped," "fetch" for "fetched," "drug" for "dragged." Multiple negatives, "I hain't never done that no time no place," and tandem superlatives, "the curiousest, sassin'est, long-headedest, don't-carin'-fer-nothin'est youngin in seven counties," abound.

Mountain folk generally omit the final *g* in -ing verb forms and prefix the Middle English preposition *a-*, as in "a-goin', " "a-comin'." Fond of *r*, they use it generally to close words which end with open diphthongs: "widder" (widow), "sorrer" (sorrow); and anticipate the *r* in shaping the mouth for the preceding vowel or diphthong: "wire" (war), "fire" (far).

Rhythms and patterns in mountain speech are melodious and intonations lack the nasal quality of Midwestern speech. Mountain people who have gone to school generally update their grammar and idioms but retain the traditional rhythms and intonations, which are soft and musical.

Mountaineers, whose first ancestors in the mountains often were educated Scotch-Irish pioneers who carried books with them into the wilderness, have a traditional respect for learning and generally are proud of the accomplishments of their children in school. However, they resent too obvious changes in the diction and language of their children and counsel them not to "get above their raising," for the leveling spirit of frontier democracy remains strong in Appalachian communities.

6

Heritage, Values, Reading Interests: Chicanos, Puerto Rican Americans, Those for Whom English Is a Second Language

THE CHICANO OR MEXICAN AMERICAN READER

Elizabeth Martinez Smith's concentration in her studies at the University of California has been on Mexico and public library service to Chicanos or Mexican Americans. She holds a degree in library science from the University of Southern California. She is lecturer at the School of Library Science, California State University, Fullerton, and regional administrator in the Rio Hondo Region, Los Angeles County Public Library System. She has traveled widely in Europe, Japan, Hawaii, Mexico, Panama, and Spain.

From 1968 to 1972 she worked tirelessly in Los Angeles to upgrade library collections and produce programs for ten libraries serving the Spanish speaking of the Mexican American public; she also served as systemwide consultant on library programs and multimedia materials. As regional administrator of Libraries in Institutions, she took charge of service in fourteen libraries in Los Angeles County jails, hospitals, rehabilitation camps, and juvenile halls. She is active in sharing her knowledge and beliefs with librarians in state and national committees,

The contents of this chapter were generated under a grant from the U.S. Office of Education, Department of Health, Education, and Welfare, and is therefore in the public domain. However, the opinions expressed do not necessarily represent the position or policy of that Agency and no U.S. Government endorsement should be inferred.

conferences, and institutes. She has been active in the Chicano Task Force, Social Responsibilities Round Table of the American Library Association, and the Committee to Recruit Mexican American Librarians (Los Angeles).

Ms. Martinez Smith brings together her personal knowledge and experience and her professional library interests and activities. This concentration is to the advantage of the Chicano population and library service. In the following report she focuses on factors that she sees as essential in providing library service to the millions of Chicanos in the United States.

Libraries, like most institutions [Elizabeth Martinez Smith says], have reflected and perpetuated the life style and ideologies of the dominant culture with standards for the basic book collections provided by organizations such as the American Library Association to ensure uniformity of service. The particular needs and interests of minority people were denied, or, at best, ignored.

Within the last decade, this condition was formally recognized—following demands by minority people—and programs were instigated aimed at correcting the neglect of the past. Soon library administrators were vying with each other for available federal funds to set up an "ethnic" library; in this case, a "Chicano" or "Mexicanized" library.[1] Federal funds have been a determining factor in establishing these libraries since few systems would redistribute budgeted monies for "special projects."

As the programs gained momentum a few discoveries were made. First, the lack of Chicano librarians, who were essential, since most federally funded programs required the involvement, in an advisory capacity, of members of the target minority group. Second was the lack of information on Spanish-language and Chicano materials. Third was the lack of readily available knowledge about the Chicano public.

After much discussion and delay, library schools set up minority fellowships and institute programs, libraries compiled bibliographies on materials, and librarians sought a clue to possibly successful programs by searching for the background, beliefs, attitudes, and values of Chicanos in historical and sociological studies.

---

[1]*Chicano* and *Mexican American* are used interchangeably in this book unless otherwise indicated. This does not imply, however, that the terms are synonymous. The fact that there are so many labels—Americans of Spanish surname, Spanish speaking, Hispanos, Mexican Americans, Chicanos, etc.—attests to the differences and diversity of the people.

Background

Conservative figures, which were based on an inadequate (random sampling) 1970 population census, estimate that about 10 million Spanish-speaking/surnamed people live in the United States.[2] Sixty percent, or 6 million, are Mexican Americans; the other 40 percent are Puerto Ricans, Cubans, and other Latin Americans. Eighty percent of the Mexican American population are located in the five Southwestern states of Arizona, California, Colorado, New Mexico, and Texas. The remaining 20 percent are scattered throughout the United States, with heavy concentrations in the Chicago area and along the various migrant agricultural circuits. Eighty-five percent of the Mexican American population are native-born citizens of the United States of America.

Chicano history is the experiences of the community of peoples of Mexican descent within the United States: first, in an indigenous Southwest/Northern Mexico culture and society; later, as a result of the Texas War of 1836 and the United States–Mexican War of 1846, as a society within a society—a conquered people. The Treaty of Guadalupe-Hidalgo of 1848 guaranteed Chicanos rights of property and culture—only to be swept aside in the occupation of conquered territories. The Chicano people thus became a colonized people, a people under the domination of the United States of America—manipulated, controlled, powerless, and culturally linked to Mexico through history and continual emigration across political boundaries.[3]

Regional differences among Chicanos exist today, as among the dominant culture. Three major areas are often cited. The New Mexico and Colorado "Hispanos" evolved a distinct culture, primarily in isolated mountain villages. The border "Texas-Mexicans" suffered the South's particular discrimination and prejudice. The "Chicanos" of southern California found themselves caught up in a continuously changing urban environment.

Sociologist Fernando Peñalosa has attempted to define and characterize the Chicano population by its degrees of self-conceptions and self-identity.[4] He suggests that at one end of the spectrum are those who acknowledge their heritage but view it as neither negative nor positive because it is not of any real importance to their living. Next are

[2]*World Almanac and Book of Facts* (New York: Newspaper Enterprise Assn., 1973), p. 492.

[3]Read Rodolfo Acuña, *Occupied America: The Chicano's Struggle toward Liberation* (San Francisco: Canfield, 1972), for Chicano history from 1800 to 1970.

[4]Fernando Peñalosa, "Toward an Operational Definition of the Mexican American," *Aztlan: Chicano Journal of the Social Sciences and the Arts*, 1, no. 1 (Spring 1970).

those who are very conscious of being Mexican, and whether this is viewed as negative or positive, it is a vital part of their lives. The third group, which is the most rapidly growing, consists of those who are acutely aware of their identity, defend their "differentness," and are committed to the betterment of their people.

Although Dr. Peñalosa does not attest to their correctness, he suggests that the terms most often used to describe these three groups are *Americans of Mexican ancestry*, *Mexican Americans*, and *Chicanos*. These segments are not due to generation differences, or even to degree of acculturation, but rather to the depth of consciousness and self-identity.

Culture

The Mexican American and his culture has been a favorite study among sociologists, especially during the last forty years.[5] Ruth Tuck in 1946 wrote that "for many years the [Mexican] immigrant and his sons made no effort to free themselves. They burned with resentment over a thousand slights, but they did so in private."[6] Munro D. Edmonson's 1957 study of new Mexicans reported that the fatalistic acceptance of things which "just happen" is a source of wonder and despair to Anglo housewives with Mexican servants, but it is a precise expression of the Mexican attitude.[7] Florence R. Kluckhohn and Fred L. Strodbeck studied twenty-three Hispanos in a community of one hundred and fifty persons in 1961 to determine value orientations that were later attributed to an entire people and their history.[8]

Two popular studies within the last decade are William Madsen's *The Mexican Americans of South Texas* and Celia S. Heller's *Mexican American Youth: Forgotten Youth at the Crossroads*.[9] Both concluded that the Mexican culture accounted for a lack of drive and determination, laziness, laxity in habits, *mañana* orientation, inferiority complex, fatalism, emotionalism, and criminal tendencies.

[5]Raymond A. Rocco, "The Chicano in the Social Sciences: Traditional Concepts, Myths and Images," *Aztlan: Chicano Journal of the Social Sciences and the Arts*, 1, no. 2 (Fall 1970).

[6]Ruth Tuck, *Not with the Fist: Mexican Americans in a Southwest City* (New York: Harcourt Brace, 1946), p. 198.

[7]Munro S. Edmonson, *Los Manitos: A Study of Institutional Values* (New Orleans: Tulane Univ., Middle American Research Institute, 1957), p. 60.

[8]Florence R. Kluckhohn and Fred L. Strodtbeck, eds., *Variations in Value Orientations* (Evanston, Ill.: Row, Peterson, 1961; reprint, Greenwood, 1973).

[9]William Madsen, *Mexican Americans of South Texas* (New York: Holt, Rinehart & Winston, 1964); Celia S. Heller, *Mexican American Youth: Forgotten Youth at the Crossroads* (New York: Random House, 1968).

As recently as 1971, a paper on library and information services to Mexican Americans supported the following factors as basic to socio-cultural differences between Anglos and Mexican Americans: Mexican Americans are (a) encouraged to keep the group norm while Anglos have high aspirations for the individual; (b) present-time or past-time oriented, as opposed to Anglos' "wide time" orientation, which is coupled with a self-concept of improvement for future gains; (c) noncompetitive, while Anglos are competitive, inventive, and resourceful; (d) family oriented, in contrast to Anglos' orientation toward a technocratic society; and (e) fatalistic and superstitious/religious, whereas Anglos have no concept of fatalism and subordination to a high authority.[10]

These negative characteristics are alleged to represent the beliefs, attitudes, and values held by Chicanos. Are they valid? Are these the differences that librarians should keep in mind when planning library service to the Chicano community?

Anthropologist Octavio Ignacio Romano has succinctly denounced such sociological studies as biased and merely a perpetuation of ideas that were prevalent during the days of Manifest Destiny, when the dominant culture justified its land stealing, violence, and murder of indigenous peoples by attributing negative values to their way of life.[11] He holds social scientists responsible for giving credibility and sanction to these stereotypes, which account for the present-day negative image.[12]

Dr. Romano is supported in a brilliant critical analysis by Deluvina Hernandez, *Mexican American Challenge to a Sacred Cow*, which refutes the attempt to equate low academic achievement of Mexican Americans with the culture itself.[13] She documents the bias of researchers and the fallacies employed in constructing a "Mexican American model" which equates behavior and culture without regard for social conditions.

Educator Y. Arturo Cabrera cites three generalizations about Mexican Americans which influence character. First is the Spanish language, for, whether it is spoken or not, strands of the language can be found in the experiences of all Chicanos—if only in history, names, and food.

[10]Robert P. Haro, "Bicultural and Bilingual Americans: A Need for Understanding," *Library Trends*, 20, no. 2:256–70 (Oct. 1971).

[11]Cecil Robinson's *With the Ears of Strangers: The Mexican in American Literature* (Tucson: Univ. of Arizona Pr., 1963), is an account of Mexican stereotypes.

[12]Octavio Ignacio Romano, "The Anthropology and Sociology of the Mexican American: The Distortion of Mexican American History," *El Grito: A Journal of Contemporary Mexican American Thought*, 2, no. 1:25 (Fall 1968).

[13]Deluvina Hernandez, *Mexican American Challenge to a Sacred Cow*, Monograph Series no. 1 (Los Angeles: Univ. of California, Mexican American Cultural Center, 1970).

Language is usually credited with determining the level of culture retention; and those who do not speak the language are referred to as assimilated into the dominant society. However, this does not apply to Mexican Americans, for (according to Dr. Peñalosa's previously mentioned study) many Chicanos do not speak Spanish yet defend their identity and culture against any attempts at assimilation. What is significant is whether speaking Spanish is seen as a positive element and whether efforts are made to support and retain this cultural aspect.

Second is the highly visible *mestizaje* of the people, the result of continual mixture between the North American Indian and the explorer Spaniard throughout Mexico and what is now called the Southwest United States (but was earlier named Aztlan or Northern Mexico). The Chicano is a *mestizo*, a blend of the Indian and European, with fused cultures and histories, and indigenous to North America.

Third is religion, which is primarily Catholic. The church has been a constant influence on the Mexican American. It has been both an oppressor and exploiter of the people as well as a consolation and defender of their rights.[14]

In *Pensamientos on Los Chicanos: A Cultural Revolution*, Eliu Carranza finds that the very word *Chicano* provides a view of a people's beliefs and values.[15] He explains that the word represents antisystematic stereotypification. It implies a brutally honest self-examination, intolerance to the dehumanization of people, and reaffirms the historical link to Mexico. *Chicano* means that one is not alone but belongs to the family of *La Raza*, or all Hispanic people. It stands for self-determination, self-examination, and self-evaluation.

The question now is are the generalizations cited by Cabrera and Carranza valid, and, if so, what are their implications for library service? It is the contention of this writer that not only are the findings of Cabrera and Carranza of significant importance but also that they may well be the factors librarians should consider, lest we become supporters of sociological studies which are being questioned and refuted by Chicanos.

The Spanish language, the *mestizaje* of the people, religion, Mexican history, and the desire for self-determination must be incorporated into viable library collections, programs, and services. The employment of bilingual, bicultural librarians in decision-making positions is essential,

[14]Y. Arturo Cabrera, *Emerging Faces: The Mexican-Americans* (Dubuque, Ia.: William C. Brown Co., 1971), p. 55.
[15]Eliu Carranza, *Pensamientos on Los Chicanos: A Cultural Revolution* (Berkeley: California Book Co., 1969).

for they can provide the understanding and commitment that are needed for success.[16]

THE PUERTO RICAN AMERICAN READER

Dr. Samuel Betances was born in Harlem, in New York City. He spent his early youth in Puerto Rico and the South Bronx. A sociologist, he holds degrees from Columbia Union College and Harvard University. He is author of "The Latin Diaspora" in *New York* magazine. His series of articles, "Race Prejudice in Puerto Rico," appeared in *Rican*. He has lectured at universities throughout the country. He is currently professor of sociology at Northeastern Illinois University in Chicago and publisher of *Rican: Journal of Contemporary Puerto Rican Thought*.

He presents some basic facts and insights about the Puerto Rican in the United States. He is a sympathetic and keen observer, and sees clearly the problems and obstacles which prevent Puerto Ricans from having access to appropriate reading materials.

Learners in search of culturally relevant materials constitute a reader group for which libraries—whether school, public, or academic—can provide those relevant materials.

In the United States [Samuel Betances says], Puerto Ricans are an important constituency among the reading public. They are learners in search of culturally relevant materials. They also form part of the new, impatient, vocal, cultural ethnic groups, such as blacks, Chicanos, and native Americans. Puerto Ricans see education (particularly higher education) and the reading which complements school assignments as of strategic importance in their struggle for identity and survival.[17] Independent of reading related to schooling, Puerto Rican youth are hungry for information about their history and culture, as well as island-mainland politics. Puerto Rican readers who also might be interested in general topics will find that libraries have—if any—only very limited amounts of books, periodicals, and media-center resources which speak to them.

The purpose of this discussion is to provide an overview on the Puerto Ricans in the United States to librarians, educators, and others who make decisions about dispersal of resources to serve new readers. Problems of identifying, purchasing, and holding onto materials which

[16]Further implications for library service are discussed in more detail in chap. 9.
[17]Fred E. Crossland, *Minority Access to College* (New York: Schocken Books, 1971), p. 4.

focus on issues of interest to Puerto Ricans as a particular reader group will be discussed later.

Puerto Ricans in the United States

Puerto Rican migration to the mainland goes back many years, before the United States claimed the island as war booty at the end of the Spanish-American War in 1898. As far back as the 1860s, Puerto Rican patriots, such as Ramon Emeterio Betances, the undisputed leader of the independence movement; Lola Rodriguez de Tio, the author of Puerto Rico's national hymn; and Eugenio Maria de Hostos, outstanding intellectual and teacher, spent time in New York seeking support for the independence of Puerto Rico from colonial Spain or as political exiles. They were, as one writer put it, "a colorful, militant group, many of whom were disappointed when the United States annexed the island in 1898 instead of granting it the independence for which many of them had struggled."[18]

Under American rule, Puerto Ricans began to trickle to the mainland in small numbers for a host of reasons, in which study and the search for economic opportunity played an important role. By 1908 records began to be kept on the outmigration from the island. For the most part, Puerto Ricans who came to the United States settled in New York, the city made famous by the influx of newcomers through the years.

In 1917, on the eve of World War I, Puerto Ricans were declared by the U.S. Congress citizens of the United States.[19] This new status meant that Puerto Ricans who came to the mainland could not be legally or technically considered immigrants or foreigners, but rather migrants. Joseph P. Fitzpatrick, sociologist from Fordham University and author of the most comprehensive and scholarly book on Puerto Ricans in the United States, says: "Actually, since Puerto Ricans are citizens of the United States, their migration to the mainland is part of the general movement of U.S. citizens from one part of the country to another."[20] It is estimated that 5 million such citizens migrate from one part of the country to another every year.[21]

[18]Joseph P. Fitzpatrick, *Puerto Rican Americans* (Englewood Cliffs, N.J.: Prentice-Hall, 1971), p. 10.

[19]For a Puerto Rican response to the proposed action of the U.S. Congress to make American citizens of the inhabitants of Puerto Rico, see the speech of Luis Múñoz Rivera before the House of Representatives, in *Congressional Record*, May 5, 1916, 64th Cong., 1st sess., p. 10.

[20]Fitzpatrick, *Puerto Rican Americans*, p. 10.

[21]Joseph Monserrat, "Puerto Rican Migration: The Impact on Future Relations," *Howard Law Journal*, 15, no. 1:17 (Fall 1968).

Migration from the island was cut off by German submarines during World War II. For every practical purpose, the great migration by Puerto Ricans to the United States took place between the late 1940s and mid-1960s. The migration of great numbers of Puerto Ricans coincides with the economic reality in Puerto Rico, where farming was abandoned in favor of an industrialization program. Cheap air transportation to the mainland and the hopes of Puerto Ricans for better employment in the industrial Northeast and the farmlands of the Northeast and Midwest are factors one must consider when reviewing the bulk of migration from the island to the mainland. Although Puerto Ricans, as U.S. citizens, could come to the mainland and leave at will, their legal status as fellow citizens did not prevent a hostile reception from the larger society. Ethnocentrism and racism awaited the new strangers, betraying Clarence Senior's notion that Anglos have been historically "a friendly, neighborly, hospitable people."[22]

When compared with white Anglo-Saxon Protestant (WASP) values, Puerto Ricans are a culturally different people. They speak a foreign language—Spanish as opposed to English. They are perceived to be Catholic—as opposed to Protestant. And to a large degree their different shades of color are in conflict with the popular definition of who is "white" in American society. While a workable theory of migration may not be available, as Monserrat suggests, it is nevertheless clear why Puerto Ricans continued to migrate to the United States, and why they will continue to migrate in great numbers in the future.[23]

> Unemployment drives them north. Official statistics put unemployment in Puerto Rico at 12.2 percent, but it is in fact much higher. As Congressman Herman Badillo has explained, "In realistic terms, unemployment approaches 25–30 percent when you consider those who have become so discouraged that they are no longer seeking work." These figures would be even more staggering had the 446,800 Puerto Ricans who migrated here between 1960 and 1970 stayed at home.
>
> Moreover, Puerto Rico is a Catholic country, and despite the sterilization and birth-control frenzy of the last decade, the population—currently approaching 3 million—is expected to double within the next 30 years. It is hard to imagine what steps would have to be taken to improve the employment outlook in such circumstances, and New York should anticipate continuing heavy migration from the Island.[24]

Because of the legend of success built around Operation Bootstrap, the program adopted by the government of Puerto Rico to industrialize

[22]Clarence Senior, *Strangers Then Neighbors: From Pilgrims to Puerto Ricans* (New York: Freedom Books), p. vii.
[23]Monserrat, "Puerto Rican Migration," p. 15–17.
[24]Betances, "The Latin Diaspora," p. 27.

and diversify the economy, it is difficult to see that in some respects the very program which was designed to solve the economic ills of Puerto Rico is in part responsible for causing one-third of all Puerto Ricans to abandon their homeland. Professor Robert Anderson writes: "A 'refuge' peculiar to the Puerto Rican is the economic escape of free emigration to the United States. The high point of net migration from the island to the mainland was reached in 1953, when almost 75,000 Puerto Ricans left the Island."[25]

It is not true that Puerto Rico is "fully industrialized,"[26] as one writer put it. Anderson indicates that "in terms of employment of the labor force, agriculture is still dominant, though there were numerically fewer agricultural workers in 1963 than there were in 1940."[27] In effect, many of the impressive statistics which have come out of Operation Bootstrap cannot conceal the miserable conditions which still exist in the island, where one out of every three Puerto Ricans is living in poverty. Gordon K. Lewis cautions students of the "progress" of Puerto Rico to be aware of the "glowing optimism in the official literature of the Commonwealth promotional agencies."[28]

Much of the industry that came to Puerto Rico can be classified as "marginal." Instead of heavy industry, Puerto Rico was flooded with needlework factories and undergarment jobs, which provided employment for women but disturbed the social patterns of the society, forcing migration of a high proportion of the young male population to the mainland. As this writer put it in another article:

> The massive number of Puerto Ricans who have migrated to the United States belies the attractive, New York–like picture that Puerto Rico's image-makers have painted of San Juan, and the legend they have woven around Operation Bootstrap. For the international entrepreneurs, who have "industrialized" Puerto Rico with brassiere and nylon factories, the Island's climate, political stability, tax advantages, and plentiful supply of cheap labor have earned it the reputation of "a perfect place for work and play." It is less perfect for Puerto Ricans themselves. One out of three still lives in misery. They are the poverty-ridden, the busboys of paradise, who eventually board—almost a cruel joke—sleek jets to JFK or Newark, leaving behind their "viejo San Juan."[29]

[25]Robert W. Anderson, *Party Politics in Puerto Rico* (Stanford, Calif.: Stanford Univ. Pr., 1965), p. 7.

[26]Alfredo Lopez, *The Puerto Rican Papers: Notes on the Re-emergence of a Nation* (New York: Bobbs-Merrill, 1973), p. 67.

[27]Anderson, *Party Politics in Puerto Rico*, p. 7.

[28]Gordon K. Lewis, *Puerto Rico: Freedom and Power in the Caribbean* (New York: Harper Torch Books, 1963), p. 133.

[29]Betances, "The Latin Diaspora," p. 27.

Migration will continue to play an important role in Puerto Rican society. New York and other cities of the Northeast, as well as Gary, Milwaukee, and Chicago, will continue to receive the refugees from Puerto Rico's "silent revolution."

Puerto Ricans have come to this country at a time when a strong back and willingness to work does not suffice for the advanced technological needs of modern American society. Employment which has real opportunities for upward mobility is not readily available to Puerto Ricans as it was to other groups who immigrated generations ago to the land of opportunity. Nathan Glazer, co-author of *Beyond the Melting Pot*, has suggested that perhaps Puerto Ricans have arrived in America "at the wrong time."

It's tragic to realize that although Puerto Ricans make up 14 percent of the population of New York City (1.3 million out of a total 8 million inhabitants), they make up 40 percent of the welfare statistics.[30] Puerto Ricans are a poor people. A recent report from the federal government indicated that approximately half of all Puerto Ricans on the mainland live in seven low-income areas of New York City.[31]

One must not think of Puerto Ricans as a monolithic group. There are differences in generations and length of time spent on the mainland, as well as class differences, which need to be taken in account when planning strategies and programs to serve Puerto Ricans.

First-generation Puerto Ricans are those who grew into adult life in their island home before migrating to the United States. Their experience is different from that of the "bridge-generation," who, although born in Puerto Rico, have spent a considerable amount of time and schooling in acculturating experiences on the mainland. Living in Puerto Rico is part of the framework of the "bridge-generation."

The second generation, or the "new Puerto Ricans," as one writer has labeled them, are Puerto Ricans who were born and raised in the United States. For the second generation, Puerto Rico is an idea. This group speaks primarily English and its knowledge of Puerto Rico consists, perhaps, of a rare two-week visit to Puerto Rico, as well as what their first- and bridge-generation relatives discuss in their presence about the island.[32]

---

[30]See the article "Badillo before Congress" in *The Rican: Journal of Contemporary Puerto Rican Thought*, 1, no. 2:13 (Winter 1972).

[31]Federal Interagency Committee on Education, *Task Force Report on Higher Education and Chicanos, Puerto Ricans, and American Indians* (Washington, D.C.: Dept. of Health, Education, and Welfare, 1973), p. 13.

[32]The terms, as applied in this report to the differences in generations among Puerto Ricans in the United States, have been adapted from Monserrat's presentation at the Howard University symposium "Puerto Rico in the Year 2000." But

To a large extent it is the second-generation Puerto Ricans who make up the new reader group in the United States. For that reason it is necessary to understand how second-generation Puerto Ricans survive in the urban centers of America. Two specific problems face the second generation in American society: (a) attempting to get an education and (b) fighting for a positive Puerto Rican identity.

Education

For Puerto Ricans, education is a crucial avenue toward upward mobility. Most Puerto Ricans in positions of responsibility agree that a college certificate is essential to getting out of poverty and the welfare dependency cycle.

A glance at the dropout rate for Puerto Ricans quickly shows how miserably the school system is failing the children of the first airborne migration into American society. The Coleman report indicated that between the ages of sixteen and seventeen, "when dropping out of schools first occurs in large numbers," youths who are Puerto Ricans were most likely to be out of school, when compared to the rates of other race minorities.[33] Dr. Isidro Lucas, who made an invaluable contribution with his study *Puerto Rican Dropouts in Chicago: Numbers and Motivation*, found dropout rates were 72.2 percent for Puerto Rican youths in Chicago.[34] In New York City the rate is close to 68 percent. But the figure for New York is even worse than what it appears to be, because a good percentage of the youths who stayed until high school graduation ended with a "general high school diploma," which did not prepare them for college or immediate skilled employment.

Cleveland has had a dropout rate of 90 percent, and Boston has failed Puerto Ricans in an even worse way. Boston had at least 7,800 school-age children, mostly Puerto Ricans, out of school—out of a total Spanish-speaking population of 32,000.[35] Between 1966 and 1969 the Boston public schools graduated four Puerto Rican students. A new record was set in Boston in 1971, when seven Puerto Rican students graduated from public schools and four from Catholic schools.

---

the reader should be aware that such terms as *Ricans* and *Neo-Ricans*, as well as *Niuyoricans* (from "New York Ricans") and *Chicago Ricans*, also have been applied.

[33]J. S. Coleman, *Equality of Educational Opportunity* (Washington, D.C.: Govt. Printing Office, 1966), p. 449.

[34]Isidro Lucas, *Puerto Rican Dropouts in Chicago: Numbers and Motivation* (Washington, D.C.: Office of Education; ERIC, ED-053-235, 1971).

[35]Task Force on Children Out of School, *The Way We Go to School* (Boston: Beacon, 1970), p. 18.

The Lucas study documented an important factor on which Puerto Ricans were most likely to drop out. It has been assumed that those students who have a "language problem" would be "turned off" by schooling and eventually leave the classrooms. But Lucas confirmed that it was the students who faced "problems of self-concept caused by discrimination, difficulty in relating to their parents and progressive estrangement from the school, which were important factors in influencing the rate."[36]

Puerto Ricans who had spent all their lives in the United States, and understood English, understood better than their recently arrived Spanish-speaking counterparts the many ways in which Puerto Ricans are led to believe that they are worthless. Lucas found that "dropout statistics were highest among Puerto Rican students who had lived in the United States ten years or more."[37]

A report published by the President's Cabinet Committee on Opportunities for Spanish Speaking People reported that "half as many Puerto Ricans drop out or interrupt their college careers when compared to the general college population."

In spite of school system failures at the precollege level, one finds (from 1970 figures) at least 20,000 Puerto Ricans enrolled in colleges throughout the United States. In order for Puerto Ricans to achieve proportional representation on college campuses, the figure would have to be increased by 225 percent, or by another 45,000. If the college-age population is used as the base, rather than the general population (because Puerto Ricans are a younger group), the rate would have to be greater than 225 percent.[38]

Identity and Race

The search for identity among the Puerto Rican second generation is complicated by several factors. First, the second generation is "neither Puerto Rican in the Puerto Rico sense nor fully American."[39] The islander in Puerto Rico at times will consider the second generation as "Puerto Rican" because in Puerto Rico the Spanish language is an important criterion in determining who is Puerto Rican. But Lopez writes:

---

[36]Task Force on Education, "National Research Project on the Dropout Problem: Spanish Speaking America" (Washington, D.C.: Cabinet Committee on Opportunities for Spanish Speaking People, Mar. 28, 1973), p. 23.

[37]Ibid., p. 11.

[38]Crossland, *Minority Access to College*, p. 16.

[39]Monserat, "Puerto Rican Migration," p. 25.

Although there are signs of the people of the island losing much of the edge in their Spanish, the main loss of language among Puerto Ricans has been in the United States. There are some Puerto Ricans, second-generation, who don't speak Spanish at all. The great majority of second-generation Puerto Ricans speak Spanish in an incorrect and completely insufficient way. A young Puerto Rican will begin a sentence in Spanish, then switch to English when his Spanish vocabulary fails him. Or he will use Spanish to communicate short, often-used concepts like "claro" (term of agreement), "Yo lo se" (I know it), and so on. When it comes to communicating full concepts and holding a conversation, the Spanish of the second-generation Puerto Rican often proves completely inadequate.[40]

In his book *Hot Land, Cold Season*, the Puerto Rican novelist Pedro Juan Soto captures the essence of the second generation's struggle to have a positive identity, and ultimately describes "an outcast, an American, a Puerto Rican, a clown doing a tight-rope act, a dweller in no-man's land."[41]

Second, in the area of race relations the second generation is neither fish nor fowl. Piri Thomas, whose *Down These Mean Streets* is the first book written by a second-generation Puerto Rican, tells about the dilemma he faced in coming to terms with the race problem. As a dark-skin Puerto Rican he felt "hung-up between two sticks." Having one parent who was a dark-skin Puerto Rican and the other more European looking made his problem even more complicated. Faced with more than his share of the mythical "one drop" of black blood, which is enough to make a person black in this country, Thomas was very confused. He gives a hint of his intensive struggle when he speaks about his parents: "It wasn't right to be ashamed of what one was. It was like hating Momma for the color she was and Poppa for the color he wasn't."[42]

Puerto Rican young people in the United States feel very confused about their identity as it relates to the issue of race and color. The confusion and psychological trauma experienced by second-generation Puerto Ricans are caused partly by conflicting social definitions that place Puerto Ricans in a "no-man's-land," neither black nor white. This crisis, while sometimes masked, causes ambivalence, anxiety, and bitterness which often turn against the self.[43]

[40]Lopez, *The Puerto Rican Papers*, p. 195–96.
[41]Pedro Juan Soto, *Hot Land, Cold Season* (New York: Dell, 1973).
[42]Thomas, *Down These Mean Streets*, p. 129.
[43]Samuel Betances, "Puerto Rican Youth: Race and the Search for Identity," *The Rican: Journal of Contemporary Puerto Rican Thought*, 1, no. 1:4–13 (Fall 1971).

A study conducted by the author in 1970 found that members of the second generation feel apprehensive about how they may be perceived by blacks in the United States. One response from a young man is revealing:

> When Blacks need an extra pair of feet to march, they welcome the Puerto Rican cooperation. When they need an extra voice to shout against injustice, they welcome Puerto Rican cooperation. When they need another head to bleed in the struggle, cooperation is welcome from their "Latin Brothers." But when as a result of the shouting, the marching, and bloody head, there is an extra pocket to fill, the Puerto Ricans are suddenly not Black enough.[44]

In its determination to learn about its historical and cultural roots the second generation has been influenced by the writings of *independistas*, the propagandist group from Puerto Rico that has designed many kinds of networks to reach young English-speaking people in the United States. The issue of political status in Puerto Rico is not resolved, and second-generation Puerto Ricans are very interested in reading and understanding the political debates in the island.[45] Their desire for self-determination in the United States is naturally transferred to similar demands for Puerto Rico. These two issues help illustrate the magnitude of the problems, aspirations, and contradictions which the second generation confronts in America.

READERS FOR WHOM ENGLISH IS A SECOND LANGUAGE

Gladys Alesi has been involved for twenty-one years in full-time adult education programs conducted by the New York City Board of Education. During this period she served as teacher in the English-to-Foreigners Program, teacher in charge of the English and Citizenship Program in Coney Island, administrator of all evening classes, director of Operation Second Chance, and director of the Work Incentive Program. During a two-year leave of absence Ms. Alesi set up a job-related adult education program for the Port of New York Authority. Since 1973 she has served as supervisor of basic education for the Manpower Development Training Program.

Her contributions to adult education are extensive. She has developed curriculum materials and supervised their use in adult basic education, including English as a second language. She is the author of six text-

[44]Ibid., p. 11.
[45]See Gordon Lewis's perceptive essay "The Problem of Political Status" in his book *Puerto Rico: Freedom and Power in the Caribbean*, p. 350–77.

books in this field, including *First* and *Second Book in American English*, which were written with Dora Pantell. She is also one of the authors of the *Federal Textbook on Citizenship* series, which is currently available to immigrants and programs serving immigrants through the U.S. Department of Justice.

Ms. Alesi discusses the subject from the point of view of the teacher. Individuals are described in the several case studies which bring specific persons to the librarian's attention. She examines the attitudes, beliefs, and some major value orientations of new readers who, as adults, are students of English as a new language. These adults are mainly newcomers to large urban areas and are enrolled in programs conducted by the public school and by quasi-public community groups, with or without federal government funding or subsidy.

Attitudes, beliefs, and values [Gladys Alesi says] derive from the norms set by the groups to which these adults originally related. They change and are otherwise influenced by social contacts in the new environment as these newcomers interact and react to new situations. It is important to consider these various stages of adjustment, particularly because most programs of English for speakers of other languages rightly begin with the kind of survival English that enables a newcomer to cope with the essentials of life here—traveling, shopping, finding housing, working, taking advantage of community services. Newcomers who use these language skills ultimately achieve at least token integration into the life of an American community as functioning, participating members.

Another point, possibly an obvious one, also requires mention. Students of English as a second language, even those in one class level or group, are a heterogeneous group. At one time the director of adult education for the New York City Board of Education identified ninety-two countries of origin for the 30,000 adults enrolled. The students ranged from those who were functionally illiterate in their native tongues to highly trained professionals; ages ranged from eighteen to eighty; work history ranged from domestic to physician.

While it is indeed elementary to review all the differences, biological and human, among these students, an attempt will be made to break these differences down, to classify and categorize typical students with a view at arriving at some conclusions. Although we will look at several individuals, the multiplicity, complexity, and interrelatedness of factors affecting characteristic attitudes and beliefs may become evident.

Three basic groups who have been in the English-as-a-second-language category may be identified:

1. Migrants who have been in the United States for twenty years or longer. Some of these people have lived in native-language enclaves for many years. A desire for U.S. citizenship may have stimulated their desire to learn their new language.
2. Recent migrants of limited educational background. Some of them are U.S. citizens.
3. Recent migrants of advanced educational background. Some are in the United States to study.

Early Migrants

A classic example is Hyman Kaplan, described by Leo Rosten, first in *The Education of H*y*m*a*n K*a*p*l*a*n* and later in *The Return of Hyman Kaplan*. Hyman Kaplan had enormous respect for the establishment, for his teacher, and for what he was taught. He struggled and succeeded in realizing the American dream.

Case studies of the American Immigration and Citizenship Conference indicate that the truth may be as interesting as these fictional accounts. While each adjustment is different, there are identifiable characteristics among the following individuals.

A Hungarian farmer, age fifty, driven from home by the revolution, arrived in the United States with a wife and five daughters. He succeeded in getting unskilled, heavy factory work, at which he spent long hours, and attended school after work. As his daughters learned English, they were able to get jobs at various types of small assembly work. The earnings of all family members were placed in a family bank account. The father remarked proudly on opening this account: "I know that I can be a successful American."

Despite this statement, the social life of these seven adults confines itself almost entirely to the family and Hungarian relatives and friends. They are quite critical of American family living; they don't understand it.

They are otherwise "integrated" into American life. They work hard, take advantage of available opportunities, and want to be "good" American citizens.

Another family group, arriving in the United States as penniless refugees from Yugoslavia, at first tried to work for a chicken farmer in upstate New York, before going to an urban community. With the help of a church group, the father obtained a job, where he advanced to skilled machinist. One daughter became a secretary and one son joined the army. They have become proud citizens and voters, and are union members, but they live very much by Old World values.

The head of the family describes life here as the best he ever had. He has responded strongly to the norm of advancement by economic competition. Except for school and work, he and his wife have had little social participation beyond their ethnic community; nor have they accepted American values in family life, use of money, or recreation.

One young man, who has been in the United States for more than two years, came to New York from Cuba at the age of twenty-seven to seek work, after losing his job in Cuba. He studied English and supplemented his study with English-language records and correspondence courses. He started work as a handyman, worked hard, and rose to supervisory rank in his company. He married a Cuban girl and raised a family. They live in a neighborhood where many other Cubans live.

Though he speaks English well, Spanish continues to be spoken at home. He follows Cuban customs in the home. His associations with Americans are mainly occupational. And yet, like the others, he is responding vigorously to the "American way" of working hard and bettering himself. He feels that this is a good way and that he will get even further ahead. This is a source of great satisfaction to him.

Recent Migrants

Recent migrants have diverse educational backgrounds but they share an inability to speak English, with the resultant anxiety of trying to get along in an unfamiliar environment. Living in a country where an unfamiliar language is spoken creates intense feelings of loneliness and isolation, especially if the break with the homeland is permanent and irrevocable. It is natural for the newcomer to seek the company of others from his native land, not only for survival but also for identity. The newcomer wants to adapt to a new way of life, learn the language, make a living in terms of the new environment; but he also wants the comfort of companions, newspapers, and movies that he can understand.

For the young person of advanced educational background, this period of adjustment may not be very long. Professional qualifications, for example, make him occupationally mobile. His strongest motivation is to learn English so that he may take his place on the career ladder of his profession as soon as possible.

The person of limited educational background may need to keep old contacts longer. The employment that is available to him may not make it possible ever to move out of the neighborhood. Having less familiarity with the bureaucracy of his old country, he is uncomfortable with agencies of government here. He may treat their representatives with fear, suspicion, and hostility, and this will impede his adjustment.

Two examples of recent migrants in the first category are a brother and sister, ages twenty-eight and thirty, from Cuba. Both had been trained as teachers. They are living in New York City with relatives who arrived earlier and have already reached the adjustment described above. The brother and sister are tremendously anxious learners, who want to speak "perfect English" as soon as possible. The young man, in fact, told his teacher that he begged his relatives to speak to him only in English. The young woman hopes to qualify as a bilingual teacher. The young man wants to go into business, perhaps banking.

A third example, a political refugee with a Ph.D., had an important government position. In order to support his wife and young children, he works at two jobs. He attended English classes, where he sometimes fell asleep. He was described by a teacher as exhausted and depressed.

Still another example, a doctor who attended a special class for foreign physicians, must learn English as soon as possible in order to pass qualifying examinations for the medical profession. He works in a local hospital. He is learning a kind of functional English so that he may understand what patients are trying to tell him. He studies the technical language he needs for the examination at home.

Another example is also a Cuban. Jose R. arrived in New York last year from Cuba via Miami. His background was originally agrarian. In Miami he worked in a hotel and in New York he is employed in food services by a hotel. The union provides released-time English instruction for him. He lives with other Cubans. His expressed hope is to return to Cuba some day "if it is all over." In the meantime he works hard, studies hard, enjoys dancing and baseball, and likes to have a good time because he can "never save enough to put money in the bank anyhow."

Other newcomers in this group are represented by a Puerto Rican family of four. The mother and father attend English classes sporadically; though other concerns come first, they realize they need English instruction. In class they are shy and reticent. The mother feels uncomfortable with the school her children attend. As the children learn English, tension between them increases. Both father and mother are conscious of a responsibility to the school, but they are not convinced that either the school people or the parents' association would welcome any of their ideas. They work busily to keep an apartment in Brooklyn, where they both work.

Another student of Puerto Rican background attends a class for Aid to Dependent Children recipients. This woman shoulders the full responsibility of raising five children. Her welfare budget does not allow her enough money over the necessities of food and clothing to permit participation in school-connected activities. There is no way for her to save for the future. Her goal is to learn enough English to enter a job training program and "get off welfare." She speaks of working toward a better life for her children.

Other students in this group can be characterized as overly pragmatic. Some have devalued the concept of book learning, others have main interests and daily pursuits that are outside the mainstream of American life. They have many strengths: love of children and the extended family, a sense of humor and a respect for beauty in every form, and ability to relax and enjoy. Even under the stress of poverty, there is great motivation to live a good life in terms of home, family, and community. Like others, they have a need for success, security, purpose, affection and respect, particularly if they are parents of school-age children who are being stimulated by new peer-group relationships.

In fact, each group has pluses and minuses that affect the integration of these adults within the larger community. For example, students of English as a new language (categorized in group 3, the Newcomer of Advanced Educational Background) may be attending designated publicly supported classes, classes conducted at the colleges, or classes operated by special groups like the Junior League Volunteer Program. Their teachers find that their previous learning experiences make teaching them easier. Their need to work or to be certified at their previous levels of employment also exerts a powerful influence on their response to instruction. This ability to learn the new language quickly is a tremendous advantage. However, some of these students continue to look upon themselves as emigrés, living in the midst of their communities but not a part of them. Older students, schooled in traditional ways, may find it difficult to have a satisfying life in a community which calls for a good deal of active, purposeful cooperation and competition.

At most, these are generalizations from which other assumptions are constantly made, so that programs may better serve the needs and interests of adult students in school programs.

In its broadest sense, a curriculum is the sum of everything that is learned in the instructional program. It may include newly acquired skills, information, concepts, or insights. It must necessarily be adapted to the identified needs of class participants (some of which are delineated in the previous descriptions).

In all English-as-a-second-language programs, an audio-lingual approach, emphasizing hearing and speaking, is the method of instruction. This presumes that reading, as part of the curriculum, is secondary to the spoken form of language. In class, initial reading is based on familiar material, such as—for example—dialogues and conversations that already are part of the spoken language of the students.

Linguists are generally in agreement that instruction in reading should begin when the sounds and patterns of English have become fairly well established. Indeed, it is obvious even to the untrained observer that children can speak their native tongue several years before they can read its symbols.

Reading and the Library's Role

To the student who has progressed beyond the beginning level, wide reading outside the limits of the curriculum is essential. It means a great deal in developing concepts, in helping the adult understand the cultural norms of the new community, in overcoming internal feelings of hostility that arise because of a lack of knowledge. Through wide reading, too, are gained impressions of structural and spiritual values. The reader gets a more extensive vocabulary with which to express these new ideas and can understand the newspapers and what the sellers of wares—even politicians—are trying to say.

In every area of living the adult newcomer needs to read to find the answers to questions that the individual frequently cannot ask. What is sought may be at hand, but because of lack of time and of experience in using community resources, the newcomer needs help to get started. It is clear that the person whose childhood education—or lack of it— failed to make a reader isn't a frequenter of libraries. Similarly, the person who has associated libraries with a bureaucratic structure may have no conception of what an American library is like.

The instructor of English-as-a-second-language classes who helps students become aware of the accessibility of informative and interesting materials is widening their experiences as well as facilitating their language learning. As soon as oral language fluency develops, the instructor should not miss the opportunity to stimulate students by promoting leisure-time reading.

7

Reading Collections
for the Adult Reader

Although aware of the relativity of all the various life
styles which have given meaning to human striving, the
possessor of integrity is ready to defend the dignity of his
own life style against all physical and economic threats.
For he knows that an individual life is the accidental coin-
cidence of but one life cycle with but one segment of
history; and that for him all human integrity stands or falls
with the one style of integrity of which he partakes.[1]

ADULTHOOD

Reading collections for the adult reader are to be looked at from the
point of view of the adult roles the individual has at various periods
during the cycle of life. What are the adult roles? What are adult developmental responsibilities and tasks? What needs of adults generate
the pragmatic and pleasurable uses of information and ideas that are
transmitted in various print forms? What is adulthood?

Several conceptual schemes describe the process of human development. The complexity of the problem and the concepts excludes the lay
person from full understanding. Nevertheless, the psychologists and social scientists who conceive of stages and crises in human development
present schemes for the practitioner which may be interpreted in the
context of the human institution that has been created to serve men
and women in their human development. Although the theoretical knowledge is general and technical, the identification and definition of adult

[1]Erik H. Erikson, *Childhood and Society* (2d ed.; New York: W. W. Norton,
1963), p. 268.

developmental tasks and life crises give the librarian in adult services a guide, developed through inferences and interpretation, that incorporates the concept of the public library as a social institution that has been created to serve the human population.

The conceptual schemes in the writings of Robert J. Havighurst and Betty Orr,[2] Abraham H. Maslow,[3] and Erik H. Erikson[4] have particular significance in the development of library services to adults. For many years adult educators, adult services librarians, and library school educators have applied Havighurst's analysis of adult needs and developmental tasks.

The years of adulthood are years of transition, crises, problems, new roles, and new learning. These years are as much a developmental period as those of childhood and adolescence. It is recognized that the social roles a person is expected to fill and the person's quality of living is dependent on the person's ability to carry out successfully the basic tasks of living at the adult stages of life. The mature adult is judged, and judges herself or himself, according to the expectations and values of the society in which he or she lives, and according to the individual's personal values and aspirations.

Havighurst and Orr gave concrete meaning to the adult role in defining significant social roles and the kind of activity that constitutes each role. They described several areas of behavior in which the adult faces new tasks to meet new responsibilities and assumes new social roles for the first time. These areas relate to the parent, spouse, child of an aging parent, homemaker, worker, user of leisure time, church member, club or association member, citizen, and friend. The developmental tasks required in each role are interpreted by socially defined behavior.

The concept that new roles demand new information and behavior to meet new responsibilities remains valid. Many of the norms of behavior defined by Havighurst are confined to a middle-class bias. The role expectations are regarded as permanent rather than changing. (Changes in values and norms of behavior are recognized more clearly in a later work, *Society and Education*, by Robert J. Havighurst and Bernice L. Neugarten, in which changes in society are related to the

---

[2]Robert J. Havighurst and Betty Orr, *Adult Education and Adult Needs* (Chicago: Center for the Study of Liberal Education for Adults, 1956); Supplement, 1960: *Adult Education for Our Time.*

[3]Abraham H. Maslow, *Toward a Psychology of Being* (2d ed.; Princeton, N.J.: Van Nostrand, 1968).

[4]Erikson, *Childhood and Society.*

changing roles of teachers; the pluralism of society and multi-ethnic cultures are taken into consideration.[5])

On the whole, the theory of developmental tasks defines the adult learning role as adaptation to culture. For example, the highly rated responsibilities for a female in creating a home are running the house—planning, buying, housekeeping, cooking, sewing. The chief interest is homemaking, which the female accepts and finds enjoyable. Women in transition are faced with quite different roles—divorce, single parenthood, economic support, financial problems, psychological burdens, equal and civil rights.

The question of new roles, of changing social roles, and the recognition of changes must be raised. New expectations and aspirations are evident for persons of all ages.

The 1960s saw a rejection of many of the earlier values and the development of a counterculture. In the 1970s attention has been directed toward the recognition of change as a predominant fact in living. Various proposals for alternative responses in adaptation, countercultures, and radical changes for control and direction to meet change have emerged. The conflicts between the status quo and change, between generations, and the differing cultures within society destroyed the beliefs in permanency and absolutes. Basic beliefs are overturned, and political disillusion, economic failures, and the problem of environmental survival indicate confusion.

Maslow's hierarchical theory centers on human needs and interests. His conceptual scheme suggests action and generates a pattern for the personal and social life of the adult. The points of congruence of library resources and services at critical points in satisfaction of these needs and as aids in achievement of satisfactions can be identified and acted upon. At the same time, the need for research in such areas is essential, and new facts should be watched for constantly. "Maslow emphasizes that the need for self-actualization is a healthy man's prime motivation. Self-actualization means actualizing one's potential, becoming everything one is capable of becoming."[6] On the whole, an individual cannot satisfy higher-level needs unless lower-level needs are first satisfied, as shown in figure 3.

Several of Maslow's basic propositions about the growth and self-actualization psychology seem to have implications for adult service in libraries:

[5]Robert J. Havighurst and Bernice L. Neugarten, *Society and Education* (4th ed.; Boston: Allyn & Bacon, 1975).
[6]Malcolm S. Knowles, *The Modern Practice of Adult Education: Andragogy versus Pedagogy* (New York: Association Press, 1970), p. 24.

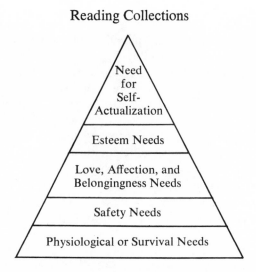

Figure 3. Maslow's hierarchy of human needs. (Reprinted, by permission, from Malcolm S. Knowles, *The Modern Practice of Adult Education: Andragogy versus Pedagogy*, p. 24. New York: Association Press, 1970.)

Agreement exists that self-actualization means "acceptance and expression of the inner core or self," "full functioning" of capacities and potentialities which "implies a minimal presence of ill health, neurosis, psychosis, of loss or diminution of basic human and personal capacities." Rather than force growth, people should let people grow and help them grow.[7]

Self-fulfillment comes through basic need gratification rather than frustration. This gratification means that basic needs are taken care of in that the person has protection, safety, and security; a feeling of belongingness, as in a family, a community, a clan, a gang; has friendship, affection; love; gains respect, esteem, approval, dignity, self-respect; and freedom for fullest development of talents and capacities, that is, actualization of self.[8]

Growth has not only rewards and pleasure but many intrinsic pains and always will have.[9]

The human being needs a framework of values, a philosophy of life, a religion or religion-surrogate to live by and understand by, in about the same sense that he needs sunlight, calcium, or love. This I have called "the cognitive need to understand".[10]

[7]Maslow, *Toward a Psychology of Being*, p. 197.
[8]Ibid., p. 199–200.
[9]Ibid., p. 204.
[10]Ibid., p. 206.

A society or a culture can be either growth-fostering or growth-inhibit-ing.[11]

Libraries, as educational agencies and sources of information and educational resources, can be part of the environment that fosters growth. Library resources offer one source of information that is neces-sary to solving problems, making decisions, and achieving self-knowledge and understanding of the world. The program and activities of the pub-lic library can be "growth-fostering." Men and women will find in the resources of the library the knowledge about the past and future, the current and historical, and will use what is helpful in growth. As Maslow says, the future "*now* exists in the person in the form of ideals, hopes, duties, plans, goals, unrealized potentials, mission, fate, destiny, etc."[12] These personal elements—ideals, hopes, duties, tasks, plans, goals—can be explored with adults in the library community without invasion of privacy and can be considered in planning and organizing adult service.

Educators and psychologists, in looking at human development as stages in the life cycle, see the human being as going through progressive changes from infancy to death. Attention has been directed primarily to early childhood and adolescence, for which the tasks and expectations in each developmental period have been described. The conceptual scheme conceived by Erik Erikson includes infancy, young adulthood, and adulthood. His conception of eight developmental stages in human development contributes a framework for understanding and for appli-cation in particular circumstances, as in this context of library adult reading service.

Erikson charts the sexual stages discerned by Freud with the physical and cognitive developmental stages. He states, "The chart [figure 4] formalizes a progression through time of a differentiation of parts. This indicates (1) that each critical item of psychosocial strength discussed here is systematically related to all others, and that they all depend on the proper development in the proper sequence of each item; and (2) that each item exists in some form before its critical time normally arrives."[13]

Erikson describes the span of human development as eight ages of man. He identifies ego qualities which emerge at each stage from critical periods of development, and the accompanying developmental crises and tasks to be mastered. Stages I to V relate to infancy and adolescence, stages VI, VII, and VIII to young adulthood, adulthood, and maturity.

---

[11]Ibid., p. 211.
[12]Ibid., p. 214.
[13]Erikson, *Childhood and Society*, p. 271.

Each stage influences the developmental tasks in subsequent stages. Each stage serves as a foundation for subsequent tasks. In the three stages of adulthood the adult usually is concerned in some way with children and youth (described in the earlier stages).

The stages of development not only have progression and depend on sequential development from one to another, but each part exists in some way in each stage. At certain critical steps, progress or regression, integration or retardation take place. The "positive" senses are not formulated as an achievement scale. Equally important are the "negative" senses—mistrust, shame, doubt, guilt, inferiority, role confusion, isolation, stagnation, despair. They are the dynamic counterpart of the positive senses. New inner conflicts and changing conditions are always influential factors (table 4). The epigenetic chart (figure 4) illustrates this concept—a system of stages dependent on one another.

"The italicized words [in table 4] are called *basic* virtues because without them, and their re-emergence from generation to generation, all other and more changeable systems of human values lose their spirit and their relevance."[14] They are hope, willpower, purpose, competence, fidelity, love, care, and wisdom. Erikson thus formulates "a blueprint of essential strengths which evolution has built both into the ground plan of the life stages and into that of man's institutions." The basic virtues are the lasting outcome of the favorable ratios described in the psychosocial stages.

At the Intimacy vs. Isolation stage the adult communicates or does not communicate, depending on what is sensed of others' needs. Erikson sees here a direct relation in cultural group relationships. Strengths of each racial group represent the need to be preserved for the sake of all people. True equality means that each has the right to be uniquely creative, and each depends upon the other for the development of their respective strengths. One respects the other's freedom of choice, and refrains from forcing the other to identify with one's own style of life.

At the Generativity vs. Stagnation stage Erikson points out two areas of special concern: (1) whatever is going to happen to the next generation, in any country, is our problem today and (2) the need to work toward elimination of discrimination based upon race and national origin and to avoid excluding oneself from efforts to eliminate discrimination. A primary concern is the establishment and guidance of the next generation.

The dominance of action directed toward others within the important Generativity vs. Stagnation stage of adult development is found in the

14 Ibid., p. 274.

Table 4. ERIKSON'S PSYCHOSOCIAL STAGES

STAGE	TASKS	BASIC VIRTUES
I. Infancy/oral sensory Basic trust vs. mistrust	New experiences	Drive and *hope*
II. Early childhood/muscular-anal Autonomy vs. shame and doubt	Assert self. Strive for autonomy	Self-control and *willpower*
III. Play age/locomotor-genital Initiative vs. guilt	Be more responsible for one's own undertakings	Direction and *purpose*
IV. School age/Latency Industry vs. inferiority	Master learning tools and skills	Method and *competence*
V. Entrance into life Adolescence/puberty Identity vs. role confusion Youth begins	Establish what kind of person one is in a world of confusion about one's identity. Search for and insistence on identity	Devotion and *fidelity*
VI. Young adulthood Intimacy vs. isolation Young adult	Fuse identity with others. Develop true genitality and ethical sense. Communicates or does not communicate, depending on other's needs. Treats persons as whole persons, respects other's freedom of choice, and refrains from hindering the other choosing for self	Affiliation and *love*
VII. Adulthood Generativity vs. stagnation Central point in adult life	Generativity is primarily the concern in establishing and guiding the next generation. Includes productivity and creativity, that is, care of others and what is produced. Generator of products and ideas; when enrichment fails stagnation results. Mutual task maturity needs guidance and encouragement	Production and *care*
VIII. Maturity Ego integrity vs. despair Final stage of integrity	Find ego identity. Find order and meaning "descriptive of one's one and only life cycle." An emotional integration, permits fellowship and leadership	Renunciation and *wisdom*

Source: Adapted from "Eight Ages of Man," p. 247–74, in Erik H. Erikson, *Childhood and Society* (2d ed.; New York: W. W. Norton, 1963).

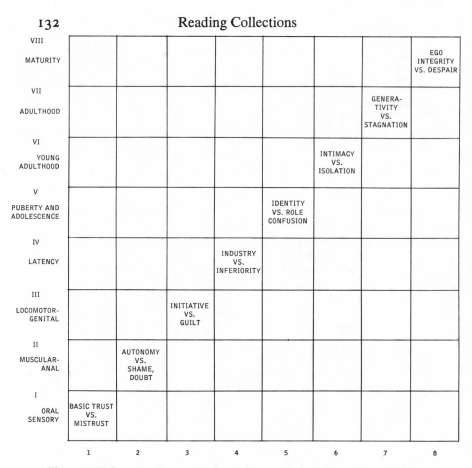

Figure 4. Epigenetic chart. (Reprinted, by permission, from Erik H. Erikson, *Childhood and Society*, 2d ed., figure 12. © 1963 W. W. Norton & Co., Inc.)

preponderance of developmental tasks required. The adult relates to others in three ways which are fundamental to a mature human relationship: by supporting the other's freedom to be himself and accepting him as he is; by listening and attaching importance to what the other has to say; and by sharing responsibility and authority (or power) with the other according to the other's developmental needs and abilities.[15]

In the final developmental period, Old Age vs. Despair, health, income, housing, social relations, and retirement planning are uppermost. At this time the adult gives meaning to life and to choices that have been made by means of the value system he or she has developed

[15]Lois Emily Whitman's "Adult Developmental Tasks: A Study of the Writings of Erik H. Erikson" (master's thesis, Univ. of Washington, 1968 [p. 77–78]) is concerned with this application of Erikson's theory.

throughout the life span. It is time to recognize accomplishments and limitations, to rejoice in the achievements and accept disappointments.

These basic virtues, which are identified by Erikson, are built on a foundation that is developed in earlier psychosocial stages. The virtues continue to be vital parts of human development throughout life, from infancy to maturity. They are, it would seem, equally vital to relationships between the library and the community it serves.

For librarians who want to demonstrate trust and reduce mistrust among residents of the community that the library serves, the following tasks have an immediate relation. Essentially, such actions require consultation, involvement, and interdependence. They require that all concerned

1. Share in decision making, and refrain from disregarding the other's right to participate.
2. Communicate intentions, and avoid excluding the other from one's plans.
3. Abide by decisions, and refrain from disregarding one's commitments.
4. Accept the other's grievances, and avoid ignoring the other's dissatisfactions.
5. Communicate one's grievances, and avoid ignoring one's own dissatisfactions.
6. Act justly, and avoid acquiescing with regard to one's own principles.
7. Insist that the others do what is just, and avoid acquiescing with regard to the other's own principles.[16]

Erikson's scheme is an accurate creative explanation and description of the process of human development. The library, an agency within a society which tends to safeguard and encourage human development, has a role and technical potentiality to assist in that development. Reading materials and programs for adults may be directed to the kinds of problems and interests inherent at each stage of growth. Insights and sensitivity to the complexities of personal, political, and social interrelationships are gained as understanding deepens in regard to adult fears, anxieties, restraints, pressures, intolerance, and conflicts, as well as positive senses of trust, identity, industry, generativity, and integrity.

The librarian need only use to the maximum the communication resources and bibliographic aids which bring to the adult information, ideas, success, and inspiration to assist in developing the sense of iden-

[16]Ibid., p. 23–24.

tity. Erikson points out how the problems of today threaten that identity and cultural solidity. Worldwide industrial revolution, wider communication, standardization, centralization, and mechanization threaten the identities which man has inherited from primitive, agrarian, feudal, and patrician cultures. Loss of identity leads to irrational motivations and actions. Librarians must find ways to provide and transmit information adults need in guidance of the young, for work, for love, and for citizen participation in local, national, and world affairs. Adults are faced with a need to make choices and decisions in all these areas as well as in areas of immediate daily problems.

Important nonintellectual factors must be taken into account, as well as the intellectual and psychological factors. Adult development follows no carefully defined line. Tasks and responsibilities overlap and are accomplished at different rates. Significant relationship exists between self-concept and learning achievement.[17] Many obstacles are in the way of progress. Many barriers exist in adult learning. Schools and libraries represent failures and obstructions to many young adults and adults. Frustration and fears which are the results of past experience deter adults. The rigid rules of libraries and fixed classroom styles are further deterrents. Staffs of libraries who lack understanding of human relations, knowledge of resources, and do not have language competencies other than English are handicapped and limit service. The concept that library service is only for children or students poses obstructions. The idea that libraries and reading are meaningless for real life is a major deterrent. The library's resources may fail to be of interest or at a level that is easily used by adults. Adults are excluded from decisions regarding the policies, the resources, and the organization and evaluation of programs. The recognition of these problems, and the obstruction, coupled with vision and imagination, can assure their removal.

This analysis results in an emphasis on the humanistic interpretation of adulthood and focuses on the library's role in relation to adult roles. This approach in no way ignores the science-oriented and technology-dominated world. It suggests a counterbalance to exclusive emphases on information and so-called knowledge business, and to sources of information and opinion gained exclusively from commercial mass media. It in no way implies or concedes that librarians are to act as psychologists, religious guides, or social workers. These professionals, in the very nature of their work, demonstrate the need for concern with adult problems created by mechanized global society. That man does not live by

---

[17]Clemmont E. Vontress, "Adult Life Styles: Implications for Education," *Adult Leadership* (May 1970), p. 27–28.

bread alone may seem self-evident. Today the very language recognizes that money is "bread." However realistically information-centered adult needs are defined, the humanistic, inspirational, consciousness-raising, cultural, and personal identity search is not to be disregarded, and continues to be of fundamental importance.

Needs and interests as well as attitudes and values direct the human being's attention to one thing or another. What distinctions can be made about such motivations or intentions? How can librarians bring to the attention of the adult the written materials that in themselves are distinguished by type of literature, subject, style, treatment, format which makes them useful and interesting to the potential reader?

Over the years adult educators and librarians, as well as social scientists, have stressed the importance of satisfying the needs of human beings to reduce tensions and arrive at a static state of inactivity. As important as it may be to meet needs such as those defined in Maslow's hierarchy or specified in life- or coping-skill categories, the place of interests and values in generating human behavior of another kind is a paramount consideration.

Distinctions between need and interest are necessary in order to distinguish the influence which may be exerted and to select reading materials of subsequent interest. In the emphasis on meeting needs, interests frequently are overlooked; yet, because interests provide a positive, strong basis for the adult's motivations and intentions, they are of particular importance.

Definitions which distinguish the meanings inherent in *need* and *interest* are made in *Webster's Third International Dictionary*. A *need* is a force, a necessity, a want for something desirable and useful. A need drives one toward something which may be physiological, intellectual, and psychological. Needs may be differentiated by their intensity of degree.

A need is described as *necessary*, that is, more pressing; as *required*, that is, an imposed requirement; as *indispensable*, something that cannot be done without; and finally as *essential*, which implies inherent necessity. Reading skills are necessary in society today, are required for schooling and handling daily affairs, are indispensable in getting and keeping a job, are essential to life skills and action.

A need forces or drives one toward something. These drives are satisfied by learning, problem solving, and thinking.

Interest means a concern, something of importance, a feeling that accompanies or causes special attention to an object. Often interest is curiosity. When a thing is *interesting*, it engages one's attention; it is capable of arousing interest, curiosity, emotion. The degree of interest may be defined in terms of intensity. An interest with power to divert and hold attention is *engrossing*. An interest that holds one's attention utterly is *absorbing*, such as favorite authors, biographies, and mysteries. Interest, insofar as it arouses curiosity, fascinates, and challenges, is *intriguing*.

The definitions suggested by Getzels in his discussion of the problem reinforce the importance of this understanding. He sees need as "a disposition or force within a person which impels him consistently toward one type of activity as against another." It looks to the achievement of goals and the establishment of equilibrium when tension drive is reduced. "An interest is a characteristic disposition, organized through experience, which impels an individual to seek out particular objects, activities, understandings, skills, or goals for attention or acquisition."[18] Such a definition assumes that a human being seeks stimulus, tends to explore and experiment. The new and unknown intrigue and challenge.

The interest that adults have in adventure, science fiction, the origin of man, strange places and unknown people, either in fact or fiction, supports this conception. The librarian who sincerely seeks and finds what is or may be interesting to the adult will find a response. Expectations of both reader and librarian will be raised.

It is necessary to concentrate on factors that cause loss of interest as well as on the nature of interests. Many factors in the environment depress not only the range of interests but the capacity to be interested. Frustration and failure in learning to read, boring materials, unhappy experiences in libraries and schools disturb and turn away persons of all ages. Some vital ingredients in development of interest are librarians' expectations that adults have interests, that new horizons are opened by the kind of materials suggested, that damaged capacity to be interested can be repaired. Beyond these expectations, librarians must have confidence and competence. The right materials and information and reading services can interest adults who are disenchanted or ignorant of resources.

INTERESTS AND NEEDS FOR KNOWLEDGE AND INFORMATION

The interests and needs of adults, particularly adult new readers, require learning materials in print or other media that center on ethnic and cultural experiences and life skills. Literacy and adult basic educa-

[18]J. W. Getzels, "The Problem of Interests: A Reconsideration," in H. Alan Robinson, ed., *Reading: Seventy Years of Progress*, Proceedings of Annual Conference on Reading at Univ. of Chicago, 1966 (Chicago: Univ. of Chicago Pr., 1966), p. 97–105.

tion must be defined broadly in terms of the life-coping skills as well as basic literacy skills.

What are these life-coping skills? What types of materials and content areas have been identified? Coping skills have been defined as the skills and knowledge needed to interact effectively in one's environment.

In a continuing education program for adults, the Rural Family Development (RFD) demonstration project at WHA-TV (the television center at the University of Wisconsin–Madison) developed a curriculum design for adults to learn reading, writing, and computation skills through a system of coping skills that represent pressing needs. The "content centers" that were devised for the improvement of the adult's quality of life and self-determination related to the adult roles as a person, in relation to others, to himself as a worker and consumer, and as a citizen. The adults participating in this program were middle-class, rural residents with some literacy skills. Those who used the RFD's telephone service were concerned chiefly with food, home maintenance, consumer problems, family finance, gardening, health service, home crafts, employment, legal assistance, entertainment, and crafts. Other areas of interest were home renting, pest control, transportation, and wildlife. The materials that were developed for the RFD participants (and have been published) draw on several bodies of knowledge. They combine much visual content with text. The general topics, in the main, are oriented around the family, the community, and the concerns of daily living in relation to work, family, home, and money.

The area of life-coping skill needs has been broadened extensively for the Library–Adult Basic Education Demonstration Project conducted by the Appalachian Adult Education Center at Morehead State University. The categories and subcategories identified in the Life Coping Skills List include advocacy, aging, children, community, consumer economics, education, family, health, housing, insurance, jobs, leisure, relating to others, relocation, self, taxes, and transportation. The subcategories (which number over 450) provide great range and preciseness. The health category alone includes more than forty subcategories. Advocacy subcategories include arrests, civil rights, consumer rights, and legal aid. Cross-references are helpful guides; for example, "consumer rights" has a reference to "consumer economics: consumer rights." The daily informational needs are many and highly individual.

Subjects of interest to adult new readers, which were identified in the Library Materials Research Project study, are classified under broad categories: personal development, learning, education, family role, citizenship, work role, group role, and leisure role. In turn, subcategories are identified in each area. For example, specific subjects under "personal development" include alcoholism, drugs, friendship, hate, health, love, personal identity, self-preservation, sexuality, social poise, and survival.

The life or coping skills were represented in the Library Materials Research Project and RFD study collections by materials on the following subjects: animal and insect control, aging and retirement, clothing, Better Business Bureau, conservation, consumer economics, education, emergencies and disasters, family planning, planning, farming and related jobs, health and disease information, housecleaning, household appliances, household furnishings, housing and home improvements, insurance, jobs, money management, personal care and grooming, nutrition, pollution, Social Security, taxes, telephone calls, and transportation. Program learning materials were related to basic skills of reading, writing, spelling, mathematics, the history of the United States, science, jobs, and social studies.

How are the information needs of a population to be defined? Childers' recent study contributes some concrete data on the needs of disadvantaged persons as related to their universe of information.[19] Childers comes to his identification of knowledge/information needs of the disadvantaged by observing the need "indirectly, through its traces," that is, traces that are found through a review of various literatures. He concludes that the disadvantaged person has information needs which differ both in degree and in kind from the information needs of the general adult population.

The two kinds of information needs may be described as kinetic and potential. "Kinetic" needs are dictated by a given situation or condition in the life of the individual. They relate to a specific problem. They are crisis and noncrisis oriented. For example, "Where can I get a job?" "A rat bit me; what do I do?" There is an immediacy to the situation. "Potential" needs are determined by longer-range anticipations of the individual. They are apt to be unconscious, and based on impulses and values which influence behavior. For example, "Who is my senator?" "I need the name of a bail bondsman." Potential information is for use later or not at all.

The areas of information need identified by Childers confirm and extend the findings of the RFD program, the Library Materials Research Project, and the Appalachian Adult Education Center demonstration. The need for coping information to meet basic life problems is uppermost. The seventeen areas of information needs identified include health,

[19]Thomas Childers, assisted by Joyce A. Post, *The Information-Poor in America* (Metuchen, N.J.: Scarecrow, 1975).

nutrition, family planning, venereal disease, drug abuse and alcohol, mental health, sickle cell anemia, home and family, consumer buying, housing, employment, welfare programs, law, political process, transportation, education, and recreation. Information needs about social agencies and law are paramount needs. Childers documents the need for information about such subjects as arrests, bail, trials, marriage, divorce, infringement of human rights.

Paradoxically, it is in these same areas that Childers' review of the literature shows a lack of information, either to a greater or lesser degree. The literature offers little evidence that the available resources or information sources provide the type of material that is needed or can be useful. The lack of information, combined with ignorance or disillusionment based on painful experiences, creates a void for the adult who is searching for relevant materials.

SPECIFIC APPEALS AND FACTORS IN USE

Each adult reader is distinctive. One's reading, one's reading skills, one's background and experience are individual and in some ways unique. Although it is possible and important to develop general categories of reading interests and needs, and group characteristics, in no way must this result in stereotypes.

The fixed pattern of reading from childhood to adulthood has proved to be only one way for developing the reading habit. The cycle can be entered at any stage. A crucial stage is reached when the adult is able to read with some ease, is partially literate, and finds pleasure and satisfaction in reading. A new awareness grows of the experiences of other people, the world, and ideas and facts. All that has been locked away in "unreadable" print becomes a "light to travel by." It is at these critical points in the development of the adult's reading competence and his realization of the value of reading that the librarian and the teacher have the unique opportunity to make accessible the kind of materials which are meaningful and rewarding to daily living and nurture and satisfy reading development. Although reading and library-use studies indicate the importance of education as a major influence, it is recognized that formal education does not assure reading competence or create lifetime reading habits, nor does it assure maturity in reading or comprehension and understanding of what is read. At some point in their lives mature readers acquire strong motives and experience the pleasure and inspiration that are found in literature. Adult new readers in adult basic education and library reading development programs report finding a recent and sudden appreciation and satisfaction in ideas and information. As their competence in reading developed they experienced real benefits to their lives, whether as practical help which qualified them for jobs or as inspirational help which opened new horizons and the experiences of others through biographies and records of current affairs. They saw themselves as able to communicate better with others, develop confidence, and acquire greater security in personal and social relationships.

Cultural and ethnic materials influence the comprehension and the reading responses of adult readers who are in the process of developing reading and basic education skills. Two special studies related to the Library Materials Research Project investigation focus on reading materials that center on the cultural backgrounds of ethnic groups. These studies were carried out as doctoral dissertations by Deligdisch[20] and Sherrill.[21] Deligdisch gathered information on competency in reading in relation to use of the material by adult new readers. Sherrill gathered data about the influence of ethnic or cultural factors on the reading responses.

Deligdisch's study aimed at identifying characteristics of materials needed by the adult new reader in making the transition from regular use of print for daily life and work situations so that he understood and found their use rewarding, and would be encouraged to regular use. He validated his hypothesis that "adult new literates read with better comprehension materials that reflect their own cultural background." The hypothesis was tested in a series of subhypotheses in terms of reading comprehension defined as a process at three levels of understanding: literal, implied, and applied meaning. The sample of adult new readers consisted of two groups: blacks and Mexican Americans, with distinct cultural backgrounds, who were enrolled in literacy programs. A selection of culture themes was made, reading materials were developed which expressed these themes, and test materials were constructed and administered in the classrooms.

Culture themes that distinguished the Mexican American group included family concept, man's role in the family, woman's role in the family, extended family relationships, the roles of the man and the woman in society, the community, work ethos, fatalism, and time orientation. Themes that distinguished the black American included artistic expression and creativity, the matriarchal family, and man-woman relationships.

[20]Deligdisch, "Reading Comprehension of Adult New Readers in Relation to Their Ethnic Background."
[21]Sherrill, "Affective Responses of Ethnic Minority Readers to Indigenous Ghetto Literature."

Deligdisch found evidence that publications centering on these culture themes of the ethnic group may improve the adult new reader's ability to apply and use what he reads. The higher comprehension of each group of his own material at the level of literal and implied meaning is statistically significant ($p > .01$). On the level of applied meaning, the two groups, blacks and Mexican Americans, scored significantly higher on their own culture-related material than on the material related to another culture.[22]

Sherrill's study was concerned with the measurement of the affective reading responses of black and Puerto Rican readers to literature by black and Puerto Rican authors. His hypothesis is that the intensity of response will be greater when the subjects read literature which reflects their own cultural background than when they read literature which reflects a different culture. Sherrill states, "The racial orientation in reading response is the focus of this study, and its influence upon both the literature and the readers studied is profound, pervasive, and varied."[23] He measured the positive and negative responses in the reaction of the black and Puerto Rican readers toward a highly specific type of literature which reflects the ghetto experience. *Literature* is defined as personal experience, that is, literature exemplified in imaginative writing—fiction, drama, and poetry—and in factual literature—biography, autobiography, belles lettres, and possibly history. Categories of some common life styles and value orientation were developed.

For purposes of measurement, a reading form was devised which consisted of eight passages of literature, four each from black and Puerto Rican authors. The passages were chosen according to the expression of personal values, as nearly as they could be determined. The subjects responded to each unidentified passage on four scales of the semantic-differential, a total of thirty-two sets of responses. The subjects were participants in Adult Basic Education and General Education Development programs. The results were programmed and subjected to computerized statistical analysis for observing the intensity of response agreements. Indexes of the affective response agreements of the two ethnic groups of readers were calculated from the group responses registered on thirty-two semantic-differential scales to eight sample passages of literature that were representative of the two cultures.

Sherrill validated his hypothesis:

[22]Deligdisch, "Reading Comprehension of Adult New Readers in Relation to Their Ethnic Background," p. 69.

[23]Sherrill, "Affective Responses of Ethnic Minority Readers to Indigenous Ghetto Literature," p. 3.

When adult members of two ghetto ethnic minority cultures respond to samples of literature indigenous to each culture, and members responding to literature from their own culture as well as from the other culture, then the members of each culture will demonstrate greater agreement of affective response (higher response intensity) toward their own literature and lesser agreement (lower response intensity) toward the literature of the other culture.[24]

In addition to the matched median statistics supporting his hypothesis, Sherrill was able to develop histograms of the frequency distributions of the group responses of the black and Puerto Rican readers across four intervals of the semantic-differential scale. He also includes a gauge of literal comprehension which represents how much of the sample passage the reader thought he understood.

Sherrill concludes that among the highly motivated group of readers in his study, cultural factors, both in the readers and in the personal-experience literature they read, are a significant element in the process of evaluation by the reader. These factors significantly influence preferences and interpretation of what is read. He concludes, further, that the "cultural factors in the readers' backgrounds are powerful determinants of the intensity of the affective response to what they read, and that the intensity of the affective response is greater when they read personal-experience literature by authors who share their cultural background than when they read personal-experience literature by authors from a different culture."[25]

Both Sherrill and Deligdisch suggest that cultural factors are strong determinants of the cognitive and affective reading responses of ethnic minority adult readers. A major conclusion from the Library Materials Research Project study has been that the recognition and evaluation of values and attitudes through the analysis of the content are essential to the selection of materials and to informed reading guidance.[26]

Literacy skills may be used in many ways in social, political, educational, cultural, and economic activities. They are necessary to a person's participation in these activities. Without the appropriate skill, the adult is severely handicapped and unable to participate. The literacy skills required for a specific work and for performance on the job have direct economic consequences. The aspirations of individuals are as important as the existing situation. As many as 60 percent of the respondents who were interviewed in the Library Materials Research Project indicated

[24]Ibid., p. 62.
[25]Ibid., p. 81.
[26]Helen Huguenor Lyman, "Reading and the Adult New Reader," *Library Trends*, 23, no. 2:203–5 (Oct. 1973).

a desire to get into other work. Aspirations relating to getting into other work showed a radical shift from less skilled, lower-salary work to service and professional work in the more highly skilled blue-collar, technical, and professional occupations. Such aspirations for upward mobility have economic, social, and educational implications.

Language and vocabulary have important implications and impact on reading skills and learning in any area. Every person has the right to express opinions, through the vote and otherwise, about political affairs. Failure to have information and literacy skill to read and to interpret political activities and the political process places restrictions and controls on an adult's daily life. The sheer complexity and number of political, social, and economic problems prevent participation in areas that most affect the individual's life. The aesthetic pleasures and appreciation in artistic and cultural aspects of life require a level of literacy of another kind. Closely allied to the values which such appreciation can bring to brightening the adult's life are those satisfactions that can be gained by creative activities. Literacy skills enable the adult to express her or his own experiences, ideas, and thoughts in writing poetry, autobiography, stories, and essays, as well as speech.

The need for legal information is common to everyone. The law is pervasive and relates to every aspect of daily life. The ability to know and understand legal aspects which impinge on an individual's activities requires vocabulary and discourse skills of a specific kind. One analysis alone illustrates the commonness of this aspect. Virtually every topic identified in Childers' analysis of information needs for disadvantaged persons has legal aspects. The same need is common to more advantaged persons. The law bears upon a person's life from birth to death—and after. The commonness of this information need and the corollary need for literacy skills in this area of reading warrant a listing of the twenty-four concerns which Childers identified:

1. Consumer products; advertising frauds
2. Contract liability: warranties, service pacts, mortgages, etc. (including treaty rights of American Indians)
3. Credit financing; borrowing
4. Bill collecting; garnishment of salary
5. Bankruptcy
6. Workmen's compensation
7. Job security
8. Landlord vs. tenant: eviction, rent raise, withholding rent, violations of housing codes or leases
9. Relocation due to urban renewal or public construction
10. Welfare entitlements: medical care, financial assistance, food stamps, public day care, etc.

11. Arrests (especially right to counsel before hearings, in the case of a misdemeanor)
12. Bail
13. Trial, including undue postponement of trial and right to court-appointed counsel
14. Criminal records
15. Appeal of convictions (for example, "legal checkups" for convicted persons, so that their cases can be reviewed in the light of relevant new laws and court decisions)
16. Probation
17. Commitment to mental institutions
18. Torts (slander, libel, and other wrongful action that is not a misdemeanor)
19. Automobile and domestic liabilities
20. Divorce, separation, annulment, non-support
21. Adoption, guardianship, child custody, paternity
22. Death and burial
23. Estate, wills, and probate
24. Infringement of human rights (for example, racial and ethnic discrimination or illegal search and seizure).[27]

One of the most practical and realistic summaries of the kinds of subjects or topics young people and adults require from materials was developed for a research on assessment of reading literacy.[28] The domains and categories of content material developed to assess whether students could "read what they are expected to read" included over two hundred discrete types of reading materials. The content indicates not only what is expected but (undoubtedly with a few exceptions) what adults would read and want to read in order to find the reward of usefulness in solving daily problems. The list suggests materials and formats which belong in library collections. It also suggests areas and types of material needs that librarians can identify in a careful analysis of the community and the residents who are to be served. These materials require the skills and comprehension of a "mature reader" who is reading at seventh to eighth grade level.

The daily informational reading needs of adults can be translated into specific types of reading materials. Such materials, usually in pamphlet and leaflet formats, are available from various community and governmental agencies. They are at fairly advanced levels of readability,

[27]Childers, *The Information-Poor in America*, p. 73.
[28]Lee H. Hansen and Karl D. Hesse, "An Interim Report of Results of the Pilot Assessment of Reading Literacy," p. 11–13. Mimeographed. (Conducted by Office of Research and Testing in Dept. of Curriculum Development, Madison, Wis., public schools, Apr. 1972, in cooperation with the State Dept. of Public Instruction and the Univ. of Wisconsin Instructional Research Laboratory.)

and may need to be rewritten at fifth-, sixth-, or seventh-grade levels and republished. They have high interest value and yield immediate practical return. Sources for such materials are shops, stores, industrial plants, supermarkets, banks, highway departments, police and fire departments, department stores, and citizens groups.

Materials to be acquired describe these categories:

Automobile—promotional literature on new cars, auto insurance promotion, automotive license manual, automotive driving tips, operator's and owner's manual, and penalty point literature

Citizenship—the United States and state constitutions, voting instructions, national and international as well as local news, referenda statements

Leisure-time activities—rulebooks for various sports, directions for assembling toys, state recreation department bulletins, directions for games, television guide, Boy and Girl Scout manuals, directions accompanying sewing patterns

Occupational—courses and schedules offered by vocational schools, instructions on job applications, civil service test applications and examinations, armed services promotional literature and manuals, prospective career promotional literature, instructions for filling out forms, college catalogs

Reference materials—road maps for city, town, country and cross country, telephone directories, encyclopedias, and other reference books such as dictionaries, atlases, reading indexes

Safety—fire department literature, airplane emergency literature, civil defense instructions, bicycle, motorcycle, and pedestrian rules, fire evacuation rules, hunting and fishing rules and regulations, warnings on commercial packaging, heart, cancer, and other health and disease information, American Red Cross literature, directions for using power tools, plant safety signs, road signs, street signs

Consumer material—junk mail, messages on packages, catalogues, contractual agreements, banking promotional literature, banking forms, financial planning forms, advertisements and want ads in newspapers, magazines, promotional literature, conservation and ecology literature, consumer magazines, appliances

Reading aids—material on how to use the library and library reading aids, such as indexes and reviews, book lists

Adult basic education materials in language, reading, social studies, science, mathematics

Relationships with others—friendship, sexuality, sex education, marriage, divorce, child care, child development, birth, death.

Another area of interest to adults of all ages is participation in voluntary associations. Group affiliations not only shape interest but determine tasks and responsibilities for the person who participates actively as a member, officer, or committee member. The person who aspires to leadership in voluntary organizations of any kind must acquire reading, writing, listening, and speaking skills to achieve desired goals. Information about the organization and the subject areas of concern is equally important. The need for facts and information about the conduct of meetings, human relations, working together in a group, and discussion techniques stimulates the interest and demand for learning. Respondents among adult new readers in the Library Materials Research Project reported membership in a variety of organizations—labor unions, religious groups, parent associations, neighborhood improvement organizations, fraternal and civil rights groups. Memberships also were held in ethnic, sports, veterans', and political organizations.

In summary, one can only repeat that collections for adult readers must reflect interests and needs, must consider adult roles and human development, and must recognize the attitudes, values, and beliefs pertinent to the situation. Above all, it is essential to create imaginative and dynamic resource collections that are meaningful to real life and a human vision of life.

SPECIFIC NEEDS OF SPECIFIC GROUPS

A common characteristic of the majority population of the United States is mobility and the migration of individuals and whole population groups from one place to another. "Moving on," and the consequent continual change, are true for all ages of the population. The resultant problems generate a variety of new problems that require similar and dissimilar informational and educational needs that are distinctive to the migrant situation and the cultural ethnic differences.

Librarians can respond more adequately to persons who face these complex problems and changes if they know and understand the two places of movement: the client's origin (where one comes from) and destination (where one is now). Migration is the social process which links these two systems of social organization.[29] Knowledge about both systems is essential for understanding the social dimensions of the migration phenomenon in order to develop and interpret appropriate li-

---

[29]Harry K. Schwarzweller, James S. Brown, and J. J. Mangalam, *Mountain Families in Transition: A Case Study of Appalachian Migration* (University Park: Pennsylvania State Univ. Pr., 1971), p. xiv.

brary collections. Such collections will meet the immediate need and support the individual's ethnic cultural background.

It is an absolute necessity to take into account, in the sociologist's terms, the *recipient system*, that is, the social system which receives them at the place of destination, and the *donor system*, the background from which they come, the place of origin. It may be assumed that, generally, librarians have more knowledge about the community to which the migrant or immigrant comes than about their place of origin.

Librarians who study the two systems are in a better position to formulate library programs to help such groups not only relocate and meet problems of ethnic rural or urban living but also to preserve and maintain their individual culture, as they desire. The librarian who comprehends and appreciates the patterned responses and changes that adults make to modernization and changes in the world about them will be better able to find, supply, and interpret the communication media and resources.

Some members (frequently *many* members) of each reader group that is focused on in this discussion move within a state or community; migrate from state to state, region to region; or emigrate between countries. Native peoples have moved from reservations to metropolitan areas. Blacks have moved north from rural to urban communities, and in some areas are part of the farm workers' group. Mexican American or Chicanos move on seasonal migrant paths and from rural areas to cities. Puerto Ricans move from Puerto Rico to the mainland's urban centers. Appalachian mountaineers move from mountains and hollows into large cities. Immigrants from numerous countries around the world continue to reach the United States.

Among the migrant groups whose way of life is continuing movement from state to state or within a state are the farm workers of the West Coast, particularly in California. They have gained national recognition in their struggle for better living and working conditions. They have distinctive informational and social needs, somewhat different, at least in content if not in nature, from other groups. Library centers, to serve their needs and interests, would disseminate survival information and recreational materials, provide information for community leaders, and act as a recording and depository point for the history and cultural contributions of the farm workers.

Zonligt identifies specific types of needs.[30] Survival information requires answers to such questions as "Where do I get food, shelter, legal

[30]Martin J. Zonligt, *Library Services to the Farmworkers: The Need for a Survival Information Center* (Chicago: Office for Library Service to the Disadvantaged, ALA, 1974).

assistance, work?" "Where do I learn English so as not to get taken by my boss or contractor?" Farm workers need information and assistance regarding unionization, filling out forms, translating letters, and the use of videotapes and films. They need to learn about local issues, medical care, voting records of politicians, information on labor contracts. They need to learn how to establish cooperatives and food-buying clubs. They need assistance in areas of "friendly concern," such as introduction to Anglos and other community contacts, to sources of scholarship funds, and referral to tutorial programs.

Survival information centers would have information on housing, medical aid, employment situations, current pay, child-care facilities, crop conditions, and harvest time. The centers would serve as the community resource for information about other agencies, farm workers' educational programs, and social services. They might serve as a center for all agencies and as a follow-up point for other agencies' clientele.

What happens to the Appalachian who moves from familiar mountains to strange cities is recorded in fiction and nonfiction in such novels as *The Dollmaker* (by Harriette Arnow) and such studies as *Mountain Families in Transition*. Appalachian culture is portrayed in the writings and music of such artists as Earl Thomas, Muriel Miller Dressler, Jane Stuart, Kathy Kahn, and John Gagliardi.

Let us return to the needs of disadvantaged adults with less than a high school education and to the implications for library services as identified during seven years of intensive study by the Appalachian Adult Education Center (AAEC).[31] Four groups with distinctive characteristics in economic, social, and education areas show a progressive decline in economic security, education, self-direction, and use of public services. (The four groups have been described in chapter 2.)

Individuals who are economically and personally secure are easier to reach than those who are impoverished and troubled. They can learn in more formal group situations. They have literacy skills and faith in education. They can be reached through mass media. They will learn to use the library. They tend to function at high levels of skill, which enables them to use programmed and General Education Development (GED) materials from the library collection. Even more advanced groups require service, that is, those persons who are engaged in a College-Level Examination Program (CLEP) of independent learning.

Individuals who are somewhat less secure are underemployed, have less schooling and lower literacy skill, but are reached fairly easily. They profit from self-instruction methods and materials. They achieve their

[31]Drennan, "The Nature of Disadvantaged Adults."

goals quickly and are able to change their economic level and life styles. They need more individualized assistance than the more secure individual, and library schedules that are adjusted to make it possible for them to use the library.

Persons with little or no economic and personal security have limited or no literacy skills, little or no faith in public service. They require individual formal service. They tend to be people oriented. Because they have little mastery of literacy skills or self-direction, they need clearly articulated subgoals toward which they can work. They can be reached by well-designed one-to-one recruitment campaigns and person-to-person service.

Persons who are unemployed and without literacy skills or education have the highest information needs. They are not likely to interpret problems as information needs. They are less inclined to use mass media, seek answers, or attempt change. Mere survival requires all their energy. Yet AAEC studies show that they can go from nonreader through high school completion in four years when they are approached through the appropriate delivery system. Initially they must be served in homes. Traditional "come to the library" concepts must change radically to bring service to this group.

It can be seen that, in order to provide the opportunities suited to their needs and literacy skills and knowledge, library resources and continuing education for disadvantaged adults must be distributed differently. Those adults who have skills require fewer services and can make use of more traditional materials. Those adults who have little schooling, many problems, and a history of disappointments require direct personal service, carefully selected materials of immediate use, and more referral services for a longer period of time.

A much needed change in library service involves serving the former as economically as possible and conserving a large portion of monies so as to offer the same quality of services to the latter. It involves setting priorities for developing collections of materials in areas of adult basic education, ethnic appeals, and varying readability levels—and from untraditional sources as well as in varying formats. Such policies are a radical departure from the usual practice of allocating or dividing available service dollars strictly by the number of persons served, or by service function such as reference, or for acquisition of traditional material in demand. Figure 5 attempts to demonstrate that, to provide an equal *quality* of service to all potential clientele, the *quantity* of money spent on individuals or individual service must vary.

In what ways can libraries achieve improved service for Chicano or Mexican Americans in their communities? Elizabeth Martinez Smith

GROUP	SOME MAJOR CHARACTERISTICS	DESIGN OF SERVICE
1 More economically and personally secure than other three groups; more education and steadier employment.	Belief in rewards from education, library and other agencies. Belief in self stronger than that held in other groups. Requisite energy for learning tasks. Literacy skills.	Can be recruited fairly easily through usual channels. Responds to group services fairly successfully. Uses communication media and other formal sources of information. Uses print. Studies for credential certification. Requires less financial support.
2 Less security and more problems than group 1 because of under-education and lack of continuous employment; more secure and fewer problems than groups 3 and 4.		
3 Less secure and more underemployed than groups 1 and 2 due to lack of high school study and to sporadic employment.	Little faith in educational system or self. Little energy to give to learning because of poverty and deprivation. Lack of income. Lack of literacy skills. People-oriented.	Must be recruited on one-to-basis. Needs face-to-face tutorial service. Requires supportive services, such as home service, transportation, child care. Uses nonprint media more easily than print. Has high information needs. Requires more financial support than with groups 1 and 2.
4 Fatalistic, unemployed because of lack of education and other obstacles; little or no schooling or security.		

Figure 5. Relationship between the individual characteristics of adults with less than high school education and the design of delivery systems for public services. (Adapted from a model developed by the Appalachian Adult Education Center in *Annual Report, 1973*, v. 2, p. 5. Washington, D.C.: HEW, Bureau of Libraries and Learning, June 1973.)

makes specific suggestions. First, the Spanish language, the *mestizaje* of the people, religion, and Mexican history must be an integral part of the library collection. Chicanos must be part of the decision making in determining policies, services, and programs. They must take part in the selection of materials and personnel. The employment of bilingual, bicultural librarians in decision-making positions will help to assure the understanding and commitment needed for success. Communication and credibility are made possible when Spanish and English are used. Spanish-language media—television, radio, newspapers, and magazines —can be used. If a bilingual staff is available at all times, it will not be necessary to resort to sign language and rely on a few Spanish words and a smile.

The library resources will determine the quality and extent of service rendered. A library which serves the Chicano community, or for that matter any Latino community, must maintain three collections: English, Spanish, and bilingual. The collections will include all types of materials —books, pamphlets, documents, periodicals, games, recordings, and films. An abundance of material can be found by using Spanish-language distributors, publications from Mexico, Latin American countries, and Chicano publishers in the United States. The guiding principle is that the Spanish and bilingual collection must be as diverse and encompassing as the English-language collections.

The *mestizaji* of the people can be reflected also in the atmosphere of the building. In the Southwest, buildings in Mexican-Southwest architectural style will be inviting. The familiar symbols of Mexican heritage, such as pictures, displays, music, and flags, can create a friendly, inviting environment.

Programs can be centered around many historical and religious events. Holidays of significance to Chicano people are *Cinco de Mayo*, when the Mexicans defeated the French in 1862, and *16 de Septiembre*, Mexico's independence day.

Librarians must have realistic expectations, and patience. Well-organized and relevant service can create respect and use for the library. After all, there is a library tradition of one hundred years or more for the dominant English-speaking public. Chicanos cannot be expected to flock to libraries, expressing gratitude and wholehearted support, when they have been ignored for so long.

The same principles and practice apply to any reader group. The history, culture, expectations, and aspirations, as well as their own communication resources, must be recognized, respected, and included through the service of the library, whether school, public, academic, or special. The many individuals and groups who make up the rather amorphous group, euphemistically categorized "persons for whom English is a second language," will respond to recognition of their backgrounds and interests.

What follows is a discussion on some of the implications which being Puerto Rican has for those who must respond to the second generation in identifying a new reader group. Dr. Betances sees many problems in identifying, purchasing, and holding on to materials of interest to Puerto Ricans as a particular reader group. These same problems also apply to other reader groups, and particularly the Mexican Americans and native Americans.

A major obstacle in the acquisition of materials for the new reader group is determining where one finds adequate materials. Institutions of higher learning have relied on departments, instructors, and catalogues for hints on titles the library needs to have. Some adult education programs rely more on administrators than teachers and librarians. Few institutions include the readers.

These traditional ways will not serve the reading and media needs of Puerto Ricans. Institutions of higher learning have ignored the reading needs of the few Puerto Rican students who have enrolled in such institutions in the past. For example, in such areas as ethnic and race relations, curricula planners, educators, and librarians have assumed—often erroneously—that when the black/white issue is covered in lectures and readings, in some way this coverage is sufficient for the students to appreciate and understand American race and ethnic group relations.

Few people realize that, to a great extent, the established publishing houses determine what kinds of books will be written and purchased. That factor alone means that few books will come out on the Puerto Rican, because the absence of a profitable market has been assumed by publishers for such books. A formula used by some companies in determining whether they will contract with a writer to supply a manuscript is whether the potential book will sell 10,000 copies the first year. It is very difficult to convince such firms that "solid" books (for example, on the political status issue in Puerto Rico or the individual needs of mainland youth) will sell 10,000 copies the first year, but such books, which are of great importance to students of the Puerto Rican experience on both sides of the ocean, may well make a profit for a company.

Large publishing houses plan their sales for the whole continent, and in their marketing consider the international market. It is difficult for sales representatives, writers, or librarians to convince the publishers that a Puerto Rican market exists. It is thought inconceivable that a people who are poor, who often are excluded from educational institutions, whose homeland is only the size of Connecticut, who may speak a language other than English, and whose image to the larger society does not go beyond the Hollywood portrayal of *West Side Story* can really be taken seriously as part of the reading public.

Puerto Ricans, who number close to 2 million on the mainland (taking into account the first, bridge, and second generations), have in recent years demanded courses, faculty members, and ethnic study programs and departments in higher education that are relevant to the Puerto Rican historical cultural experience. It is true that many read Spanish and are fluent in English as well. Because reading materials are not found in traditional bookstores and libraries, Puerto Ricans either must do without vital materials or start bookstores in the barrios (as has been done in the Northeast and Midwest). Actually, a great hunger exists for reading materials and information. Libraries, above all, ought to have the materials needed to serve the Puerto Rican reader. Priorities should be given to publishing books in subject areas of interest to the students of Puerto Rican experience to enrich that population's hunger for knowledge.

Some publishing companies are becoming aware of Puerto Ricans as a particular reader group. For example, Frederick A. Praeger, Publishers, has begun to respond to the Puerto Rican market by contracting Kal Wagenheim to write and edit books of great interest to Puerto Ricans. Companies in Puerto Rico that publish pertinent books (at times in English) of interest to the mainland reader have not taken into account the market which the second generation represents. Although this problem is changing, because Puerto Rican educators and community leaders are receiving lists of books that are published on the island, other problems remain.[32] The island companies usually publish one edition of a book, and they publish far too few copies (3,000 copies is the average). Consequently, some important books go out of print before they become available to the market outside Puerto Rico. Puerto Rican publishing firms, if they want to become competitive, will have to send sales representatives to outlets which serve the second-generation reader in the United States. They will have to publish larger editions and translate some works for wider distribution in this country. Libraries on the mainland will have to make use of reading lists and order books from the island with a sense of urgency.

---

[32]An example is the list provided by Editorial Edil of Rio Piedras, Puerto Rico, *Nuevos Libros de Puerto Rico: Catalogo* (1973/74).

Because Puerto Ricans are close to their homeland in terms of language and customs, libraries must have works in the Spanish language. At the same time, development of such collections becomes almost impossible because of the shortage of bilingual librarians. It may be advisable for institutions of higher learning and libraries to create ad hoc committees of Puerto Ricans, who may meet several times a year with library staffs to recommend what may be worth acquiring to serve Puerto Rican readers.

Beyond some general interest in the Puerto Rican reader, some libraries will want to develop comprehensive collections. In order to develop a serious collection of works, it may be necessary to reprint works from the Puerto Rican collection at the University of Puerto Rico or the Library of Congress. Tomas Blanco's *El Prejuicio Racial en Puerto Rico* is an example of why it makes sense to have books reprinted. Although only 1,200 copies of Blanco's book were published in 1938, the book is of particular importance to the second generation because the race issue is of great importance on the mainland. Many pamphlets, articles, essays, monographs, and books also could be made available in this way for the new reader.

The *San Juan Star*, Puerto Rico's leading English-language newspaper, is of interest to the Puerto Rican readers, as is *Claridad*, a newspaper which has an English supplement. *Claridad* is published by a political party which hopes to see Puerto Rico become an independent republic. Its perspective often takes the mainland into account, and Puerto Rican students enjoy reading it.

As an ethnic group in American society, the Puerto Ricans stand to gain substantially by knowing "who they are" and "where they came from." The host society also will gain by coming in contact with still another diverse and culturally rich group of people. Libraries can help the process by providing essential services to this new but permanent reading group. The larger society (and other ethnic groups) will read and learn about themselves in the context of learning about the Puerto Ricans.[33]

Gladys Alesi points out the importance of a coordinated effort by teachers and librarians to help students in English-as-a-second-language

[33]Books of interest to Puerto Rican readers include Kal Wagenheim and Olga Jimenez de Wagenheim, eds., *Puerto Ricans: A Documentary History* (New York: Praeger, 1973; Doubleday, 1975); Francesco Cordasco with Eugene Bucchioni, *The Puerto Rican Experience: A Sociological Sourcebook* (Totowa, N.J.: Littlefield, Adams, 1973); Paquito Vivo, ed., *The Puerto Ricans: An Annotated Bibliography* (sponsored by Puerto Rican Research Center, Washington, D.C.) (New York: R. R. Bowker, 1973).

classes find reading materials. She describes several instances of cooperative efforts. Obstacles faced by students in the use of libraries have been overcome in many programs in New York City.

One of the first cooperative efforts between the public adult schools and the public library was launched in Brooklyn, with the impact coming from the Brooklyn Public Library. As a result of this initial success, adult class visits to libraries today are taken for granted. The books that are displayed for the class visits are selected because of interest level, psychological attraction, and instructional power. Librarian and teacher, planning the first visit, discuss specific students and their needs and interests so that the display table may be attractive to everyone in the group. In this discussion, the teacher describes a student's need to know about home repairs, getting a driver's license, information on baby care, and works in the native language. The display table should include many books in self-help categories. In the first visit, students are shown around the library and note many special features—the community bulletin board, the file of civil service notices and examinations. Students obtain library cards so that they might leave with library books of their choice. In class, students dramatize the experience of asking for specific information.

Cooperative programs stimulate reading interests and habits for English-as-a-second-language students. Fear, sensitivity, and suspicion—characteristics of misunderstanding among adults who have been uprooted and transplanted—disappear as people find they are responsible for themselves in a supportive atmosphere that has respect for their personality, needs, and traditions.

Rarihokwats pleads, cajoles, and "orders" that autonomy be passed to native peoples, who are the only ones who are competent to make decisions. The librarians are in a position to advise and place their professional technical knowledge at the service of this reader group.

Dudley Randall would have library service focused on the younger population—the young adults. Surely the adult population among blacks is vitally and actively interested in education and the library's role. Public, school, and academic libraries have a deep responsibility to provide the kind of reading collections that this reader group (and librarians) can point to with pride and can use with profit.

The response to the reading needs and interests of the black population and many Afro-American studies in the curricula at all levels of education has resulted in a vast amount of materials in print and other media, published by new black publishers and traditional publishing houses. Here the problem becomes identification of sources and selective acquisition. Librarians will find the extensive collections of the book-stores in the ghetto communities of the largest cities—Boston, New York, Baltimore, Washington, Los Angeles, San Francisco, Chicago—are the most accessible sources of supply.

It can be noted here that the phenomenon of topical bookstores (similar to that of the paperback) requires study. Subjects of current importance to all groups are to be found in the bookstores that specialize in current interests, such as the women's movement, the occult, whole earth and natural foods, and the "small press" and "underground" publications.

The need to involve the community in the structure and goals of libraries cannot be stressed enough. Many of the community groups, Chicanos, Native Americans, Puerto Ricans, and others do see the library as unnecessary to their survival, a fact history will uphold. What Elizabeth Martinez Smith points out in relation to Chicanos is relevant to other parts of the population. She points out the value of the celebrations such as the Christmas pageant of "Las Posadas" and Easter celebration of the "Blessing of the Animals" which are significant to the Chicano public. She stresses the need to involve the Chicano public in the structure and goals of libraries. Success will be virtually impossible, at best miniscule, if local organizations—from the established and conservative to the grassroots and radical, community centers, churches, schools (all levels)—and individual *jefes* and *jefas* (leaders, important people, chiefs; an affectionate term for those people who are aware of all that goes on within a given neighborhood) are not included in the planning and implementation of library services. Personal contact in the form of door-to-door visits, written invitations, and talks at group meetings are essential. The library must be presented as a service-information center that belongs to the community and is governed by its needs, wants, and desires.

A word of caution: Librarians will need patience and must be able to tolerate criticism. After all, there is a library tradition of one hundred years or more for the dominant English-speaking public. Chicanos and others cannot be expected to flock to libraries expressing gratitude and wholehearted support when they have been ignored for so long.

8

Evaluation of Reading Materials

The dynamics of library service to adult readers depend to a great extent on successful and imaginative evaluation of reading materials. Objective and subjective evaluation makes possible the choice and recommendation of appropriate reading for intellectual and practical use by adults and adult groups. Complete analysis of a written work, either of a general or specific nature, is essential to the development of library collections that are adequate and satisfactory to the circumstances of adult roles and life styles. Criteria for evaluation measure the source of the message, and the message itself, in terms of the ideas and information communicated, as well as the treatment or style of presentation. The facts and insights gained through analysis of the material are a foundation for selective and informed reading guidance. The evaluator envisions more accurately the potential reader or receiver of the message. This process in no way denies choice and personal selection by the reader, who makes the final judgment in the act of use and in terms of satisfaction and impact for oneself or one's group.

Four major elements that are basic to the evaluation of reading materials for adult readers and reader groups (with which this discussion is primarily concerned) are:

1. The characteristics, interests and needs, and life styles for the reader groups and individuals among the residents of the library community
2. The nature of adulthood, adult roles, the society, and the environment, as well as the daily responsibilities and problems which are adult concerns

3. The nature and characteristics of a library's collection, selected to meet principles and standards established in terms of adulthood and an adult community's interests and needs, as well as professional and ethical requirements
4. A philosophy of library service.

The interaction among these elements—philosophy, adulthood, life styles, interests and needs, the ideas and information contained in resources of the library—creates the dynamics of adult library service. The analyses about adults and adult reading in the first part of this book and the principles and standards for selection, which are to be proposed, are to be applied in the context of use. The philosophy and criteria for analysis of reading materials require careful reading and examination of the material which is being evaluated and comparisons with other resources. The character of the four elements and their interrelationships, and decisions regarding them, can be determined only by the residents and the library staff, who are in a "real" situation.

During the past decade, several research studies and experimental adult education and library reading development programs have added knowledge about adult reading and furnished new facts and insights for the development of adult reading programs and library services. They are referred to in other parts of this book, and specifically in chapter 9. The conclusions reached by Fader; MacDonald; the staff at the Appalachian Adult Education Center, Morehead State University; Barss, Reitzel and Associates; and Lipsman are noted. The findings of various researchers—Harman, Hilliard, Laubach, Freire, Goldberg, Brooks, Brown and Newman, Clift, Otto, Ford, Keller—have been reviewed in some detail under "Previous Research and Studies" in Lyman's *Library Materials in Service to the Adult New Reader*. Also in that volume, in "Five Cities in the LMRP Population Study," are brief descriptive accounts of the library reading development programs in Baltimore, Cleveland, Los Angeles, New York, and Philadelphia. Continuing research and experiences bring further data about reading interests and needs and evaluative criteria for the selection and analysis of reading materials.

Until recently, major determinants for the addition of an item to a library's collection have been demand from individuals or groups in the community, availability from the publishing world, and quality (sometimes defined as value). These criteria, which incorporated mainly values and literary standards of a middle-class dominant white culture, created what has been described (endlessly) as middle-class basic library collections. Demand-oriented philosophy results all too often in restrictive practices. Acquisition of materials is dependent on expressed approval or disapproval. The opinions of a limited but vocal number of persons justify selection. Admittedly, demand that means use is an important criterion in any library; but the quantity of unexpressed demands and relevance to everyone must also be considered.

The "balanced" collection all too often becomes bland and mediocre, "safe," and restricted to the past or uncontroversial current items. Conversely, the gathering in of everything permits usefulness in a narrow area of knowledge and little or no usefulness to some of the needs of many persons. Quality frequently means literary merit in which content is supportive of values held by dominant groups in society, or a local community, or by librarians. Literary merit, as the decisive test of quality, ignores the range of expressions, plurality of styles, the communication media available in the contemporary world.

Quality, of course, *is* important. A collection of quality, with quantity that can satisfy single and multiple demands, is the goal of librarians in all types of libraries. It is striven for in relation to an entire collection as well as to its parts. It it not to be circumscribed and fashioned by a narrow or biased acquisition and selection policy.

· What is meant by quality? It is difficult to define—is frequently intangible, is formed by tastes, opinions, values, and study. It may be judged by everyone, particularly in regard to works in humanities and outside factual or scientific information. Quality may be a literary factor, a style, an honest or accurate statement, whether found in a factual pamphlet of information or a sophisticated, complex work of literature, an elementary introduction to a subject or a scholarly treatise. In the context of today's problems and scientific and humanitarian knowledge of the twentieth century, quality certainly means more than literary merit or content supportive of values or beliefs held by dominant or powerful groups, by censorious minorities or self-selected censors. Quality indicates originality in excellence and superiority.

The issue, then, becomes agreement on what quality is or what other factors may be more important. Opinions and judgments differ. Personal and public tastes and values lead to different decisions. Librarians are faced with the necessity of defining excellence and its distinctive characteristics. Well-differentiated attributes in the reading material will be considered within the context of the community to be served and the variety of communication resources. The recognition of pluralism becomes paramount. Both expressed and unexpressed demand are important. Recognition of changes in society and adult life and thoughtful appraisal of the elements in the educational, recreational, informational, and inspirational functions of the public library bring to the fore the important factor of diversity. A diverse population with different beliefs and values, a technology for global communication that brings peoples of the world closer together, and new tastemakers with command of a variety of printing methods require collections that are tailored to specific interests and needs and are, at the same time, intellectually stimulating.

A critical assessment of the population, community resources, and library resources will reveal the many interests and informational needs which only a diverse collection will satisfy. This significant aspect of evaluation is performed in the depth and precision of the analysis. Its extent depends upon the content, type, and quality of the material. The usefulness of the criteria to a library's program of reading guidance service depends also upon the philosophy of service and the competence of the staff.

Librarians develop collections that are thought provoking and responsive to residents of the library's community if they are close to changes and try to understand both past and present. The philosophical bases for developing library collections, based on criteria of balance, literary merit, the uncontroversial and the tested, result in quite different collections when libraries recognize the various modes and media of communication, the range of ideas and literary treatment in communication, and the "alternative press" as well as the traditional publishing houses. With such recognition librarians will combine knowledge of expressed and unexpressed demand, sensitivity to various values and life styles among residents of the community, and facts about the informational and educational needs of the population. Attention will be given to materials about controversial areas of ideas, beliefs, politics, sexuality and human relations, issues and problems. Open discussion of hitherto forbidden and secretive social matters will be reflected in the variety of resources.

EVALUATOR AS MATURE READER

The evaluator who judges materials for the library's collection must be a mature reader. Maturity is not an achievement or point of equilibrium. It is an ongoing process and growth—a process of becoming. To become a critical reader requires years of experience. The librarian is in an advantageous position to enjoy that development and, at the same time, carry out professional responsibilities. The least experienced staff member has competence and abilities in some area of study and experience. Some stage of maturity has been reached in the mere fact of reaching adulthood.

What characteristics distinguish the mature reader? The question has been answered by various researchers, such as Huse, Philbrich, Adler, Center, and Strang, and summarized by Gray and Rogers.[1] These same characteristics are relevant to the librarian evaluator and are to be interpreted here in a professional context of library service.

Of primary importance, as Stella Center emphasized over twenty years ago, is a genuine enthusiasm for reading, an "irresistible compulsion to read," and the habit of reading for "intelligent delight." Let no one take the responsibility for reading and evaluating ideas and content, accuracy of information, factual or imaginative writing, who has no enthusiasm for the subject or the task. This keen enjoyment of reading and breadth of reading interest, which are characteristic of the mature reader, are all the more essential for the selector of reading collections.

Secondly, the mature reader reads a wide variety of materials that contribute pleasure, stimulate creative thinking, and include serious materials which promote understanding of social, economic, and political problems of society and problems of an ethical and moral nature. Few individuals can achieve range and depth in many areas. The mature reader who, as librarian, attempts a range of reading, at the same time reads seriously—in depth at a high level of critical evaluation—in one or more subject areas. Insofar as the librarian gains this in-depth knowledge and is thoroughly informed about a particular subject or type of materials selection, it is possible to make a more critical and dependable selection and interpretation of those reading resources.

Third, the mature reader has the ability to translate words into meanings, to understand the ideas presented, and to sense the mood and feelings communicated. In this respect the librarian correlates knowledge of the material in the context of use by potential readers. Comprehensibility and style are related to the writer's intended audience or to the reader whose interest has been identified by the librarian. In brief, the librarian can act as liaison between the author and reader.

Fourth, the mature reader has the

ability to perceive strengths and weaknesses in what is read, to detect bias and propaganda, to think critically concerning the validity and values of ideas presented and the adequacy and soundness of the author's presentation, views, and conclusions. This involves an emotional apprehension, either favorable or unfavorable, as well as a penetrating intellectual grasp of what is read.[2]

[1]Gray and Rogers, *Maturity in Reading*.
[2]Ibid., p. 54.

This ability is of particular significance for the librarian who identifies the attitudes, beliefs, values and adult roles that are presented in the material.

Fifth, the mature reader has a tendency to fuse new ideas (acquired through reading) with previous experience, which may result in clearer understanding and broader interests, improved "patterns of thinking," and personal growth. Librarians may wish to attain such abilities for personal benefits. Professionally, such abilities sharpen librarians' judgment in developing collections of substance and stature about social problems and in anticipating reading interests and issues in new and frequently controversial areas of information and ideas. They further aid in achieving an objective and fair position which can be recognized by the residents of the community.

Sixth, the mature reader has a capacity and habit for making use of all one knows or can find out in interpreting or construing the meaning of the ideas read. This has important implications for librarians in situations of reading guidance and in activities for interpreting the materials. In this respect the librarian, as a mature reader, has the capacity to adjust one's reading pace to the needs of the occasion and to the demands of adequate interpretation. Limitations of time and energy and (what is more influential) restrictions because of other demands set limitations on the librarian's achievement of this goal.

With such a background, the librarian evaluator develops the ability to:

1. Critically evaluate and use the opinions and judgments of others, such as critics, specialists, library users, and understand and take into account their biases and values.
2. Recognize and respect the various attitudes and values within the community's populations.
3. Read and select materials which meet the cultural needs and interests, the life styles, of groups in the community who are less dominant, fewer in numbers, and different from the majority group, as well as for the latter, whose members have more similarities.
4. Translate the understanding of ideas and attitudes into meaningful information and reading guidance techniques for the benefit of individuals and groups in the community.
5. Develop wide experience in publishing and published materials, which enriches one's knowledge and understanding.
6. Continue building and strengthening special subject areas that are determined by professional and personal areas of interest and need.
7. Develop resources and knowledge of the information and educational resources that are available to adults at the local, regional, and national levels.
8. Read with expertness, skill, comprehension, and assimilation, at a rate suitable to the material read.

In the last quarter of the twentieth century, books are only a part of a library's collection. Electronic media and audiovisual formats are pervasive transmitters of information. At the same time, books take on new forms—paperback, audio tape, computer—and comprise a basic medium of communication. The arts of book selection and book reading are set forth with great knowledge and sensitivity, and literary style, by Haines in *Living with Books*[3] and Adler and Van Doren in *How to Read a Book*.[4] Haines' principal theme continues to be pertinent: "Those who select books for library service can develop proficiency and vitalize their work only by themselves 'living with books.' "

Twenty-five years later, the choices are extended to innumerable formats, subject matters, and changing environments. Criteria change but the essential principles remain. Haines and Adler suggest tests and ways through which selection can become an art. Haines' tests for nonfiction, which are in the form of questions, consider subject matter, authority, qualities, physical characteristics, and values for the reader. She adds several specific tests for fiction, and definitions of each area.

Librarians continue to find the following tests for nonfiction and fiction useful (as outlined by Haines):

TESTS FOR NONFICTION

SUBJECT MATTER

What is subject or theme?
What is scope? Complete? Partial? History of the subject, or discussion of certain aspects or conditions?
Additional subjects covered?
Is the book brief? Exhaustive? Selective? Balanced?
Is the treatment concrete? Abstract?
Is it popular? Scholarly? Technical? Semitechnical?
Is it for general readers? Students? Specialists?
Date (usually important in relation to subject matter).

AUTHORITY

What are the author's qualifications? What is his education? Experience?
Special preparation for writing this book?
Has he used source material? If secondary material, is it reliable?
Is his work based on personal observation or research?

[3]Helen E. Haines, *Living with Books: The Art of Book Selection* (2d ed.; New York: Columbia Univ. Pr., 1950).

[4]Mortimer J. Adler and Charles Van Doren, *How to Read a Book* (rev. and updated; New York: Simon & Schuster, 1972).

Is it accurate? Inexact?

Does he understand thoroughly the period, facts, or theories with which he deals?

What is the author's point of view? Partisan? Fair-minded? Conservative? Radical?

QUALITIES

Does the work show any degree of creative power?

Is the form appropriate to the thought?

Has it originality of conception? Of expression?

Has it a clear, graphic style? Readability? Charm? Profundity? Imaginative power?

Has it vitality? Interest? Is it likely to endure as a permanent contribution to literature?

PHYSICAL CHARACTERISTICS

Is there an adequate index?

Are there illustrations? Maps? Charts or graphs? Bibliographies? Appendixes? Any other reference features?

Has the book clear type? Good paper?

VALUES FOR READER

Information?

Contribution to culture?

Stimulation of interests?

Recreation or entertainment?

What reading relationships does it offer?

To what types of readers does it appeal?

TESTS FOR FICTION

(Some of the tests previously cited are also appropriate for fiction.)

Is it true to life? Sensational? Exaggerated? Distorted?

Has it vitality and consistency in character depiction? Valid psychology? Insight into human nature?

Is the plot original? Hackneyed? Probable? Simple? Involved?

Is dramatic interest sustained?

Does it stimulate? Provoke thought? Satisfy? Inspire? Amuse?[5]

The insights and enduring values of this exemplary text continue to serve as guides and inspiration for the library school student and the librarian. The principles set forth in the context of library service in a field of librarianship devoted to discriminating judgment and the application of the potencies of books to the enrichment of life continue to be valid and useful.

Adler and Van Doren discuss in a straightforward, logical way the art of reading a good book for understanding. They see the goals of

[5]Haines, *Living with Books*, p. 53–54. Reprinted by permission.

reading to be information, understanding, and entertainment. Although the three goals are frequently inseparable, the authors focus on reading for understanding, that is, analytical reading for comprehension and enlightenment. Reading is an active process and an act of discovery.

How to Read a Book is a practical guidebook, a manual with rules for the achievement of an art. The first step is skimming and inspectional reading to determine the general theme or idea, comprehend the book's structure, and interpret generally the contents. Active reading requires a "demanding reader" who asks what the book is about, what is being said, how it is said, is it true in whole or in part, and what is its significance.

Their rules for intelligent reading may be summarized briefly. The active reader will try to find out the theoretical and practical structure of the book, determine the author's messages (meanings, propositions, and arguments), criticize the book fairly and reasonably, and follow certain criteria for disagreement and agreement.

Then the general rules are translated into guides on how to read different kinds of reading matter—practical books, imaginative literature, stories, plays, poems, history, science, mathematics, philosophy, and social sciences. Finally, they discuss how to analyze and compare different books and authors, that is, to read syntopically.

The Adler and Van Doren methods may not appeal to everyone, but their rules are extremely helpful and a matter for consideration for the mature reader.

Traditional criteria frequently interpret authority and reliability of authors and publishers insofar as they are well known. Criteria emphasize elements which are difficult to define and agree upon, such as quality, literary value, permanence, moral tendency, proper language, orthodox beliefs and values. In some instances demand becomes the sole consideration. Such criteria are not to be discarded, but in the context of this subject they are inadequate. Although they may be interpreted more broadly, other criteria are necessary. The diversity of interests among potential readers and in available publications is to be recognized and taken into account.

Criteria are expanded to include principles and standards that encompass new and unknown authors and publishers, a variety of formats, controversial subjects, differing beliefs and values, the ephemeral and immediate as well as the enduring, a range of literary treatment, and language appropriate to the content. The relevance and reality of the content and the style and attitude with which a work is presented, as well as the information and ideas contained in the work, are key elements in use or nonuse by adult men and women. Unreal or false situations, unfamiliar language, derogatory phrases, disrespectful attitudes to a culture, untruths and false pictures of history and events are as important to identify and judge as the true, the respectful, the familiar, the real. In this connection the six speakers describe (chapters 5 and 6) the reality, as they see it, faced by minority populations within the United States. Fortunately, library programs have changed somewhat in recent years. The identification of materials which present strengths and contributions of each group, as well as meet the group's problems and needs, is recognized as important.

The detailed analysis, precise description, and critical evaluation advocated are desirable and possible. One instrument, developed expressly for this purpose, is the guide *MAC Checklist—Materials Analysis Criteria: Standards for Measurement.*[6] Although this instrument of evaluation developed in the Library Materials Research Project was designed to evaluate materials for a specific group, identified as adult new readers, the application of the MAC checklist to a wide range of materials proved that the instrument can be used in the evaluation of adult materials for various types of readers who have a range of reading skills. The subsequent discussion follows the concepts and procedure of the MAC checklist.

MATERIALS ANALYSIS CRITERIA

The first step in analyzing the book, magazine, newspaper, or pamphlet is naturally to read it. For a complete analysis of any type of writing, the entire work must be read. For some types, a careful examination and skimming may suffice. The kind of material, the simplicity or complexity of the ideas, information, and treatment are major considerations. On the assumption that, because of careful reading, the evaluator knows the material, the analytic process proceeds. The depth and precision of the analysis rests on the knowledge, judgments, and decisions of the evaluator.

The general areas for evaluation include bibliographic evaluation, content analysis, measurement of readability, appeal to readers, and quantitative evaluation. The information gained in the analysis of these five areas serves as a basis for a descriptive summary for each of the

---

[6]The development of the MAC checklist is described in the research report *Library Materials in Service to the Adult New Reader*, part IV. The MAC checklist is on p. 492–511 of the first (1973 ed.) and second (1974 ed.) printings. The second printing is recommended because of the corrected sequence in the checklist.

five areas. This summary record and the specific facts learned in the analysis become the basis for a descriptive, critical annotation. Essential facts about the material and a well-balanced presentation of tangible and intangible aspects of the work, comparisons with other materials, and recommendations are recorded for use in acquisition and reading guidance.

Bibliographic Evaluation

The analysis begins, as in any evaluation, with critical evaluation of the bibliographic aspects. These aspects include author, title, illustrator, publisher, quality of the series and the edition, the language of the text, price, date, physical format, and type of literature. Each bibliographic aspect must be considered separately but in relation to the other aspects. Any one aspect may be the determining factor in an acquisition decision.[7]

Layout and format make a difference. Acceptance or rejection of material by the adult new reader may be influenced by the visual appeal of the cover and inside pages of the material. The judgment to read or not to read may depend on the use of color, presence or absence of illustrations on the cover, or a book jacket. The motivation to read may depend entirely on external factors. The desire to continue to read may depend on the accuracy and honesty of the motivating factors. When they mislead or confuse, the content may not be "satisfactory."

Assessment of the authority and integrity of the source is a major consideration. Are the authors and editors well known or unknown or anonymous? Frequently a search for facts about the source must be made. Reference aids and indexes are necessary. Specialists in subject areas, professionals, and community residents can assist in evaluation. The publisher's announcement, book-trade announcements, reviews, and book notes provide clues and opinions. Some authors have local significance. Because much of the material may originate from sponsored sources or indigenous sources outside the regular trade channels and review media, frequently judgments about authors and publishers must be made on the basis of the content itself.

The publishing house whose publications are known to be dependable is usually reliable. Publishers who can be relied upon for timely and useful works that will meet standards of excellence include Doubleday;

---

[7]The reader is referred to the perceptive, detailed discussion in Haines, *Living with Books*, chap. 9: "Books in Their Textual and Physical Aspects," and chap. 11: "Editions, Series, Translations." Her definitions of terms and points to observe in selection are valuable.

Follett; Harcourt Brace Jovanovich; Holt, Rinehart & Winston; McGraw-Hill; New Readers Press; Noble & Noble; Reader's Digest Services; Scholastic Book Services; Scott, Foresman; and Steck-Vaughn, to name only a few.

But the range and diversity of interests and needs are far from met within the usual channels. The lesser-known, obscure, and small ethnic presses which are outside the regular trade channels and have a limited number of publications are difficult to find and evaluate. They are major sources for ethnic materials, new writers, and authentic authoritative voices of the population group about which they write. Minority publishers and alternative presses are becoming better known, and have increased within the last five years.

The recent list, *The Wild and Free Press*, compiled by the Social Responsibilities Round Table of the American Library Association, includes access tools, review media, and distributors for the alternative, underground, little magazines and small presses. The SRRT *Directory of Minority Third World Publishers and Dealers* (1974) included forty-eight publishers and eight dealers and distributors. The *Directory* includes about thirty publishers of black materials and literature, at least twelve Chicano publishers, one publisher of Indian materials, and two of Asian American materials.

Much of the pamphlet material in the area of coping skills is produced by agencies and organizations, business and industry. Evaluation of the content of such material in relation to the biases and self-interest of the source is mandatory. Special attention to readability levels is also required. A seemingly easy manual for a driver's license, published by the state for its residents, may be written at a reading level that is unintelligible to many adults who must depend on it for necessary examination information.

Editions are a problem because of changes that may occur. To judge whether an edition is original, abridged, partially or entirely rewritten, or an authentic version of the original requires comparative examinations. Old and new editions, particularly of classic, enduring titles of great writers such as Twain, Shakespeare, Dickens, and current writers such as Ellison and Baldwin, must be examined carefully to identify abridgments, rewriting, or other changes.

Facts on copyright dates and reprint editions are found on the reverse of the title page, in the preface, or in a blurb, promotion note, or review. Paperback and hardcover editions present problems of accuracy on publication dates. The once-accepted practice of publishing paperback editions as reprints is no longer followed. The paperback edition may be published simultaneously with, or even preceding, the hardcover edition. The reprint date may not indicate the first edition date but only the current publication date.

Comparisons of editions or opinions of reviewers who have made such examinations of different editions can help to decide whether revisions result in sufficient changes that the later edition supersedes the earlier editions or are so minor that the earlier editions are acceptable. It may be important to keep both (or several) editions because of valuable material such as critical interpretative introductions, useful factual information, or different translations.

The quality of the series, individual titles within a series, and various editions can be determined only by comparisons and detailed examinations. It is wise not to accept or reject a series as a whole because one or more titles are known and evaluated as acceptable or nonacceptable. Furthermore, some titles in a series may be more or less appropriate. The needs, interests, and reading abilities of the potential users, as well as the type of library collection and objectives and other factors implicit in the local situation, will determine the appropriate additions to the collection.

Titles of reading materials have significance and direct implications for selection and use. In the evaluation of a work the title should be looked at from the point of view of what it says. The title is the name by which the item is known; it may or may not indicate what the content is, that is, the subject. It may give clues to the character of the work or it may mislead. It may have promotion value. It may deter rather than create interest. It may be imaginative, factual, uninspired, or pointless. Cover illustrations, bindings, and promotion blurbs have similar significance. They, too, become indicators of content and give clues to the nature of the material. They are to be evaluated for accuracy and authenticity as well as informational and promotional value.

The date of copyright and publication is an important indication of the time and period of writing and data collection. Of course, for any factual and scientific informative material it is essential that the date be taken into account for its historical, chronological, and accuracy significance. In many instances the information must be up to date, or at least the time of reporting must be identified. The "timeliness" of material is not the only factor; material may be timeless in various aspects—ideas, values, and quality. The story, novel, or biography may have universal quality, irrespective of time and place, and the author may speak to readers of any age, time, or place. New editions, reprints, and old editions may stand the test of time and be relevant to the contemporary scene. The appeal may be as great or greater as at the time of first publication. Authors may be ahead of their times, and popularity, appreciation, and appeal may come at a later time. The important factor in evaluation is that the evaluator be aware of the date and its significance and judge it accordingly.

Format is a critical element in terms of cost, appeal to potential users, accurate up-to-date information, character of content, type of use, library function, processing, and accessibility. Major priorities should be given to the content in terms of appeal to potential users and need in the collection. Is it a format that will be most used—paperback, newspaper, magazine, leaflet? Is it for use as reference material, for loan to individuals or groups, for historical and research purposes, for study and instruction? Is it permanent or is it expendable or consumable? Does it require special attention in preparation for use and to make it readily accessible? Is it available in different formats, for example, hardcover and paperback or broadside and leaflet? Is it to be used temporarily or for a long period? Does it meet library acquisition and selection policies and principles? Does it need to meet them? Different formats need to be compared for quality and usefulness in relation to purposes. Diversity in the physical format of materials (as well as content) is of particular importance. The usual book and newspaper sources are likely not to contain the type of content found in pamphlets, magazines, or workbooks.

Variety in physical format helps to assure variety in content. The various formats, other than the book in hardcover, usually make possible an extension and broadening of the library collection. Paperback books make it possible to have titles and authors from the past and present. They continue to widen the range of choices for readers. Their popular appeal, ease of handling, economy in cost, and spacesaving value offer special advantages. Newspapers and magazines are essential for current, up-to-date information. Local publications contribute local news and information of particular interest to a community and ethnic groups. Pamphlets, leaflets, forms, and booklets are a primary source for much of the coping-skill materials. Publications by governments, social and educational agencies, business and industry, labor, and vocational and professional organizations are valuable additions which are worth the search and trouble they entail; they are likely to be the only source for information on daily problems such as Social Security, legal procedures, consumer economics, adult educational opportunities, health, job and home responsibilities, housing, leisure-time activities, disaster aid, military service, and tax reporting. Newspapers and newsletters, broadsides, and posters are often community-indigenous products and of special interest to residents. They communicate information on local problems, events, and issues which can be found nowhere else. Readers, textbooks, and workbooks are characteristic aids for instructional programs. Such material frequently is consumable or expendable. Otherwise it is subjected to restrictions of reference and consultative use.

"Type of literature" is a category in the criteria for defining broad general areas that are descriptive of types and styles of writing on any subject. The types of literature are defined as autobiography, biography, historical accounts, scientific accounts, and travel; the essay of information and factual reference; the novel, personal essay, play or drama, poetry, and short story; folklore, how-to-do-it accounts, and tracts—religious, moral, political. The variations and genres can be determined only in relation to the literature under consideration. More precise descriptions, such as historical fiction, psychological novel, and other categories, depend on the nature of the writing.

Library materials may require other distinctive categories that are descriptive of the medium, form, or use—for example, atlases, maps, globes, charts, dictionaries, income tax forms, drivers' manuals, checkbook forms, talking books, and computer printouts.

Accurate assessment of the bibliographic aspects of material that is being analyzed depends, as does the application of any criterion, on the professional knowledge, critical abilities, and professional skills of the evaluator.

Content Analysis

In the analysis of reading materials the central part of the analysis is the content. Content occupies the central position in the communication process. It is the *what* in the classic sentence—*Who says what to whom, how,* with *what effect.* The construction of a system of categories to fit innumerable subjects, and within practical spatial limitations, defies the evaluator. Traditional classification systems (represented by Dewey Decimal and Library of Congress systems), which have been devised to classify and catalog knowledge, result in innumerable subject headings. For specific purposes, the librarian may turn to various lists that are organized around the subject categories: the Sears list of subject headings (although an abridgement of the LC headings, it may also be too extensive) or the shorter lists of various subjects identified for the Library Materials Research Project and refined for the MAC checklist, and the coping-skill list compiled for the Library–ABE Project, Appalachian Adult Education Center, Morehead State University. They are useful to the extent that they can be adapted to the immediate purpose and local situation.

What is most important in content analysis and recognition of the integral relation between content and other parts of the analysis (as classified under bibliographic evaluation and measurement of readability) is that the analysis be accurate and objective, result in insights and understanding, and give meaning to the subject and its treatment. All of this can be stated in the summary and annotation. The criteria impose a structure and assure that key points, necessary to overall judgment, are considered specifically as well as generally. Haines' tests, Adler and Van Doren's rules, the concepts in *Starting Out Right* (see below), and Lyman's criteria for analysis of reading materials have the advantage of providing a procedure that is systematic. Such procedures permit a thorough analysis of a book or other materials according to an orderly plan or scheme. They are based on certain principles and a complex of intellectual and social assumptions.

Although this method poses explicit or implicit questions that cannot always be answered, in most cases it is possible to answer them or find answers. The criteria for the analysis of reading materials suggest a procedure backed by the knowledge and experience of the person who judges the written work. If the librarian-evaluator masters the skill of actively reading a long and difficult book, he or she is also able to read shorter, easier writings—short stories, magazine or journal articles, current news reports, and new and unorthodox matter as well as the traditional and familiar.

In reading for the ideal and complete analysis, the procedural performance is not applied to every book, as the authors of the methods are the first to recognize. An approximation may be achieved, and parts are to be described, to a greater or lesser degree, dependent on importance and use. Application of the criteria to the analysis of a written work leads to a skill which, once acquired, will be applied naturally, consciously or unconsciously, and in relation to its value and use in regard to the writing under consideration.

Protesters to these kinds of procedures point out that no one person will make the same judgments. How can agreement be reached, except in the most superficially obvious ways? Each reader takes an individual meaning. Although these objections are valid at a very complex, sophisticated level, certain assumptions are applicable to all studies of content analysis. The content analysis scheme which was developed by Berelson and others "is a research technique for the objective, systematic, and quantitative description of the manifest content of communication."[8]

[8]Bernard Berelson, *Content Analysis in Communication Research* (Glencoe, Ill.: The Free Press, 1952), p. 18.

Berelson stresses that quantitative analysis should be undertaken only when relative frequencies of content categories are relevant to the problem at hand. Quantification requires precise and accurate counts of categories and has a high degree of objectivity. Such a procedure can be applied easily in such instances as counting the number of times pejorative and stereotype words are used in describing such groups as native Americans, blacks, and women—words no longer acceptable in the socially conscious and sensitive society of today.

Although the content analysis procedure outlined in the MAC checklist does not use the quantitative technique, three general assumptions, as defined by Berelson, are relevant and appropriate in the context of the MAC checklist procedure. Berelson states:

1. Content analysis assumes that inferences about the relationship between intent and content or between content and effect can validly be made, or the actual relationships established. We say "inferences" (i.e., "interpretations") because most studies utilizing content analysis have been limited to inferences; . . . . This assumption that knowledge of the content can legitimately support inferences about noncontent events is basic to a central contribution of content analysis, namely, to illuminate certain noncontent areas. Content analysis is often done to reveal the purposes, motives, and other characteristics of the communicators as they are (presumably) "reflected" in the content; or to identify the (presumable) effects of the content upon the attention, attitudes, or acts of readers and listeners. . . .

2. Content analysis assumes that study of the manifest content is meaningful. This assumption requires that the content be accepted as a "common meeting-ground" for the communicator, the audience, and the analyst. That is, the content analyst assumes that the "meanings" which he ascribes to the content, by assigning it to certain categories, correspond to the "meanings" intended by the communicator and/or understood by the audience. In other words, the assumption is that there is a common universe of discourse among the relevant parties, so that the manifest content can be taken as a valid unit of study.

[The major question which arises is whether meanings derived from the content will be understood differently by different readers. The psychological predispositions of the reader distort his comprehension of the "manifest content." To some degree this may be true. The various kinds and levels of communication content influence the meanings that can be understood. Readers are likely to get the same meaning from factual news event description but various meanings from a poem. The more simple and direct the content the more likelihood there is of identical meanings by readers. Certain uniformity of comprehension and understanding is possible.]

3. Content analysis assumes that the quantitative description of communication content is meaningful. This assumption implies that the frequency of occurrence of various characteristics of the content is itself

an important factor in the communication process, under specific conditions.[9]

Thus it would seem that librarians, in gaining knowledge of the characteristics of items and resources for a collection and in evaluating effects and appeals of the material, are able to prejudge, as it were, before the reader makes a final choice and judgment and to interpret these characteristics to the potential reader. In such an application the basic assumptions are extended. It is assumed that:

1. The inferences or interpretations made by the librarians on the one hand about the communication (subject, values, and other characteristics) and about the author's purposes, motives, and other characteristics and on the other hand the presumed effects upon the attention and responses of the reader are possible.
2. The meanings librarians ascribe to the content will have the same or similar meanings to the reader.
3. The frequency with which words, phrases, ideas, and attitudes occur in the content is a valid indicator for determining the characteristics of the content and for making judgments on what is said, to whom, and how well. Instead of speculating on what the author might have said or intended to say or should say, it is of first importance to see what, in fact, the author did say.

Analysis of the content of what is being communicated is the most important and crucial aspect in evaluating materials. This central part of the criteria presupposes agreement on the basic assumptions in regard to similar understanding of interpretations, meanings, and frequency which make content analysis possible. The framework includes five broad areas: the social roles that adults may have during the life cycle; subjects with which the writer deals in the writing being analyzed; the attitudes and values which are identifiable in the writing; the structure of development, that is, the intellectual challenge and treatment or manner of presentation; and the measurement of readability. The major categories and subcategories are directed to the reading needs and interests of adults, particularly the adult new reader.

The subject of the book or writing—what it is about—is a first concern to the reader and consequently to the selector of reading materials. The structure and development of the author's method of writing, the genre and the characteristics of the writing—language, style, plot, and character development, as well as ideas presented—are analyzed.

[9]Ibid., p. 18–20.

Social scientists and educators have identified a variety of social roles learned by individuals in the socialization process by which one becomes a member of the group and assumes certain ways of life. Learning to read and write is one aspect of such socialization and a means to that end. A social role is a pattern of behavior that is expected of persons who fill a certain position or place in society. Every person fills a number of, or even many, social roles. As the individual goes through life, social roles, relationships, and interaction between other individuals and groups become more and more complex. All roles contain contradictory elements. Expectations vary in regard to what behavior fits a role. One need not be a researcher or sociologist to observe that adult roles are multiple. The adult woman or man is a daughter or son, a sister or brother, a mother or father, a wife or husband, a worker, a friend, a neighbor, a member of an ethnic group, a church member, a club or organization member, a citizen.

But human beings fail to fit into neat categories and refined definitions. Patterns of behavior vary. Social change continues. Current publications transmit, reflect, and challenge social patterns. A changing society and changing values lead to changing roles and countercultures. Changing values and cultural pluralism are bringing to the fore cultural differences and new emphasis on ethnic and national groups in the United States.

Equally important, and subject to diverse research findings and opinions, is the social structure of society in the United States. Some sociologists see a hierarchy of class stratification; others feel that no definite class distinctions can be made in a mobile, open society, based on equality for all. Social scientists present a basic five-class structure in which a given class varies in size, depending on the type of community. The five social classes are lower working, upper working, lower middle, upper middle, and upper.

In analyzing materials, social roles may be identified. It seems unnecessary to try to identify social class; rather, it is more appropriate to analyze and describe the material under consideration in a detailed, descriptive way. For example, inferences about class are to be left to the reader. The accurate description is a more objective guide and will "place" the writing so that the librarian and reader can make an assessment of its use and interest.

The social roles of adults are delineated in the first section of the criteria to provide a framework in which the content of the written work may be scrutinized and judged in terms of adult lives and adult interests and needs. Both subject and values are integrated into the same social role structure. These aspects of the content analysis are based on the ideas and conceptual theories of human development and the place of information and intellectual resources in the lives of individuals. Obviously, not all writings will be concerned with adult roles—autobiographies, biographies, literature, history, political affairs, and philosophical and spiritual guides are more likely to reveal these social characteristics than how-to-do-it manuals, science, or factual material.

Adults are living these social roles and are concerned with the behaviors involved in such roles. It therefore seems relevant, in the process of content analysis, to identify the category or categories of roles portrayed in the writing. To classify the role or roles described as a dominant or secondary matter permits further clarification.

Seven categories are defined: the role of the person in one's own development, the role in the family, the role of the person in the group, the role of the person as a participant in political and social life, the role of the person as a participant in education, the role of the person in work, and the role of the person in one's leisure. The personal development role would include such factors as growth and self-development that enables one to meet individual and social expectations at various periods during life. Subjects relevant to personal development are individual identity, religious and spiritual beliefs, social relationships, health, understanding the arts, literature, nature, science. The role of the person in work is illustrated in works that relate to choice, preparation, and work in an occupation that brings satisfaction and income. Subjects relevant to the work role include employment, job applications, vocational and professional careers, labor and industrial relations.

Subjects of interest to adult readers with common or similar backgrounds have been identified in chapter 7. Significant factors that influence interest in various subjects, in addition to role responsibilities, are environment, ethnic background, life style, language, and educational background.

The concept of adult roles and the categories of roles are correlated with subject and value classifications. The matching of subject interests and value categories with the life tasks and psychosocial stages of development provides a connective link to be used in the selection and interpretation of the reading materials. For example, subjects that are classifiable under "group role" are membership in various types of groups—ethnic, neighborhood, peer, political, religious, responsibility to others, and survival. Attitudes and values related to "group role" include advancement, alienation, conformity, group identity, and survival.

Subjects of particular interest which were identified in the Lyman Library Materials Research Project were survival—environmental, political, personal—and survival for the individual, the group, and the government. Self-identity is a recurring subject of interest in personal, family, group, political, and work roles. Erikson identifies these same concerns—survival and identity—as major problems which adults face in today's society. Other significant subjects were health, law, and dissent. Civil rights, consumer problems, housing, and legal aid are of vital interest to minority groups of young adults, the black community, Chicanos or Mexican Americans, Puerto Ricans, and the native peoples. Personal identity, ethnic culture and heritage, practical information for daily living, popular best sellers, selected classics, the occult, and current events appear to be subjects of perennial interest. No list can identify the many and varied subject interests or anticipate future demands. The alert, perceptive librarian keeps abreast of the current needs and interests of the clientele.

Subjects are evaluated as authentic or inaccurate. The scope of the material and the timeliness are further elements to consider. In some instances the evaluator may be unable to judge, and uses other sources for opinions—resource specialists, critical reviews, and subject experts. Authenticity and accuracy, whether in scientific, factual, or imaginative works, are desirable and necessary qualities.

The importance of identifying at least the main attitudes and values presented in the content has been pointed out. Attitudes and values expressed in the material are difficult to determine, in contrast to the usually clear distinction which can be made in regard to subject or themes in a work. The identification and evaluation of this aspect of content take on a complexity in direct relation to the depth and complexity of the work. Although in many instances certain values in a work bear no importance, to the type of reader in other instances they may be critical facts in motivation to read and in appeal or lack of appeal. Misunderstanding and misleading information or ignorance of points of view may lead to complete rejection of all library service by the disillusioned or offended reader.

Why is it so difficult to analyze attitudes and values, and to determine whether the characteristics are promoted or supported, criticized or rejected, or presented in an ambivalent or neutral manner? Attitudes and values are not clear cut in many instances. They are not always stated explicitly. They may be concealed, consciously or unconsciously, by the writer. Differing points of view may be presented in the narrative or through the action of characters. The evaluator finds it difficult to decide which value is important. The evaluator's own attitude and values may get in the way, or he may read into the content unjustified conclusions. On the other hand, the evaluator's opinions may make little difference.

One brings to mind the judgments and disagreements about values portrayed toward war and about the cultures of nations in such works as Kurt Vonnegut's *Slaughter-House Five* and Frances Fitzgerald's *Fire in the Lake*. One thinks of the various levels and complexities about personal and social values in the novels of Charles Dickens. *Our Mutual Friend* may seem a simple story and a satire on wealth, and yet it is a complex study of family relations, of greed, hypocrisy, corruption, as well as honesty, good will, and friendship among multiple relationships at various levels of society. The same biases and prejudices involved in values and attitudes interfere in an objective appraisal in written works, whether an information pamphlet on how to obtain the rights of tenants or grow an organic garden, or a well-known censorship controversy around innumerable titles from the past and present, such as the *Decameron, Catcher in the Rye, Ulysses, Soul on Ice,* or *Quotations* from Mao Tse-tung.

Religious beliefs, political affiliations, attitudes toward sexual matters, economic systems, fears of different or new values enter into judgments. What is desired or not desired, what is approved or rejected, what is permitted or prohibited are represented in attitudes or values that in turn represent deep-seated beliefs, vested interests, irrational and rational points of view, clear or confused principles. Old values remain while new and changing values go unrecognized or are denied consideration.

In the analysis of content it is important to identify as clearly as possible the attitudes, values, and objectives expressed in the material. The content, as it is presented in the material, is the basis for judgment. This content may or may not reflect the author's values or the author's stated purpose or intent. The evaluator takes all possible clues into account and tries to be objective. The evaluator, whether librarian or teacher, will need to determine whether the attitudes and values expressed in the writing are meaningful to individuals or to the potential reader group. The ability to do so will rest on one's knowledge and understanding of the community and potential adult reader, and will be verified or denied by the reader.

Another approach is development of criteria for the examination of literature that deals with a particular reader group: ethnic, religious, class, sex, or potential library user. Guidelines for evaluation of children's literature have been developed in a rather unique study. This self-initiated research project was conducted by six women in Madison, Wisconsin, who organized as a Children's Literature Review Board. They developed a conceptual framework for children's books that deal with blacks and formulated some guidelines for examining this body of literature. *Starting Out Right*, in which they present their views after a study of many books, is an honest record with fresh insights and new ideas.[10] Although the focus of the analysis was on children's books, the criteria have meaning for and are applicable to the analysis of adult books.

The criteria they developed were for use in judging children's books and classifying the most common flaws that occur in black-inclusive books. They define traps or "syndromes" that represent qualities they judge to be undesirable in handling the black experience. The syndrome patterns are applicable to other minorities and to images projected about them.

The criteria are in the form of questions, which are listed below in brief form without the explanatory and specific subquestions. The examples and detailed explanations are to be found in several chapters of *Starting Out Right*. It can be seen quite readily how they open new avenues of critical thought and clarify a confusing area. These standards can be applied for almost any age level and most types of books. The three main areas relate to the pictures and illustrations, the word content, and the tone and perspective set by the author.

The first question, relating to expression of the black experience, is the most important and perhaps the most difficult because of its abstract quality. The answers to this question, the review board feels, are "the final arbiter." The main questions to be answered are:

1. Is the book written so that a Black perspective has been taken into consideration? Does the author have some knowledge and appreciation of the Black experience? Are the characters placed in stereotyped roles? Are they legitimately set in situations that bring forth poverty and discrimination? Are the Black characters victimized or placed in positions of humiliation or sacrificed to White characters? Do writers deal honestly with Black-White situations? Are historical events seen from the Black perspective?

2. What is the dimension of Blackness in the book?

3. How responsible is the author in dealing with problems and issues?

4. Do the Black characters look like human beings? Grotesque characters, overdrawn figures, stereotyped features are snares to avoid.

5. Will the young reader [adult] know that he is looking at a Black person or do characters emerge "grey" in appearance to resemble Caucasians in blackface?

6. Is the Black character portrayed as a unique individual or as a representative of a group?

7. Does the clothing or behavior seem to perpetuate the stereotypes about Blacks being primitive or submissive?

[10]Bettye I. Latimer, ed., *Starting Out Right: Choosing Books about Black People for Young Children*, Bulletin no. 2314 (Madison: Wisconsin Dept. of Public Instruction, 1972).

8. Is the story romanticized?

9. Is the setting authentic and recognizable?

10. Does the author set a patronizing or a paternalistic tone?

11. Is a Black character used as a vehicle to get a point across so that the character becomes a tool of literary exploitation and acts artificial rather than real?

12. How are Black characters shown in relationship to White characters and vice versa?

13. If any dialect or slang is used, does it have a purpose?

14. How accurate is the story if it deals with historical or factual events?

15. In a biography, is the personality as well as the accomplishments of the main character shown?

16. How much does this book free the child [the adult] from the white-centered middle class world with its connotation of superiority?[11]

The syndrome patterns identified in this study constitute an original and unique approach to the classification of undesirable qualities found in books about ethnic minorities and women. Books with multiple syndromes are to be rejected. The five syndromes are Romantic, Avoidance, Bootstrap, Oasis, and Ostrich-in-the-Sand.[12]

The Romantic Syndrome is found in unbalanced situations, when books tend to glorify situations and to ignore and gloss over realities. Romanticization occurs most frequently in illustrations and biographies.

The Avoidance Syndrome denies the harsh and oppressive conditions under which blacks have functioned. Bigots and bigotry are not identified. A self-protective device, it is commonly practiced by white-oriented writers who seem unable to come to grips with reality.

The Bootstrap Syndrome maintains that success is guaranteed if one is properly motivated, if one helps oneself, and perseveres. The basis for this belief appears to be that certain personal virtues bring inevitable rewards and that problems one encounters by virtue of being black will be resolved by a system that has made blackness a handicap.

The Oasis Syndrome presents an integrated group of characters in an insignificant way. This syndrome appears in fictionalized stories, as opposed to biography or information-dispensing books.

The Ostrich-in-the-Sand Syndrome results in books which give a distorted, unreal, and oversimplified point of view on issues of discrimination, racism, prejudice. By oversimplifying an issue or ignoring a situation of prejudice, the story becomes deceitful. This syndrome appears consistently in fiction attempting to demonstrate acts of prejudice and discrimination.

[11]Ibid., p. 7–12. Reprinted with permission of Bettye I. Latimer and Equal Opportunity Office, Wisconsin Dept. of Public Instruction, Madison.
[12]Ibid., p. 13–19.

These aspects, "syndromes," and answers to the questions noted are important in a serious analysis. They form the bases for critical comments and interpretations of points of view as presented in the work itself. In a reverse situation, the criteria might be applied in judging and classifying the portrayal of whites and white characteristics in works of black writers.

Structure and Development

Structure and development, the fourth part of the analysis of content, is defined as the treatment or manner of presentation. It is primarily applicable to imaginative works—the novel, drama, poetry. It is often applicable, at least in part, to literature of fact, such as biography, autobiography, philosophy. The traditional stylistic elements of plot, setting, character development, and style are indicators of the characteristics to be evaluated. Equally important is richness of ideas—ideas and themes which convey values, insights, and understanding. They are major indicators of the intellectual challenge and literary and emotional impact of the work.

It is absolutely essential to identify these stylistic elements, the richness of ideas and intellectual challenge, the language characteristics, and emotional impact. Such an analysis of structure and development in a work permits accurate, descriptive, critical, and interpretative knowledge for librarians to use in information, guidance, and promotion techniques. It makes possible a more accurate evaluation or prediction on the appeal of the material, the kind of appeal, and to whom it appeals.

For the purposes of evaluation, the structural elements are defined quite simply. Plot is a plan of action. Setting is the time, place, environment, background, or surroundings. The form and shape the story acquires in the creative act, from the author to the audience, results in some order in time and space, and importance in which incidents of the narrative occur. The characters in the action may be part of the action and theme, and they may be developed and individualized.

The style is related not only to word choice or vocabulary, sentence structure, stylistic development, and manner but also to originality of expression, appropriateness to content, and effectiveness of the presentation.

The richness of ideas constitutes the quality of content in terms of simplicity or complexity, the originality and depth of the matter, the insights and appreciations presented. The intellectual challenge and emotional appeal of the work may be indicated through these aspects of the work. The question to answer is: Are the ideas trivial or significant? What values do they convey?

These five elements are evaluated first in regard to characteristics which answer the question whether plot, characters, setting, style, and ideas are factual, stereotyped, average, above average, original, or universal. Then the development of these same elements is looked at and described as simple, average, or complex. In their importance and relationship to each other, are they judged as of primary or secondary importance or integrally intertwined? The style in which the material is presented is characterized. Is it, on the whole, described as dramatic, factual, fantasy, or humor? Is it imaginative, journalistic, poetic? Is it popular, scholarly, scientific, technical?

The subjective judgments made by the evaluator on these same elements are of importance in gaining depth and understanding about the significance and worth of the material under consideration. The analysis of structure and development in relation to style and richness of ideas is not always necessary or even appropriate. Only the type and character of the work will determine the extent to which it applies. Innumerable examples (such as a pamphlet on household repairs and tools, a book on consumer rights, or a mathematics text) may be found which have no plot or character development, and no particular setting. In most instances the style of writing and ideas presented are vital elements and warrant some description and evaluation.

What of the language used in reading materials? It may well be that no factor is more decisive in the judgment accorded a printed work, for it is language—words, symbols—that creates this communication medium. Simply defined, language is the means by which human beings communicate through a set of symbols or words with common meanings. Patterns of vocabulary and usage characteristic of communities of various sizes and types are referred to as language, dialects, jargon. The general pattern of communication in the United States is the English language.

In the past, languages other than English (common to immigrant groups) have been recognized as spoken by first-generation foreigners. Today various languages and dialects are recognized as important because of their use by sizable populations. The Spanish language is so recognized because of large populations of Cubans, Mexican Americans, and Puerto Ricans in the country. Bilingual communities are emerging.

In the context of evaluative analysis by librarians a classification is suggested. Language may be defined variously as:

1. Argot—a language peculiar to a particular group
2. Colloquial or vernacular—spoken in various geographic and local communities—a familiar speaking style, conversational
3. Formal—standard, traditional, correct in grammar and syntax according to conventional use

4. Dialect—language of a particular social class or district, a regional speech pattern
5. Slang—informal, nonstandard (including street language), and sometimes socially unacceptable
6. Jargon—the language peculiar to a trade or profession
7. Technical—vocabulary and words that have meaning only in a subject field or a specialized meaning when applied to the field
8. Hard nontechnical words—have characteristics similar to the technical words. Less familiar and uncommon, consequently the meanings are not always clear.
9. Easy words—usually one-syllable and commonly used, but less easy than they appear because of many meanings.

The pattern of the language, once identified, can then be judged in all its multiple ramifications. At first, relatively simple questions are to be answered.

Is the language appropriate or inappropriate? But appropriate or inappropriate to what? Therein lie the complex relationships. Is it appropriate or inappropriate to the content? to the subject? to the characters? to the setting? to the ideas? to reading ease?

Will it convey meanings of interest to the library communities? What meanings does it convey? Is the language understandable? By whom?

Is it language of the street, of a certain social class, of the gang, of the ethnic group, of the job, of the profession? Is it language of the immigrant resident?

Is it language known to potential reader groups?

Is the language authentic, accurate speech, to be expected of the characters?

Is the language characteristic and essential to communication and understanding?

Is the language offensive? To whom? Why?

Is it acceptable or unacceptable for the collection?

Language—words, vocabulary—provides clues and insights to other aspects of the material and related criteria. The identification of attitudes, preferences and prejudices, likes and dislikes, values and disvalues, and philosophy is revealed in language patterns and choice of words. Cratis Williams points out the distinctive mountaineer speech of the Appalachian Scotch-Irish. Elizabeth Martinez Smith and Samuel Betances stress the need for bilingual and Spanish-language materials in New York, Los Angeles, and Chicago. Miami is a bilingual city. The Navajo language is being written and spoken on the Navajo reservation.

Pejorative words are to be looked for in ethnic materials, in textbooks, in literature and science. Words are indicators of ideas and feelings.

They can be offensive, heedless, disrespectful, depending on the context and use.

The librarian is in a professional position that strengthens and supports intellectual freedom. It is a position vulnerable to first attacks by the authoritarian philosopher, the moralist, the self-selected censor, the political, religious, or social reformer who sees in the language dangers and threats to the individual, the community, the nation. The language that is different, unfamiliar, prohibitive, new, technical, the ideological, the indigenous speech becomes accessible to everyone when in print. Doubtless it warrants the attention it receives.

"Easy" words are included here because of the emphasis on language that is made up of easy words. Wordlist compilers and readability specialists classify words by measure of vocabulary and for evaluation of readability. Some researchers question this approach. Howards points out that polysyllabic words are typically one-meaning words, whereas the so-called easy words normally have dozens of meanings. Howards demonstrates that *easy* has meant "frequently used" rather than "thoroughly comprehended."[13]

Measurement of Readability

"To me a book is meant first of all to be read. Therefore it is of greatest importance that the pages be readable."[14] The measurement of readability in the context of this analysis consists of an evaluation of several factors that may be said to affect the communication situation. These factors can be judged fairly easily by the librarian. They are influential elements; they affect comprehension and enjoyment as well as ease and speed of reading. The factors to be analyzed include physical, visual, and selected literary aspects of the printed material—typography, special features, learning aids, language, and the prediction of reading level in relation to comprehension as measured by readability formulas.

TYPOGRAPHY. The "hygienic" elements of the reading situation in relation to the elements of typography or general appearance of the printed matter that contribute to legibility include type, spatial arrangement, printing surfaces, and illustrative matter. Legibility is a measure of readability insofar as physical conditions in typographical arrangements affect or influence ease of reading. They are not a consideration in the readability formula measurements. The limitations of all such

[13]Melvin Howards, "How Easy Are 'Easy' Words?" *Journal of Experimental Education*, 32, no. 4:77–82 (Summer 1964).

[14]Alfred A. Knopf, *Portrait of a Publisher* (New York: The Typophiles, 1965), 2:85.

factors are taken into consideration and balanced with content, complexity of the message (in relation to a potential reader's abilities), language, maturity, experiential background, motivations, and purpose. Legibility—whether high, moderate, low, good, or poor—is a valid measurement in that it can promote or hinder, clarify or distort the accurate perception of letters and words, easy and rapid reading.

Achievement of the hygienic reading situation that promotes maximum ease and speed of reading, that is, optimal legibility of print, involves various factors. Legibility is a measure of readability insofar as physical conditions and other factors related to print affect or influence ease of reading. It is not a consideration in the limited readability formula measurements. Typographical arrangements of the printed matter, proper illumination for reading, and other physical attributes (such as source of light, slope of page, size of format, vibration of material, and length of reading time) are factors which affect readability. Firm conclusions about the usefulness of these factors in improving legibility are hard to find among the research studies; the methods of measurement are limited and further research is needed. Although uncertainty exists, certain facts are fairly definite, and they provide measures of some uniformity which are of practical use to librarians who are analyzing these aspects of legibility.[15] Librarians also rely on common sense, their own experiences, visual perceptions, and personal preferences to judge legibility.

It can therefore be seen that numerous elements influence legibility and, in a broader, more meaningful sense, affect readability. Although various influential factors may be identified, it is difficult to determine to what extent, and how, they are influential. Elements that are to be measured include the legibility of letters of the alphabet and 10-point digits, kinds, height and sizes of type, width of line, leading, spatial arrangements, color of print and background, printing-surface texture and color, and finally the interrelationship of all these factors. The coordination of these typographical factors affects ease and speed of reading.[16]

Other factors (outside the limitations of this discussion) which well might be considered are tradition, artistic and aesthetic appearance, printing styles, punctuation, and writing skills. An intensive analysis of all possible factors is an ideal model. Although impractical in some situations, a computer-based analysis would make the possibility of in-

[15]Miles A. Tinker, *Legibility of Print* (Ames: Iowa State Univ. Pr., 1963). The discussion relates primarily to printed material to be read by adults.
[16]Ibid.

cluding multiple factors more likely. Legibility of print and readability scores could be determined readily through machine analysis. Generally, no single method of measurement is adequate for determining the legibility of print in all kinds of typographical setups. Inadequate methods can lead to false conclusions. Yet some facts seem clear.

What are some of Tinker's conclusions about legibility factors, based on his summaries of research studies by himself and others? Legibility of letters of the alphabet shows much variability between capital letters and lowercase letters. Lowercase letters are more recognizable because they differentiate more than capitals. Capital letters have more visibility. For the mature reader, the variation in letters "is a minor factor." For immature readers, confusion of letters of similar form—as *c* and *e* or *r* and *t*—cause difficulty. Improvement of letters in terms of functional design and in regard to serifs, outline, width, special characteristics (at the same time keeping aesthetic quality) is desirable. Some digits, such as *6, 9, 3, 5,* need improvement in height-width proportions. Roman numerals are more difficult to read than arabic.

The kinds of type which may be used in print provide a range of choices. The characteristics of each type form and style which give high legibility and consequently more effective communication are many. Tinker found that type faces in common use did not differ significantly. Readers' opinions can be used to determine legibility. A close correlation exists between what readers judged pleasing, that is, as having aesthetic values, and what is legible. Readers prefer type faces that are more perceptible and of high visibility. Neither factor appears to affect speed of reading. Italic print is read somewhat more slowly than roman.

Except for visibility at a distance, all capital print retards speed of reading, in comparison with lowercase type. Thus capitals should be dispensed with in printing. Lowercase letters permit reading by word units, take less space, and require fewer fixation pauses for reading the same amount of material. Boldface type is read at the same rate as lowercase, but readers prefer the lowercase. Mixed type forms retard reading. A satisfactory measure of legibility of type faces is the speed of reading.

The size of type is of continual interest. Little agreement exists between publishers, researchers, and librarians on what is considered optimal size. Size of type must be considered along with line width and leading. These three factors must be coordinated in order to judge legibility. A wide variation in usage is found in books, magazines, newspapers. A wide diversity is seen in variations in line width (figure 6). Both single and double columns are used in magazines and journals.

9 picas

6. Mr. Smith gave a news-
boy a quarter for a paper

13 picas

6. Mr. Smith gave a newsboy a quarter for a paper and left without his

17 picas

6. Mr. Smith gave a newsboy a quarter for a paper
and left without his change. When the boy ran and

21 picas

6. Mr. Smith gave a newsboy a quarter for a paper and left
without his change. When the boy ran and told him he said he

25 picas

6. Mr. Smith gave a newsboy a quarter for a paper and left without
his change. When the boy ran and told him he said he had never

29 picas

6. Mr. Smith gave a newsboy a quarter for a paper and left without his change. When
the boy ran and told him he said he had never seen such dishonesty. 7. It was a cold day

33 picas

6. Mr. Smith gave a newsboy a quarter for a paper and left without his change. When the boy
ran and told him he said he had never seen such dishonesty. 7. It was a cold day in winter and the

37 picas

6. Mr. Smith gave a newsboy a quarter for a paper and left without his change. When the boy ran and
told him he said he had never seen such dishonesty. 7. It was a cold day in winter and the ground was cov-

Figure 6. Line widths for 8-point type, Times Roman, set solid. (Adapted from Miles A. Tinker, *Legibility of Print*, figure 6.1. ©1963 The Iowa State University Press.)

Line widths vary with type size. Diversity in the use of leading presents similar inconsistencies.

In spite of the difficulty of measuring and testing legibility, it would seem that typography can be a positive help. Design and print layout have an important place in the creation of more legible materials. Something can be learned from the studies in this area related to material for the partially sighted. Many adults have sight problems of a physical nature, and a study of print for the partially sighted confirms certain facts.[17] Two factors are taken into account. Design and provision of special reading material for the partially sighted are complementary to, rather than a substitute for, the provision of optical reading aids such as magnifying glasses and special spectacles. It is recognized that various other confusing factors affect reading ability, such as readers' education, motivation, degree and cause of vision loss, as well as literary style and typographic layout of the printed page. All such factors are to be considered in analyzing reading materials and in reading guidance.

Size of print is considered by some to be one of the most important factors in continuous reading. It is not so important in special reading situations, such as signs, labels, maps, a telephone directory, or dictionary (although the latter task is considerably hampered by small type). Weight, or boldness, of type also affects legibility, athough it is of secondary importance compared with size. Overlarge type can diminish reading efficiency. The print must be large enough to be seen, but, once it is, reading efficiency is likely to decrease by further enlargement. This loss results because of the need for more eye movements to do the same amount of work. The eye scans the text in a series of stops and starts, and reading takes place during the stops or fixations. During each fixation the eye takes in the words on either side of the most clearly focused central point. With larger type, each fixation picks up less information.

Differences in type face seemed to have comparatively little effect. Spacing, or extra space between the words or the letters or between lines, has little effect. "If all the best typographic features were combined, there would be an improvement on the order of 35 percent compared with print using all the worst features combined."[18]

Personal attitudes of the reader, such as will power, incentive, and general interest in "serious" reading, play a role as important as the physical amount of vision. It would seem that these elements should be considered equally pertinent in evaluating materials for readers with

---

[17]Alison Shaw, "The Visually Handicapped Readers: Print for Partial Sight," *Libri*, 19, no. 4:249–53 (1969).
[18]Ibid., p. 253.

normal and with partial sight. A further step is necessary to determine that normal sight exists.

Although a variety of optical magnification devices provide a means of enlarging type, the quality of the enlargement suffers. Magnifying devices, by enlarging the print, also enlarge printing defects. Some type styles enlarge grossly out of proportion. Cataract and glaucoma patients require a heavier weight or bolder type, rather than enlarged type, and magnifying regular type does not provide the blackness needed for greater legibility. Some low-vision reading aids are heavy and cumbersome. Some scratch easily. Although they are practical for limited or reference-type reading, they are tiring or lack the efficiency needed for sustained reading.

Enlargement of print by photo-offset reproduction may decrease legibility. Microscopic ink gaps and blurs become noticeable when enlarged to 18-point type size. Italics, quotation marks, and hyphens may become obtrusive when the printed page is enlarged. Large-print reproduction may result in awkward, oversize, heavy formats and poor bindings.

After several experiments and studies regarding the three interrelated factors—type size, width of line, and leading—Tinker reports that:

1. Leading has an important effect on the legibility of type. While effective for improving the legibility of all sizes of type, leading has considerably less influence on 12-point type than on smaller sizes.
2. Smaller sized type leaded is not more legible than large sized type set solid. The 10-point set solid was read as rapidly as 8-point type with 2-point leading. Readers preferred 10-point set solid.
3. "Safety zones," that is, the limits of variation in line width and leading that may be used for a given type size without appreciable loss of legibility, were defined for 6-, 8-, 9-, 10-, 11-, and 12-point type in varied widths and leading (figure 7).[19]

Although a common belief is that line width should vary with type size, it appears that there is no direct relation between variation in type size and width of line and speed of reading. Printing practice varies. Optimal type size and line width are influenced by leading and the relationships are varied and not always clear. Readers' preferences favor moderate line widths. Printing practice seems to adjust to the average reader's desires.[20]

Several findings were made on the basis of experimental study with typographical arrangements for six type sizes, readers' preferences, and

[19]Tinker, *Legibility of Print*, p. 106–7.
[20]Ibid., p. 104.

6 Point	14-pica line width with 2 to 4-point leading 21-pica line with 1 to 4-point leading 28-pica line with 2 to 4-point leading
8 Point	14-pica line with 2 to 4-point leading 21-pica line with 2 to 4-point leading 28-pica line with 1 to 4-point leading 36 pica line with 2 to 4-point leading
9 Point	14-pica line with 1 to 4-point leading 18-pica line with 1 to 4-point leading 30-pica line with 1 to 4-point leading
10 Point	14-pica line with 1 to 4-point leading 19-pica line with 2 to 4-point leading 31-pica line with 2-point leading (marginal)
11 Point	16-pica line with 1 to 2-point leading 25-pica line with or without leading 34-pica line with 1 to 2-point leading
12 Point	17-pica line with 1 to 4-point leading 25-pica line with or without leading 33-pica line with 1 to 4-point leading

Figure 7. Safety zones for six commonly used type sizes. (Reprinted, by permission, from Miles A. Tinker, *Legibility of Print*, p. 106–7. © 1963 The Iowa State University Press.)

printing practice.[21] It appears that 9-, 10-, 11-, and 12-point type are equally legible where each is printed in an appropriate line with 2-point leading. Speed of reading 8-point type is moderately but significantly retarded, and speed of reading is seriously retarded when 6-point type is employed. Some indication was found that 11-point type is slightly more legible than 10-point. Readers prefer 11-point, and the trend in printing is toward its use (figure 8).[22]

Type size, leading, and length of line are interrelated factors in the legibility of a page of print. Although 10- or 11-point type size with 2-point leading provides optimum legibility for those with normal vision, experimentation has shown that the 16- or 18-point type with 4-point

[21]Ibid., p. 102–3.
[22]Ibid., p. 70–71.

Standard: 11 point, 22 picas, 2 point leading

11. When my mother saw the marks of muddy shoes on the floor, and all over the nice clean beds, she was surprised to see how careful the children had been. 12. When the little boy next door had both of his legs broken by being run over by an automobile, we were afraid he might never be able to see again.   13.

Comparison I: 8 point, 16 picas, 2 point leading

11. Frank had been expecting a letter from his brother for several days; so as soon as he found it on the kitchen table he ate it as quickly as possible. 12. A certain doctor living in a city near here always has a very serious expression on his face. This is perhaps because in his work he meets only

Comparison II: 6 point, 14 picas, 2 point leading

11. Frank had been expecting a letter from his brother for several days; so as soon as he found it on the kitchen table he ate it as quickly as possible. 12. A certain doctor living in a city near here always has a very serious expression on his face. This is perhaps because is his work he meets only well people. 13.

Figure 8. Samples of three type sizes set in optimum line widths and leading. (Reprinted, by permission, from Miles A. Tinker, *Legibility of Print*, figure 7.2. © 1963 The Iowa State University Press.)

leading of "large-type editions" is attractive to the new reader because it "looks easier."

Less than optimum	}	9-point type 2-point leading	9-point type 4-point leading
Optimum for normal vision	}	10-point type 2-point leading	11-point type 4-point leading
Large-type editions	}	16-point type 4-point leading	18-point type 4-point leading

Some graphic designers think that the shape of the individual letter is a more important factor than size in attaining readability: "To test the success of existing typefaces, it is not the legibility (which has come to mean the recognizability of individual letters) that matters, but readability, or the way in which a typeface's individual letters are effective when they are put together into words or sentences."[23]

This does not mean that the legibility of individual characters is unimportant. However, as it is known that text settings are read not character by character but word by word or phrase by phrase, the readability of individual characters is important. The importance of readability is emphasized in this definition of reading: "a combined process of perception of collective shapes of words or word parts and the assimilation, i.e., completion of the partly perceived words by inferring the omitted parts out of the already guessed meaning of the words."[24]

Graphic designers also point out that it is the x-height of the letter which conveys the visual impact of type. ("The x-height is the height of the body of the lowercase letters, exclusive of ascenders and descenders."[25]) Consequently it appears that it is not the serifs, as has been claimed, that makes a typeface readable. The four samples shown in the foldout page, figure 9, emphasize this distinction.

Figure 9 provides a measurement guide for librarian-evaluators who wish to judge the x-height of the text settings that they are evaluating. By placing the x-height line alongside the text line, one may estimate the typeface's legibility or readability.

Spatial arrangements of the printed page relate primarily to the size of the full page, margins, single- versus multiple-column printing, intercolumnar space and rules, and paragraphing. Tradition, aesthetic principles, visual illusions, style-manual rules, and familiar practices account for many spatial arrangements. The diversity in printing practice in regard to all these factors is seen readily on inspection of books, magazines, newspapers, pamphlets. Page-size variations have resulted from variations in paper size. Large margins are unnecessarily large. Consistency in page size and more print on a page because of reduction of marginal space would result in savings of printing and paper. Inner or gutter margins should be wide enough so that the inner line is not obscured by the curvature of the paper. Curvature of printed material significantly reduces speed of reading and visibility of print. Indenting the first line of a paragraph improves legibility. Double-columnar printing is preferable to single. More and more double- and multiple-columns are being used. Many spatial arrangements have justification in aesthetics or tradition. Such measures are not to be ignored and must be incorporated into overall judgment.

[23]"Gillegibility," *Upper and Lower Case* 3, no. 1:46 (Mar. 1976).
[24]G. W. Ovink, quoted in ibid.
[25]James Craig, *Production for the Graphic Designer* (New York: Watson-Guptil, 1974), p. 200.

Printing surfaces can promote or detract from the legibility of print. Texture, color, thickness, lighting, visibility of print, and quality of paper are factors to be considered. In the past a variety of opinions were held without experimental data. Opinions were in favor of white, unglazed paper with a matte (dull-finish) surface for printing and of a thickness to prevent print from showing through on the reverse side. Experimental studies demonstrated that a rough paper surface had no advantage over a glazed surface. Material on paper with a moderately high glaze was read as rapidly as material on a dull surface, although readers prefer a dull printing surface. Extreme glare affects speed of reading. Logically, paper should be thick and opaque enough to prevent print from showing through on the reverse side.

In general, loss in legibility results from combinations of various nonoptimal typographical arrangements. Even two or more marginal factors or combinations of nonoptimal typographical arrangements—such as black print on enamel paper stock, small type, increased line length, decreased leading—affect legibility.

Newspapers and numerals present special reading problems not found in book and magazine publishing. Formulas and mathematical tables require boldface printing in part, opaque white matte paper, and avoidance of an excessive number of columns. Size of type is an important factor. An objective examination of printed numbers and tables will reveal legibility or lack of legibility.

To summarize—typography is an art of visual communication, an art which has for its materials ink, paper, and twenty-six symbols and ten digits. The methods of using these materials to gain maximum legibility constitute the science of typography. Quite simply, a legible type is one that can be read rapidly and easily. Type faces in common use are equally legible. Readers prefer a type face that appears to border on boldface, and possibly without serifs. Italic print is read somewhat more slowly than ordinary lowercase. Capital letters also retard speed of reading. Boldface type is read at the same rate as ordinary lowercase type. Material in mixed type forms markedly retards speed of reading.

In spite of the limitations, and in part because of them, librarians must use less precise observations and clues. Careful examination by a critical eye enables the evaluator to decide whether style of type, size of type, x-height, adequacy or inadequacy of margins, color of type, color of paper, illumination of printing surface, and spatial arrangement result in legibility that can be evaluated—at least in a general way—as high, moderate, low, or illegible.

Margins, page layout, spacing between headings and text, spacing between lines of the text, and length of paragraphs are aspects to be noted and rated. Broken type, blurred letters, errors in typography, misspellings, poor paper, narrow inside margins, and glossy paper influence readability. They present visual aspects that can be judged on sight in a general way as acceptable or not acceptable. Publishers can be made aware of the unacceptability of poor formats and physical defects.

The physical aspects are not final determinants in acceptance or rejection. Again, the importance of content and the availability of comparative works must be considered as well as interests and needs.

SPECIAL FEATURES. Special features, added to the text, can be important factors in providing additional and supportive information. The most common special features include maps, illustrations, diagrams, tables, charts, and graphs. General aspects to be rated are whether they are supportive of the textual content, are adequate in number, are placed logically. Illustrative, geographic, or statistical information is not always included; consequently it is important to note special features that are needed but missing or that (when included) would be better omitted.

Maps. Maps are to be rated as very good, good, poor—or by some similar rating scale—for accuracy of content, clarity of legends, clarity of symbols, color identification, consistency of scale, precision of scale, quality of reproduction, and technical accuracy.

Maps and atlases are of major importance in the daily life of individuals. Adults must depend upon maps to find their way about cities and the country, to understand other areas of the world, and to learn about the earth, its environment, and environmental development. Road and street maps, state and national maps, political and economic maps, and historical and environmental maps are essential to meet the travel and information needs about places and countries of nearly all adults. The importance for librarians to evaluate and interpret maps for users cannot be overemphasized.

What is a map? Maps represent the earth's surface on a plane—or the moon, or universe. The scale becomes a major factor in understanding or reading the map. Maps show spatial relations. As a map is flat, it necessarily distorts directions, distances, and areas of land and sea masses on a sphere. A primary method of map making is the projection, the method by which the spherical surface of the earth is flattened out. The characteristics that must be judged include method of projection, letter size and style, width of lines, colors and shadings, and design of legends.

Librarians must also judge maps in various ways: in relation to suitability to the age of the user, authority of the publisher, scope, content, arrangement, supplementary material, indexing, accuracy, up-to-dateness, type, format and scale, methods of indicating relief, and cost.

In evaluating maps that are part of a work, an atlas, or sheet maps, certain basic criteria can be applied. Of course, the reliability and reputability of the map maker and publisher are to be determined. Questions about design and content include:

1. Is the information which is shown on the map accurate?
2. Is there a date on the map? Does the date apply to the information shown?
3. Is the projection suitable for the purpose of the map?
4. Is there an adequate and easily understood grid of latitude and longitude?
5. Is the material suitable for the scale?
6. Is there a complete and easily understood legend?
7. Are standard symbols used, and easily identified and distinguished from others?
8. If color is used, is it attractive? Is the color scheme generally acceptable?
9. Does the map present a clear picture, without confusing the reader?
10. If relief is shown, is it understandable and accurate?

Quality of execution can be determined to a great extent by careful observation and examination:

1. Is line work well done ("clean")?
2. Is continuity maintained after a conflict of line and lettering or lettering and lettering?
3. Are letter faces and sizes appropriate? (They should not overpower.)
4. Is the color reproduction good?
5. Is the generalization well done (progressive elimination of detail as the scale is reduced)?
6. Is the map durable? Can it be purchased with cloth backing or laminated, or can this be done at the library?

Finally, what is the cost and is the map worth it? Above all, it is important to have consistency of scale with maps. When the scale is not consistent, this should be stated clearly so as to prevent giving unintentional misinformation. All inconsistencies should be noted in annotations so that the reader is not misled.

Illustrations. Illustrations are commonly used in all types of reading materials. They may illustrate factually or imaginatively, accurately or fantastically. They may explain, mislead, or add appeal and artistic and scientific insights. Techniques are varied—line drawings, photographs, pictures, reproductions of paintings, drawings, lithographs, etchings, cartoons. Comic books, magazines, how-to-do-it manuals, art books, novels, and all nonfiction subjects lend themselves to illustration.

Illustrations and diagrams are rated as to accuracy of content, artistic quality, quality of black and white and color, quality of reproduction, and technical quality. Evaluating the technique requires some knowledge of the illustrator's artistry and skill, as well as the printing and reproductive process.

More and more choices must be made because of the variety of illustrations in different editions of a work and diverse formats. The enduring works of authors have various editions with either traditional or modern illustrations. Does one choose Dickens illustrated by George Cruikshank, or Hablot Browne (Phiz), or by Louis Slobodkin or Hilary Knight? Are Tenniel's illustrations for *Alice in Wonderland* more appropriate and appealing than a modern illustrator's? Are poor-quality color reproductions of an artist's painting better than good-quality black and white?

With the advent of multimedia learning programs and the paperback phenomenon it is possible, and essential, to consider various formats. Are choices to be made between the paperback and hardcover edition? The paperback may omit the illustrations. Editions may be published with or without illustrations. Are comic books' presentations of old and new stories to be acquired? Phonodiscs, audio tapes, slides, films, and filmstrips may illustrate and supplement the printed text, or vice versa. Evaluation of each medium becomes critical to decisions regardless of content and purpose.

Diagrams, Tables, Charts, and Graphs. Diagrams are usually found in information-type material. Their placement in relation to the content illustrated, appropriateness, and accuracy are critical aspects to evaluate.

Tables, charts, and graphs convey important information. It is of particular importance that they be placed at logical points in the text and be legible. They support the textual content and provide additional and explanatory information. The quality of the table, chart, or graph is judged on at least seven minimal aspects: accuracy, quality of production (which is usually black and white), the printed character (that is, type, clarity and size of character, and resultant character alignment), quality of black and white and color, quality of reproduction, spacing, and the explanatory statement. The latter, which usually accompanies the table, chart, or graph, should be looked at carefully for accuracy and for its contribution in relation to clarity and information.

LEARNING AIDS. Learning aids constitute a number of special features that may contribute to or detract from the writings. They are an important feature in any work concerned with communicating information, ideas, and knowledge. Common learning aids which constitute a guide to the use of the work are the preface, introduction, table of contents, and index or indexes. Other learning aids, essential to instructional materials, include answers, appendixes, chapter summaries, exercises to test skills, explanatory phrases in the text, footnotes, follow-up projects, glossaries, question guides, reading guides, bibliographies, self-pacing techniques, and vocabulary definitions. Other aids may also be found.

The critical point is that each aid should be evaluated for its content and relation to the whole. How useful is the aid? Is it clear or unclear? Is it accurate? Is it logically placed in the work? Are questions written at the same reading level as the text? Are the answers to problems correct? Does the glossary really provide helpful definitions? Are the scholarly aspects of citations, bibliographies, appendixes worthwhile? Are the exercises, self-pacing techniques, follow-up projects relevant?

Some questions can be answered by examination; others require actual testing. The cookbook, how-to-do-it manual, highly technical textbook, and unfamiliar language book can be tested only by practice. Recipes must be used, directions for repair followed, the physics text read. The glossary and vocabulary definitions must be checked. Do they illuminate the writing? Books on crewel work, house plants, or any current popular subject must be compared.

The honest, useful presentation must be distinguished from the worthless, confused, inaccurate, and possibly dishonest. It is equally important to note what illustrations and special features and aids are needed but are missing.

READABILITY LEVELS AND READABILITY FORMULAS. The reading abilities of the adult reader are linked closely with the intellectual capacities and the intentions of the reader and the readability of materials. The librarian, in order to match these various links—that is, to find the material suitable to the adult's purposes and abilities—needs to have information in each area about the reader and the material. Let us reconsider briefly what is known about measuring literacy and readability. What do the scientists and reading specialists contribute to the solution of the problems?

How are librarians to decide whether material is likely to be readable for a reader group or individual? Librarians estimate readability on the bases of their experience and the reactions of the readers. In this sense they guess, and some are skillful in their judgments. Teachers and reading specialists, in addition to guessing, use comprehension tests. The tests may be reliable and precise but require a great amount of time and effort. The measurement of readability by judgments and tests requires participation by the readers, and is often difficult or impossible, particularly in a library situation. The use of a readability formula seems the most practical method. The readability formula, based on word and sentence counts, predicts the probability that material is readable for a particular group. Although judgments and tests are useful measurements, reading formulas, because they are predictive and may be made without the reader, are more practical.

How important is readability? Although researchers and librarians frequently disagree on the value or validity of the formulas, the problem of assessing readability remains. Librarians are faced with all types and levels of materials that require evaluation. Professional and volunteer workers in adult education (especially in adult basic education programs), students, teachers, individuals, and community agencies ask for advice in selection and for materials. Foremost is the librarian's responsibility for developing library collections to meet general and particular needs. Librarians must often accept the publishers' ratings, which frequently prove to be undependable and whose criteria for measurement are unknown. For years, writers, editors, publishers, journalists, lawyers, and reading specialists have applied readability measures to the fields of education, business and industry, newspapers, government publications, and textbooks. With the advent of mass communication in radio and television, even "listenability" formulas have been developed. A small number of librarians use readability formulas when they are involved in readers' advisory services, are selecting materials for adults with limited reading skills, or are providing materials for adult basic education programs in periods of emphasis on literacy.

Librarians are almost exclusively dependent on the authorities to assess the validity of the measurement formulas or devices. The lack of agreement among them confuses the problem. The librarian will decide what application is useful in relation to the situation. It is a well-established fact that, regardless of readability, material will not be read unless the content is of interest and relevant to the reader's needs and purposes. In the context of the dynamics of reading, materials will be selected that are culturally supportive and intellectually stimulating as well as practical and instrumental.

Librarians' concern and direct involvement in the search for readable books resulted in several important activities during the 1920s and 1930s. Research studies relating to the problems of adult reading and readability were undertaken at the University of Chicago[26] and by the

[26]William S. Gray and Bernice E. Leary, *What Makes a Book Readable?* (Chicago: Univ. of Chicago Pr., 1935).

A readable type face is characterized by: the ease with which each character is recognized, which is determined by the amount of space on the inside and outside of each character; the height of ascenders and length of descenders; the relation of heavy and light lines; and the height and weight of each character. Despite the fact that serifs sometimes detract from

CENTURY SCHOOLBOOK 12-point on 14

A readable type face is characterized by: the ease with which each character is recognized, which is determined by the amount of space on the inside and outside of each character; the height of ascenders and length of descenders; the relation of heavy and light lines; and the height and weight of each character. Despite the fact that serifs sometimes detract from character recognition, they do provide a continuity that facilitates scanning. The eye should not have any difficulty in determining which group of

10-point on 12

A readable type face is characterized by: the ease with which each character is recognized, which is determined by the amount of space on the inside and outside of each character; the height of ascenders and length of descenders; the relation of heavy and light lines; and the height and weight of each character. Despite the fact that serifs sometimes detract from character recognition, they do provide a continuity that facilitates scanning. The eye should not have any difficulty in determining which group of letters is to be scanned next. Each type face has its own limitations. They must be considered by

9-point on 11

A readable type face is characterized by: the ease with which each character is recognized, which is determined by the amount of space on the inside and outside of each character; the height of ascenders and length of descenders; the relation of heavy and light lines; and the height and weight of each character. Despite the fact that serifs sometimes detract from character recognition, they do provide a continuity that facilitates scanning. The eye should not have any difficulty in determining which group of letters is to be scanned next. Each type face has its own limitations. They must be considered by the artist or designer selecting a type so that the one chosen will be best for the job at hand.

8-point on 10

Fig. 9 (cont.). Samples of four type faces. Above, Century Schoolbook in four sizes. The size of type chosen should be appropriate to the book's purpose. For example, 12-point type is commonly selected for visually handicapped readers and for readers ages 7–10. 11-point type faces are commonly used for adult books and often for readers above the age of ten. 10-point type is used for both hard- and soft-cover books. 9-point is commonly used for paperbacks and for reference books. 8-point type may often be found in footnotes, legends, bibliographies, and indexes.

A readable type face is characterized by: the ease with which each character is recognized, which is determined by the amount of space on the inside and outside of each character; the height of ascenders and length of descenders; the relation of heavy and light lines; and the height and weight of each character. Despite the fact that serifs sometimes detract from character recognition, they do provide a continuity that facilitates scanning. The eye should not have any difficulty in determining which group of letters is to be scanned next. Each type face has its own limitations. They must be considered by the artist or designer selecting a type so that the one chosen will be best for the job at hand.

BASKERVILLE
10-point solid

A readable type face is characterized by: the ease with which each character is recognized, which is determined by the amount of space on the inside and outside of each character; the height of ascenders and length of descenders; the relation of heavy and light lines; and the height and weight of each character. Despite the fact that serifs sometimes detract from character recognition, they do provide a continuity that facilitates scanning. The eye should not have any difficulty in determining which group of letters is to be scanned next. Each type face has its own limitations. They must be considered by the artist or designer selecting a type so that the one chosen will be best for the job at hand.

10-point on 11

A readable type face is characterized by: the ease with which each character is recognized, which is determined by the amount of space on the inside and outside of each character; the height of ascenders and length of descenders; the relation of heavy and light lines; and the height and weight of each character. Despite the fact that serifs sometimes detract from character recognition, they do provide a continuity that facilitates scanning. The eye should not have any difficulty in determining which group of letters is to be scanned next. Each type face has its own limitations. They must be considered by the artist or designer selecting a type so that the

10-point on 12

A readable type face is characterized by: the ease with which each character is recognized, which is determined by the amount of space on the inside and outside of each character; the height of ascenders and length of descenders; the relation of heavy and light lines; and the height and weight of each character. Despite the fact that serifs sometimes detract from character recognition, they do provide a continuity that facilitates scanning. The eye should not have any difficulty in determining which group of letters is to be scanned next. Each type face has its own limitations. They must

10-point on 13

Fig. 9 (cont.). Samples of four type faces. Above, Baskerville 10-point with varying amounts of space between lines.

A readable type face is characterized by: the ease with which each character is recognized, which is determined by the amount of space on the inside and outside of each character; the height of ascenders and length of descenders; the relation of heavy and light lines; and the height and weight of each character. Despite the fact that serifs sometimes detract from character recognition, they do

BASKERVILLE
12-point on 14

A readable type face is characterized by: the ease with which each character is recognized, which is determined by the amount of space on the inside and outside of each character; the height of ascenders and length of descenders; the relation of heavy and light lines; and the height and weight of each character. Despite the fact that serifs sometimes detract from character recognition, they do provide a continuity that facili-

11-point on 13

A readable type face is characterized by: the ease with which each character is recognized, which is determined by the amount of space on the inside and outside of each character; the height of ascenders and length of descenders; the relation of heavy and light lines; and the height and weight of each character. Despite the fact that serifs sometimes detract from character recognition, they do provide a continuity that facilitates scanning. The eye should not have any difficulty in determining which group of letters is to be

10-point on 12

A readable type face is characterized by: the ease with which each character is recognized, which is determined by the amount of space on the inside and outside of each character; the height of ascenders and length of descenders; the relation of heavy and light lines; and the height and weight of each character. Despite the fact that serifs sometimes detract from character recognition, they do provide a continuity that facilitates scanning. The eye should not have any difficulty in determining which group of letters is to be scanned next. Each type face has its own limitations. They must be considered by the artist or designer selecting a type so

9-point on 11

A readable type face is characterized by: the ease with which each character is recognized, which is determined by the amount of space on the inside and outside of each character; the height of ascenders and length of descenders; the relation of heavy and light lines; and the height and weight of each character. Despite the fact that serifs sometimes detract from character recognition, they do provide a continuity that facilitates scanning. The eye should not have any difficulty in determining which group of letters is to be scanned next. Each type face has its own limitations. They must be considered by the artist or designer selecting a type so that the one chosen will be best for the job at hand.

8-point on 10

Fig. 9 (cont.). Samples of four type faces. Above, Baskerville in five sizes.

A readable type face is characterized by: the ease with which each character is recognized, which is determined by the amount of space on the inside and outside of each character; the height of ascenders and length of descenders; the relation of heavy and light lines; and the height and weight of each character. Despite the fact that serifs sometimes detract from character recognition, they do provide a continuity that facilitates scanning. The eye should not have any difficulty in determining which group of letters is to be scanned next. Each type face has its own limitations. They must be considered by the artist or designer selecting a type so that the one chosen will be best for the job at hand.

10-point on 11
(with 1 point of space
between lines)

A readable type face is characterized by: the ease with which each character is recognized, which is determined by the amount of space on the inside and outside of each character; the height of ascenders and length of descenders; the relation of heavy and light lines; and the height and weight of each character. Despite the fact that serifs sometimes detract from character recognition, they do provide a continuity that facilitates scanning. The eye should not have any difficulty in determining which group of letters is to be scanned next. Each type face has its own limitations. They must be considered by the artist or designer selecting a type so that the one chosen will be best for the job at hand.

10-point on 12
(with 2 points of space
between lines)

A readable type face is characterized by: the ease with which each character is recognized, which is determined by the amount of space on the inside and outside of each character; the height of ascenders and length of descenders; the relation of heavy and light lines; and the height and weight of each character. Despite the fact that serifs sometimes detract from character recognition, they do provide a continuity that facilitates scanning. The eye should not have any difficulty in determining which group of letters is to be scanned next. Each type face has its own limitations. They must be considered by the artist or designer selecting

10-point on 13
(with 3 points of space
between lines)

A readable type face is characterized by: the ease with which each character is recognized, which is determined by the amount of space on the inside and outside of each character; the height of ascenders and length of descenders; the relation of heavy and light lines; and the height and weight of each character. Despite the fact that serifs sometimes detract from character recognition, they do provide a continuity that facilitates scanning. The eye should not have any difficulty in determining which group of letters is to be scanned next. Each type face has its own limita-

Fig. 9. Samples of four type faces. Above, Century Schoolbook. The pages of this foldout show four type faces commonly used in books. (Only roman characters have been set as they are the ones most commonly used in book work.) The pages are arranged to serve as an aid in identifying these four type faces when used in other books, for verifying the size of type used therein, and in determining the amount of space between lines.

A readable type face is characterized by: the ease with which each character is recognized, which is determined by the amount of space on the inside and outside of each character; the height of ascenders and length of descenders; the relation of heavy and light lines; and the height and weight of each character. Despite the fact that serifs sometimes detract from character recognition, they do 12-point on 14

A readable type face is characterized by: the ease with which each character is recognized, which is determined by the amount of space on the inside and outside of each character; the height of ascenders and length of descenders; the relation of heavy and light lines; and the height and weight of each character. Despite the fact that serifs sometimes detract from character recognition, they do provide a continuity that facili- 11-point on 13

A readable type face is characterized by: the ease with which each character is recognized, which is determined by the amount of space on the inside and outside of each character; the height of ascenders and length of descenders; the relation of heavy and light lines; and the height and weight of each character. Despite the fact that serifs sometimes detract from character recognition, they do provide a continuity that facilitates scanning. The eye should not have any difficulty in determining which group of letters is to be scanned next. 10-point on 12

A readable type face is characterized by: the ease with which each character is recognized, which is determined by the amount of space on the inside and outside of each character; the height of ascenders and length of descenders; the relation of heavy and light lines; and the height and weight of each character. Despite the fact that serifs sometimes detract from character recognition, they do provide a continuity that facilitates scanning. The eye should not have any difficulty in determining which group of letters is to be scanned next. Each type face has its own limitations. They must be considered by the artist or designer selecting a type so 9-point on 11

A readable type face is characterized by: the ease with which each character is recognized, which is determined by the amount of space on the inside and outside of each character; the height of ascenders and length of descenders; the relation of heavy and light lines; and the height and weight of each character. Despite the fact that serifs sometimes detract from character recognition, they do provide a continuity that facilitates scanning. The eye should not have any difficulty in determining which group of letters is to be scanned next. Each type face has its own limitations. They must be considered by the artist or designer selecting a type so that the one chosen will be best for the job at hand. 8-point on 10

Fig. 9 (cont.). Samples of four type faces. Above, Times Roman in five sizes.

A readable type face is characterized by: the ease with which each character is recognized, which is determined by the amount of space on the inside and outside of each character; the height of ascenders and length of descenders; the relation of heavy and light lines; and the height and weight of each character. Despite the fact that serifs sometimes detract from character recognition, they do provide a continuity that facilitates scanning. The eye should not have any difficulty in determining which group of letters is to be scanned next. Each type face has its own limitations. They must be considered by the artist or designer selecting a type so that the one chosen will be best for the job at hand.

A readable type face is characterized by: the ease with which each character is recognized, which is determined by the amount of space on the inside and outside of each character; the height of ascenders and length of descenders; the relation of heavy and light lines; and the height and weight of each character. Despite the fact that serifs sometimes detract from character recognition, they do provide a continuity that facilitates scanning. The eye should not have any difficulty in determining which group of letters is to be scanned next. Each type face has its own limitations. They must be considered by the artist or designer selecting a type so that the one chosen will

A readable type face is characterized by: the ease with which each character is recognized, which is determined by the amount of space on the inside and outside of each character; the height of ascenders and length of descenders; the relation of heavy and light lines; and the height and weight of each character. Despite the fact that serifs sometimes detract from character recognition, they do provide a continuity that facilitates scanning. The eye should not have any difficulty in determining which group of letters is to be scanned next. Each type face has its own limitations. They must be considered by the

A readable type face is characterized by: the ease with which each character is recognized, which is determined by the amount of space on the inside and outside of each character; the height of ascenders and length of descenders; the relation of heavy and light lines; and the height and weight of each character. Despite the fact that serifs sometimes detract from character recognition, they do provide a continuity that facilitates scanning. The eye should not have any difficulty in determining which group of letters is to be scanned next. Each type

Fig. 9 (cont.). Samples of four type faces. Above, Optima, a sans serif type face, 10-point with varying amounts of space between lines.

A readable type face is characterized by: the ease 12-point on 14 with which each character is recognized, which is determined by the amount of space on the inside and outside of each character; the height of ascenders and length of descenders; the relation of heavy and light lines; and the height and weight of each character. Despite the fact that serifs sometimes detract

A readable type face is characterized by: the ease with which 10-point on 12 each character is recognized, which is determined by the amount of space on the inside and outside of each character; the height of ascenders and length of descenders; the relation of heavy and light lines; and the height and weight of each character. Despite the fact that serifs sometimes detract from character recognition, they do provide a continuity that facilitates scanning. The eye should not have any difficulty in deter-

A readable type face is characterized by: the ease with which each 9-point on 11 character is recognized, which is determined by the amount of space on the inside and outside of each character; the height of ascenders and length of descenders; the relation of heavy and light lines; and the height and weight of each character. Despite the fact that serifs sometimes detract from character recognition, they do provide a continuity that facilitates scanning. The eye should not have any difficulty in determining which group of letters is to be scanned next. Each type face has its own limitations. They must be considered by the artist or de-

A readable type face is characterized by: the ease with which each character 8-point on 10 is recognized, which is determined by the amount of space on the inside and outside of each character; the height of ascenders and length of descenders; the relation of heavy and light lines; and the height and weight of each character. Despite the fact that serifs sometimes detract from character recognition, they do provide a continuity that facilitates scanning. The eye should not have any difficulty in determining which group of letters is to be scanned next. Each type face has its own limitations. They must be considered by the artist or designer selecting a type so that the one chosen will be best for the job at hand.

Fig. 9 (cont.). Samples of four type faces. Above, Optima, a sans serif type face, in four sizes.

A readable type face is characterized by: the ease with which each character is recognized, which is determined by the amount of space on the inside and outside of each character; the height of ascenders and length of descenders; the relation of heavy and light lines; and the height and weight of each character. Despite the fact that serifs sometimes detract from character recognition, they do provide a continuity that facilitates scanning. The eye should not have any difficulty in determining which group of letters is to be scanned next. Each type face has its own limitations. They must be considered by the artist or designer selecting a type so that the one chosen will be best for the job at hand.

A readable type face is characterized by: the ease with which each character is recognized, which is determined by the amount of space on the inside and outside of each character; the height of ascenders and length of descenders; the relation of heavy and light lines; and the height and weight of each character. Despite the fact that serifs sometimes detract from character recognition, they do provide a continuity that facilitates scanning. The eye should not have any difficulty in determining which group of letters is to be scanned next. Each type face has its own limitations. They must be considered by the artist or designer selecting a type so that the one chosen will be best for the job at hand.

10-point on 11

A readable type face is characterized by: the ease with which each character is recognized, which is determined by the amount of space on the inside and outside of each character; the height of ascenders and length of descenders; the relation of heavy and light lines; and the height and weight of each character. Despite the fact that serifs sometimes detract from character recognition, they do provide a continuity that facilitates scanning. The eye should not have any difficulty in determining which group of letters is to be scanned next. Each type face has its own limitations. They must be considered by the artist or designer selecting a type so that the one chosen will be

10-point on 12

A readable type face is characterized by: the ease with which each character is recognized, which is determined by the amount of space on the inside and outside of each character; the height of ascenders and length of descenders; the relation of heavy and light lines; and the height and weight of each character. Despite the fact that serifs sometimes detract from character recognition, they do provide a continuity that facilitates scanning. The eye should not have any difficulty in determining which group of letters is to be scanned next. Each type face has its own limitations. They must be considered by

10-point on 13

Fig. 9 (cont.). Samples of four type faces. Above, Times Roman 10-point with varying amounts of space between lines.

American Library Association Committee to Study the Development of Reading Habits. At Teachers College, Columbia University, the Readability Laboratory was established,[27] and the American Library Association Subcommittee on Readable Books was organized. As a result of these activities the People's Library series was published.[28] In the 1960s, Holt, Rinehart, and Winston published the Holt Basic Education series.

Neither series was really successful, but the fact should in no way prevent other attempts. Certainly some secrets of success must be known to best-seller authors, pulp writers, journalists, and successful teachers and librarians. Certainly adults do not need or want pablum, sterile writing, and limited wordlists.

What are readability formulas? How valid are they? Do they measure what they are intended to measure? "A readability formula uses counts of language variables in a piece of writing in order to provide an index of probable difficulty for readers. It is a predictive device in the sense that no actual participation by readers is needed."[29] The general-purpose formulas are ones which librarians will find easiest to use and most suitable to their needs. These formulas, intended to cover a wide range of difficulty, may be applied manually or by machine. They are simple, two-variable formulas that are based on word and sentence counts. The criterion has been set against a set of graded passages, with the number of occurrences of a given style factor being related to the grades.

What of validity? Klare, who has reviewed the research literature up to 1960 in readability, together with an analysis of trends in 1963 and again in 1974, reached definite conclusions.[30] For predictive purposes, "the evidence that simple word and sentence counts can provide satisfactory predictions for most purposes is now quite conclusive."[31]

In spite of reservations among many librarians and complete rejection of reading formulas by some reading specialists and librarians, because they feel formulas are invalid and require an inordinate amount of time to calculate, the readability formulas are included as a measurement among the criteria recommended for evaluation of reading materials.

Primarily, a readability formula is a means of rating a piece of writing *after* it has been written. A formula indicates only the general difficulty

[27]Lyman Bryson, "Readability Laboratory," *Library Journal*, 61:445 (June 1936).

[28]*The People's Library*, Series 1–11 (New York: Macmillan, 1940).

[29]George R. Klare, "Assessing Readability," *Reading Research Quarterly*, 10, no. 1:64 (1974–75).

[30]George R. Klare, *The Measurement of Readability* (Ames: Iowa State Univ. Pr., 1963).

[31]Klare, "Assessing Readability," p. 98.

of style. Formulas measure only one aspect of writing (that is, style), and only in relation to difficulty. Difficulty in style does make a difference. The more readable written material may influence reading speed, acceptability, and understanding. Many other factors are the reader's knowledge and experience with the subject, motivation, one's value system, the strength of one's desire to learn, and the amount of time the reader can give to study and rereading.

The librarian must recognize all the limitations of formulas. At best, they offer a rough yardstick. Many reading researchers reject them entirely. Publishers and teachers and librarians in elementary, middle, and high schools use them. Librarians of necessity must be familiar with them, if only to compare and recheck reading levels presented by publishers and other evaluators.

Readers prefer a more readable version of material to a less readable one. The preference for simple style is particularly true when the subject is not familiar, is outside the reader's specialty. When readers have little experience with reading, the frustrations created by a difficult style will discourage and deter any use of that material.

Learning and comprehension, however, do not depend entirely on the readability scores. Easy readability may conceal density of subject content. The most important works are usually of a complexity and range of meanings that make possible a range of understandings. Both fiction and nonfiction authors, whether of a classic or the current best seller—Plato, Aquinas, Dickens, Lawrence, Malcolm X, Christie, Baldwin, Woolf, Michener, Solzhenitsyn—have appeals of range and complexity that are more difficult to measure than length of words and sentences.

What reading formulas are suggested? The Robert Gunning Fog Index was selected for final inclusion in the MAC Checklist, Materials Analysis Criteria.[32] Rudolph Flesch's Reading Ease Formula and Edward B. Fry's Readability Graph were tested.[33] The Fog Index, because of its ease of mathematical computation and the accuracy with which it measures the difficulty of adult materials, was chosen for routine use. The other formulas are also useful and valuable for comparative purposes. They are based on average sentence length and syllable counts in words. The estimated reading grade level is based on the compilations used in

[32]Robert Gunning, *The Technique of Clear Writing* (New York: McGraw-Hill, 1952; rev. ed. 1968); Robert Gunning, "The Fog Index after Twenty Years," *Journal of Business Communications*, 6:3–13 (Winter 1968).

[33]Rudolph F. Flesch, "A Readability Yardstick," *Journal of Applied Psychology*, 32:221–33 (June 1948); Edward B. Fry, "A Readability Formula that Saves Time," *Journal of Reading*, 11:513–16, 575–77 (Apr. 1968); Edward B. Fry, "A Readability Graph for Librarians," part 1, *School Libraries*, 19:13–16 (Fall 1969).

each formula in terms of three or more selected hundred-word samples. Several samples may yield more reliable results.

The methods used in analyzing and measuring readability are based on sentence length and vocabulary (that is, proportion of "hard words"). Readability is defined as the difficulty or ease with which it is predicted any individual can comprehend the written material. Other factors that may be considered in determining readability level are prepositional phrases, pronouns, prefixes and suffixes, references to proper names, word complexity, and modifiers. Formulas to determine readability do not consider content, style, word order, format, or imagery. Although these elements are important in an evaluation of reading difficulty, no formula has yet been devised which can analyze or measure them. They are considered in the application of various criteria developed for the MAC checklist and include structure and development of the work, analysis of style and language, and a quantitative evaluation scheme. The legibility factors, such as type, spatial arrangements, printing surface, and learning aids, can be judged according to more concrete, simpler, and objective standards.

It is estimated that, after one acquires experience in their use, the time required for computation can be considerably less. The Gunning Fog Index would require about fifteen minutes for computation, the Flesch Reading Ease twenty minutes or more, and Fry somewhat less, as it provides a graphic solution rather than a formula.

Robert Gunning's Fog Index requires the count of words of three or more syllables. The reading grade level equals 0.4 average sentence length plus the percentage of words of three or more syllables. For application of the Fog index, computer programs have been developed.

Fry uses the same variables of syllables per one hundred words and words per sentence. The user enters the counts of syllables and sentences on a graph and reads the grade score directly from it.

The Flesch Reading Ease formula is based on average sentence length in words and the number of syllables in hundred-word samples. This formula was designed for general adult reading matter and has been widely used. The grade placement refers to a 50 percent comprehension level.

The Dale-Chall formula for adult materials also has been widely used and various recalculations have been made. Some librarians use it consistently. It is not included here because of difficulty in calculating the results of the analysis and the questions of its appropriateness in vocabularies for adults.

The following guides have been developed for use in the application of the three readability measures. The Fry Graph for Estimating Readability is based on two simple mathematical procedures: syllable count and sentence count. The procedure and application for estimating readability with the Fry graph (figure 10) follows.

1. Select Word Samples. Randomly select at least three separate word samples from various sections of the material being evaluated. Each sample should contain *exactly* 100 words. *Do not count proper nouns.*

2. Sentence Count. Count the total number of sentences in each sample of 100 words. When a word count ends within a sentence, estimate the sentence to the nearest tenth. For example, if a word count ends immediately after the third word in a five-word sentence, the last phrase in the selection is counted as 6/10 of a sentence.

   Average the sentence counts and arrive at an average number of sentences for all the samples used, as illustrated in example 1.

3. Syllable Count. Count the total number of syllables in each 100-word sample. *Do not count proper nouns.* Determine the average number of syllables for all the samples used, as illustrated in example 2.

APPLICATION *Example 1*   EVALUATOR'S WORK SPACE

Number of Sentences:
   First 100-word sample*   5.6
   Second 100-word sample   6.0
   Third 100-word sample   8.8
               divide $\overline{20.4}$
                3)___   3)_____
   Average Number of Sentences   6.8

*Sample paragraphs were taken from Malcolm X and Alex Haley, *Autobiography of Malcolm X* (New York: Grove Press, 1966). Sample 1 was ¶ 1, p. 39; sample 2, ¶ 3, p. 161; sample 3, ¶ 3, p. 345.

APPLICATION *Example 2*   EVALUATOR'S WORK SPACE

Number of Syllables:
   First 100-word sample   148
   Second 100-word sample   132
   Third 100-word sample   130
               divide $\overline{410}$
                3)___   3)_____
   Average Number of Syllables   136

Average number of syllables per 100 words

SHORT WORDS   LONG WORDS

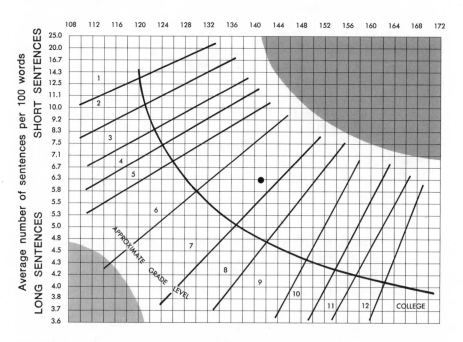

Directions:

Randomly select 3 one hundred word passages from a book or an article. Plot average number of syllables and average number of sentences per 100 words on graph to determine the grade level of the material. Choose more passages per book if great variability is observed and conclude that the book has uneven readability. Few books will fall in gray area but when they do grade level scores are invalid.

Example:

	SYLLABLES	SENTENCES
1st Hundred Words	124	6.6
2nd Hundred Words	141	5.5
3rd Hundred Words	158	6.8
AVERAGE	141	6.3

READABILITY 7th GRADE (see dot plotted on graph)

Figure 10. Fry graph for estimating readability. (Reprinted, by permission, from Edward B. Fry, "A Readability Graph for Librarians," pt. 1, *School Libraries*, 19:13–16 [Fall 1969].)

4. Plotting Grade Level. To determine the approximate grade level of the materials being evaluated, plot the average number of sentences and the average number of syllables on the Fry Graph for Estimating Readability.

The dot on the graph indicates the point at which the line for the average number of sentences (6.8) and the line for the average number of syllables (136) intersect. The graph indicates the readability level of this material at approximately seventh grade. When plotted scores fall into the shaded areas, grade level scores should be considered invalid. Figure 10 shows the Fry analysis, with the dot on the graph for a work with a 6.3 grade level.

The Flesch Reading Ease Formula is based on a count of two language elements: average sentence length in words and number of syllables in hundred-word samples. The procedure and application for the Flesch formula follows.

RE = reading ease, SL = sentence length, and WL = word length

1. Select three 100-word samples from the material to be rated—one sample near the beginning, one near the middle, and one near the end.
2. Count the number of syllables per 100 words. This is word length (WL). Count the number of syllables in symbols and figures according to the way they are normally read aloud.
3. Determine the average number of words per sentence by dividing

Table 5. PATTERN OF READING EASE

DESCRIPTION OF STYLE	AVERAGE SENTENCE LENGTH	AVERAGE NO. OF SYLLABLES PER 100 WORDS	READING EASE SCORE	ESTIMATED READING GRADE
Very easy	8 or less	123 or less	90 to 100	5th grade
Easy	11	131	80 to 90	6th grade
Fairly easy	14	139	70 to 80	7th grade
Standard	17	147	60 to 70	8th to 9th grade
Fairly difficult	21	155	50 to 60	10th to 12th grade (high school)
Difficult	25	167	30 to 50	13th to 16th grade (college)
Very difficult	29 or more	192 or more	0 to 30	college graduate

Source: Rudolph Flesch, *The Art of Readable Writing* (New York: Harper, 1949), p. 149. Reprinted by permission.

APPLICATION *Example 3*

$$RE = 206.835 - .846WL - 1.015SL$$

	I	II	I	II
EVALUATOR'S WORK SPACE				
1. WL (word length)	135			
2. Multiply WL by .846	×.846		×.846	
	114.210			
3. Subtract above from 206.835	206.835 −114.210		206.835	
		= 92.625		
4. SL (sentence length) =	16.6			
5. Multiply SL by 1.015	×1.015		×1.015	
		= −16.849		= −
6. Subtract figures in column II. This will yield *reading ease score* =		75.776		
7. Compute score for 2d 100-word sample		49.550		
8. Compute score for 3d 100-word sample		27.593		
9. Compute average of the three reading grade scores	3)	152.919	3)	
Reading Ease Score is 50.973.		50.973		
This score falls into the Fairly Difficult range.				

the number of words in the sample by the number of complete
sentences.

4. Apply these data in the RE (reading ease) formula to each 100-
word sample, as illustrated in example 3.
5. Compute the average of the three samples.
6. Determine difficulty of material by applying RE score in Pattern
of Reading Ease scale. The reading ease description of style categories may be translated into grade levels on the Flesch scale
(table 5).

The Gunning Fog Index (example 4) is based on two language factors: sentence length and hard word factor. "Hard words" are words
composed of three or more syllables. The Fog Index shows the reading
grade level required for understanding the material. The procedure and
application for use of the Gunning formula follows.

1. Select three or more 100-word samples, one near the beginning (but not the opening paragraph), one near the middle, and one near the end.
2. Count the number of sentences in each 100-word sample. Determine the average sentence length by dividing the number of words by the number of *complete* sentences.
3. Count the number of words of three syllables or more to get the number of hard words. *Do not count proper nouns*, easy compound words like *bookkeeper*, or verb forms in which the third syllable is merely the ending.
4. Add the number of polysyllabic words and the average sentence length, then multiply by 0.4, which yields the reading grade level.
5. Repeat the computation for each sample of 100 words.
6. Compute the average of the three samples.

The Fog Indexes for reading matter correlate with school grades. Second, third, fourth, fifth, sixth, seventh, and eighth grades are respectively two, three, four, five, six, seven, and eight on the Indexes; high school, freshman to seniors, are nine to twelve, and college, freshman to seniors, thirteen to seventeen.

APPLICATION *Example 4*

	I	II	I	II
1. Number of sentences in 100-word sample	6			
2. Average sentence length: 100 ÷ 6 (put answer in column II)		16.6		
3. Number of hard words (put answer in column II)		+2	+	___
4. Add figures in column II =		18.6		
5. Multiply this sum by .4		×.4		×.4
6. Reading grade level is seventh grade, fourth month, for first 100-word sample		7.4		
7. Compute the score for 2d 100-word sample		6.6		
8. Compute the score for 3d 100-word sample		22.8		
9. Compute the average of the three reading grade scores	3)	36.8	3)	___
Fog index =		12.2*		

*A rating of 12.2 indicates a level beyond high school.

Appeal to Readers

Appeal to readers is an area in which the librarian focuses the professional skills gained in evaluating the material and in analyzing the adult community to predict interest and use. Such judgments at best are generalizations and become specific only when an individual or specific group is under consideration. The final judgment will be made by the reader. The librarian who realizes the unpredictability of many interests and needs and the many variables which affect the decision will promote a wide variety of reading materials. In this way the adult's choices are widened and discriminatory abilities perfected.

The appeal of the material is dependent on many factors discussed in this work. At the very least, such factors as appeal, ethnic emphasis, special backgrounds, and purposes or effects may be identified. The importance of appeal, in terms of adult roles portrayed in the content, the subject, the attitudes and values, style, and readability, is to be considered in making predictive judgments. On the basis of the entire analysis, the appeal of the reading material to the potential reader is determined as major or secondary. Less and less are materials classified as appealing to readers because of sex or age. Nevertheless, some material is intended for or directed to particular interests of men or women or a specific age group.

In such instances it is helpful both to the reader and the librarian to have indicators of appeal. Current emphasis is on elimination of the practice of labeling materials for a particular sex or for certain age groups—a practice which may have led to discrimination and a narrowing of choices because of mistaken preconceptions. For example, *Go Ask Alice*, the anonymous record of a young girl's struggle with drugs, appeals to parents, teachers, men, and women of any age. It may have particular appeal to young women between fifteen and eighteen years of age in white, so-called middle-class society because Alice embodies these characteristics. For the same reasons, it may be rejected by readers. For convenience, the librarian will want to set scales of intervals relating to ages. In the MAC checklist the scale is:

15–18 years	45–54 years
19–24 years	55–64 years
25–34 years	65 and over
35–44 years	Any age

Special background appeal in relation to setting can have real importance. Again, in very general terms, rural, urban, and suburban backgrounds should be identified—but many inner-city residents come from rural backgrounds. Maya Angelou's *I Know Why the Caged Bird Sings* combines rural and urban, while Louise Meriwether's *Daddy Is a Number Runner* is laid exclusively in Harlem. Anne Moody's *Coming of Age in Mississippi* describes life in the South and the civil rights struggle during the sixties. Ethnic emphasis is clear—three young black women growing up in the United States of America. All are perceptive, well-written accounts of growing up as unique black experiences. Although the age, sex, and ethnic emphasis are defined clearly, the appeal to much wider age and ethnic reader groups is also clear.

Finally, what qualities in the material may attract the potential reader? Here the descriptive terms identified in analyses of readers' purposes for reading and effects of reading are useful. The qualities in the following categories are suggested. The librarian and the reader will ask the questions: Does the material have potential appeal to a potential reader because it is informational, interpretative, problem solving? Does it have aesthetic, intellectual, spiritual appeal? May it provide security in a personal and social sense for the reader? Does it provide adventure, pleasure, relaxation? Does it have any or several of these aspects? What other appeals are found?

Quantitative Evaluation

Quantitative evaluation permits a scale of numerical ratings. Such ratings are based on judgments made in evaluating the several categories related to bibliographic aspects, content analysis, measurement of readability, and their relationship to the appeal to individual readers, reader groups, and potential readers.

The numerical rating of each question is an overall, integrated evaluation of the category to which it refers. In assigning each rating it is necessary to take into account all the factors considered in the category. For example, under "bibliographic evaluation" one asks "What is the overall assessment of the reliability and authority of the material (bibliographic data)? What is the overall judgment of the material's physical format? How is the material evaluated in relation to its representation of the type of literature?"

Each question then is rated on a scale from 1 to 9 (or 0 if not applicable). The scale developed for the MAC checklist is:

1	Definitely inferior	6	Somewhat good
2	Very poor	7	Good
3	Poor	8	Very good
4	Somewhat poor	9	Definitely superior
5	Fair	0	Not applicable

The rating scores established for each of the four categories—bibliographic evaluation, content analysis, measurement of readability, and appeal to readers—serve as an index for computation of the quantitative evaluation score.

Summary and Annotation

The final, overall evaluation of the material will contain the summary of the data and insights gained in the detailed analysis. To be useful for reference and reading guidance, it must be integrated into a meaningful résumé which is based on the four major aspects of the analysis. It is a detailed, descriptive, but brief record. It is this summary, and the detailed, itemized characteristics of the checklist analysis, that form the bases for a critical annotation.

The annotation provides the basic data for decisions on selection and potential use. Above all it records all pertinent information and professional opinion about the item analyzed. The annotation becomes an advisory aid to be used in reading guidance as a selection file, a book review, or book talk for program development. It incorporates in a clear statement the subject, the authority, the content in terms of values and attitudes, the readability level and style, the relationship to adult roles and life skills, potential readership, any ethnic emphasis, and reading appeals. It will contain a comparison of its contents and significance with other publications. It will be subject to review and revision, based on reactions of users and staff and comparisons to subsequent publications. A file of annotations is a useful reference aid for a staff and a valuable collection for staff development programs.

Annotations must be well written, express factual data, and demonstrate (by description or example) the flavor and style of the work. An annotation, to be most useful, will contain critical appraisal, praise or blame, and point out strengths, weaknesses, and the opinions of others (as well as the evaluator's). It will discriminate and distinguish, both in its descriptive and critical aspects. It will suggest specific and general appeals. It will identify potential use and users.[34]

The final evaluation may be summarized succinctly through a code of symbols which are developed to meet particular objectives of the library's service to readers. The detailed analysis of any title is used to make a definite recommendation, not only on acquisition but on potential use. Such a code would have sufficient range to specify the addition

[34]A useful guide to annotation is Haines, *Living with Books*, chap. 7: "Book Evaluation and Reviewing by Librarians," and chap. 8: "The Art of Annotation." The Haines book continues to be a useful review, both for those who are familiar with it and those who study it for the first time.

to general and subject collections and for developing specific collections for use in designated reading and study programs and by potential readers. The following code is an example:

R	Recommended for general collection
RS	Recommended for subject collection
R–ABE	Recommended for adult basic education collection
R–GED	Recommended for high school equivalency collection
R–ESL	Recommended for English-as-a-second-language collection
R–CLEP	Recommended for college-level examination program
M	Marginal title that should be used only until replaceable by better title
RE–	Recommended for collections with ethnic emphasis; for example, further designation by code: A = Appalachian, B = black, Ch = Chicano, N = Native American, PR = Puerto Rican American, Chi = Chinese
NR	Not recommended

What are the benefits of a structured analysis? The value of specific guidelines, questions, and checklists lies in the organized direction they give to the evaluation of the material. Carefully defined and itemized categories provide a structured approach. The basic information is obtained for an objective analysis of the work as well as a more subjective evaluation of specific factors and an overall critical appraisal. The process of analysis is incorporated within the procedure required to follow the instrument's form. The MAC checklist provides a tested instrument and the basis for similar guides.

The organized approach to evaluation results in an organized summary of the essential and individual aspects of the content and the writing. A written record of the findings provides a permanent reference source. The analysis is an aid to gaining insights and understanding values and attitudes presented in the materials, but also in stimulating constant attention to the beliefs and attitudes among the residents of the community. The interrelationships within the material are examined through the criteria.

Library collections that are based on careful selection can represent more accurately the diversity of interests and needs and the values and opinions in the community. Collections will be developed with greater breadth and depth. Selections will be made with emphases on particular clientele, client groups, and service programs. The selection process will obviate gathering in everything or limiting the range of materials to demand, the obvious, or the traditional. Approval plans can be used more efficiently.

9

Implications for Library Services

The implications which the preceding concepts and facts have for the development of dynamic reading service are far reaching in that they touch upon nearly every aspect of library organization. How can librarians generate—that is, basically demonstrate—the value of ideas and information contained in the medium of print? How can librarians show what such information and ideas—content—can mean to the lives of adults? At other periods librarians have reached out to aid the new immigrant, the less affluent, the uneducated and less educated adult, as well as the student and the educated, more affluent population. Today, rightly, service programs are placed in the context of changing mores, new knowledge, new leadership, multimedia communication, and direct service to individual and community interests and needs.

The interrelationships between print and electronic media are a constant consideration. The media generally are more oral and visual and less verbal. An integrated use of print and audiovisual media is necessary for illiterate and literate persons. Government agencies and private organizations in various social, educational, and economic areas focus their efforts on literacy goals. Programs in industry and business, schools and libraries, job training and adult education place equal emphases on literacy skills of reading, writing, and computation—skills not to be learned alone or separately; rather, skills that are carefully integrated with information necessary to problem solving and needs of daily life. The objectives and opportunities of programs such as adult basic education, job training, reading development, equivalency and independent study, and right to read concentrate on developing the life skills and understanding necessary to adult roles in various aspects of personal, social, and political life. Today society is to be characterized not so much as illiterate but rather as nonliterate. A culture that is dominated by youth and older persons makes overwhelming demands on all adults between these ages. It is these adults who exercise much of the power and control, politically and economically.

The librarians' and clients' definition of the problem in cooperative effort will result in acceptance rather than rejection of resources that contain nonstandard speech, change-oriented ideas, extreme leftist or rightist political philosophy, literature of cultures and life styles outside and within their own cultures. Librarians, if they restrict resources to local issues or demands, do a disservice to themselves and their constituents, who include all members of the community. In the global village of today, human beings are brought close together. They are called on to make decisions extending far beyond immediate boundaries, to other peoples in other cities, states, and countries. Informational and cultural resources must embrace a wide range of local, national, and international ideas and knowledge.

The actions librarians take to assist persons to access to and use of communication resources depend on how the problem is defined. What is done or not done depends on whether the causes of the problem of use or nonuse are to be seen in the person or the system.[1] In consequence, questions to be answered will be: What changes are to be made in the library system? How can the library assist persons solve their personal and social problems with information relevant to their lives and meaningful to learning and pleasure? Are changes in the behavior of adults necessary? Who decides what the problems are? Who defines the information and learning needs of the individuals and groups in the community? What funds are to be used? Who selects the materials? What linguistic differences are to be considered? What reading skills are needed?

Most reading specialists and librarians would agree that a person is literate when that person is able to get the information and ideas he or she needs from the materials one needs to read. Certainly some specialists and librarians would agree that a person who is otherwise considered literate, even highly literate, is illiterate in certain areas of knowledge and unable to read critically and with understanding in totally new areas.

Regardless of how important each basic factor of capacity, ability, motivation, literacy levels, measurements, and readability of materials is, the librarian has primary responsibility to identify, supply, and interpret reading materials that are suitable to the inquiring adult's interests, needs, and abilities. Other major factors inherent in the situation include:

[1]Nathan Caplan and Stephen D. Nelson, "Who's to Blame?" *Psychology Today*, 8, no. 6:99–104 (Nov. 1974).

1. The importance of the content to the individual
2. The meaning the content or writer's message projects because of the individual's highly personal interpretation and understanding, which in turn are dependent on life experiences
3. The reality or believability of the writer's message and style
4. The intentions or motivations with which the adult comes to the material.

Such factors pose human aspects that are rarely considered in literacy models or easily measurable. These same factors are inherent in the written material which reflects and incorporates the intentions, abilities, background, and personality of the source of the message. The source may be a single writer, or a group of writers, and may be influenced by editors, financial supporters, publishers, and producers.

Adult readers, teachers, and librarians are aware of the unpredictable nature of matching reader and message successfully. Fader cites the story of the young man who read Hawthorne's *Scarlet Letter* because of sheer persistence and motivation. Lyman reports the instance of the young man who struggled through *Manchild in the Promised Land* because here was a man who made it. In a Southern literacy class, *The Happy Hooker* was read eagerly by the adults. Frustration and despair result both for readers and librarians when readers' advisers fail to find the information written so that it fits not only the reader's reading abilities but also the information need, and to some degree the readers' life experiences.

What are the major objectives for a dynamic reading program which meets the needs of society? Libraries are the social agency with a unique contribution to make in assisting adults achieve maturity in reading. Libraries traditionally have responsibility for developing multimedia collections that are relevant to the adult readers' abilities and interests and needs. Abilities and demands, particularly among less advantaged groups, are defined and often limited by the struggle to survive.

A first concern is to provide students and teachers and independent learners with instructional and informational materials in the areas of literacy, survival skills, coping and life skills.

Equally important is the provision of materials which may enrich the adult's life, satisfy natural curiosity about human beings and the world, and help extend the adult's experience.

Library programs for ethnic groups, or for that matter for any individual member, are to help in the rediscovery, revitalization, and strengthening of ethnic identity.

The library assists the adult realize the challenge of study, the intellectual and aesthetic satisfactions of learning, as well as the practical and instrumental values. Librarians will create situations that stimulate interest and motivate readers.

Librarians will strive to create situations where ethnic groups are independent and have a degree of control which the situation demands. Individuals from ethnic groups will be involved through recruitment, community contacts, and as personnel for programs and activities, as well as advisers and decision makers in analysis of materials and planning of services.

They will strive for relevance for any collection or program, seek out and recognize various attitudes and values among the community's residents and the library's personnel.

An overall objective is to create a library system that serves as a reliable intelligence center, an intellectual and learning resource center, and a source of pleasure and recreational reading for everyone. Such an ideal is not impossible of achievement. A total adult service for a total community, as library principles and practice currently indicate, requires a network of library systems which is made up of all types of libraries and media centers.

What are the implications for library management? What do administrators need to know to achieve such objectives, to support financial policies, and to implement programs? What do librarians and staff need to know? How may the necessary facts be collected? Obviously, fully to answer these questions requires education in library science and related disciplines. The assumption is made that, in general, librarians and staff have professional qualifications.

The administration and entire staff should, at the most, give support in every possible way and, at the least, sanction to experimental projects and services which are extended to ethnic groups. The authority and autonomy are delegated rightly to the person or persons who are directly responsible. It is equally essential to support and encourage that person or staff, as well as the development of the program. All too often a project staff is left to succeed or fail at a remote distance within the system. A similar problem arises in coordinated or cooperative arrangements with other agencies. Successfully coordinated programs are developed only if they are given constant attention.

The lack of control in acquisition, selection, and evaluation of materials by those who use the materials is resolved by direct participation in the acquisition process by reader groups: adults (literate and nonliterate), students and teachers in adult basic education, equivalency programs, language classes, and independent study as well as specialists from universities and libraries.

Members of the groups to be served are active on library boards, as liaison staff, as advisers and decision makers. They create a more sensitive staff and broader authority.

If objectives are determined in joint planning, each one learns and agrees on what is expected. Although more time consuming and difficult to organize, planning in a more democratic way lessens the tensions and misunderstandings that may result from differing expectations of the reader group and professional staff.

The lack of involvement in planning educational and training programs which leads to the rejection of programs by those for whom they are intended can be changed. Community representatives respond positively if they participate in decisions, as well as advise and counsel.

Individuals from the community who take on liaison and library responsibilities cannot be expected to be instantaneous experts. Library staff development programs or library school study are important in the training of library staff and representatives from the community.

Language differences and lack of competence in language among staff are remedied by recruitment of bilingual staff and acquisition of language competence by existing staff. Bilingual reading materials and bilingual programs of information are increasing. The advantages of a staff with different historical, cultural, and linguistic backgrounds are proved.

The lack of information which is necessary to program planning is frequently a cause of poor planning, and consequently results in failures. The library is surely a resource center for its own needs. The information and records related to library planning should be available to any staff, board members, committees, government officials, community representatives, and others who are involved.

The library will assume an active role in helping the entire community know about cultures and problems of different groups. It is important that each culturally different group learn about its own culture and that of the larger society. It is equally important that the larger society learn about the culture and aspirations of that different group. Librarians recognize the power of the author, content, style, and the significance of ideas and accurate information.

In the final analysis, the problem for librarians, who are in an agency of society that collects and stores materials for communication, is to communicate. The adult services librarian, by virtue of the position, is evaluator, interpreter, transmitter, gatekeeper. The librarian's responsibility may be primarily to teach what she or he knows. Without coercion or moral righteousness, the librarian creates situations and opportunities for adults to read and gain satisfaction through development of lifetime reading habits.

An active reading development program (as does any library service) requires careful planning, responsible involvement, and sanction and support by the public and professional makers of policy—together with that of the staff of the library, as well as strong internal assistance by technical services departments. The reading program or literacy project may be experimental, nontraditional, or a demonstration or extension of usual services, but it requires the continuing assistance of the acquisition, conservation, processing, distribution, and promotion units of the library system. It may be necessary to adapt or to ignore established processes and procedures. New policies and objectives and different clientele demands and interests may require the absorption of the increased demands or radical changes to permit the provision of new activities and the processing of a variety of formats. Public and school libraries must give as much attention to the reading development program as to the regular curricula. Even more important may be the integration of such programs into the regular services.

Current and expected trends in adult and continuing education, in recurrent education, and specifically in the training of teachers, librarians, reading specialists, and researchers will set new priorities and practices. Recent indicators of future developments are the media selection centers, learning resource centers, and the learning library-laboratory. Individual and group programs are tailored to help adults improve skills in how to learn as well as gain content and literacy skills.

Analysis of the Situation

The first step in program planning involves an analysis of the current situation to assess, as completely as possible, the facts, problems, and resources in relation to the clientele and objectives identified in a community study. Although a perceptive, well-informed staff knows more or less about the community it serves, such knowledge necessarily is limited to immediate contacts, past knowledge, and individual experience and opinion. A systematic, directed study is desirable and quite likely essential. The library staff, an outside consultant, community residents, and other qualified resource persons may conduct such a study. The process of investigation opens new communication channels, provides opportunities for getting acquainted, for learning about beliefs, attitudes and opinions, and for the recruitment of supporters, advisers, and clientele, as well as the collection of factual data. The detailed study outlines similarities, distinctions, and differences.

Basic demographic or social characteristics about the residents who live in the legally served area include facts about sex, age, origin, schooling, location, occupation, and income. Facts about cultural patterns and expectations and attitudes toward reading and the library are fundamental to the understanding of the human aspects.

Serious questions often are raised whether these psychological aspects can be identified. Is it possible to identify, let alone evaluate, beliefs and attitudes within a community? Attitude research requires highly technical knowledge and sophisticated understanding of theory and methods. It may be possible to observe and study the relationships, the interaction between individuals and the world in which they live. The adult readers' attitudes toward books, reading, libraries, and the events and people around them are important considerations in planning and providing library reading programs.

Everyone has certain characteristic ways of feeling and responding, and such ways are relatively fixed. In evaluating readers' attitudes the librarian may ask several questions. What does the adult know about the library's resources? What is considered valuable? How does the person rate the various elements, such as staff, materials, environment? How does the reader feel toward the library? How does the adult feel about a specific subject, author, or type of format? Analysis of the traditions and folklore, the historical background, reveals deep-seated beliefs and attitudes that influence sanction, support, or disapproval of library programs.

In an extensive study of the community it is quite likely that distinct groups will emerge. Groups are discovered which are actually or relatively small in number. They may have been overlooked or unknown. Groups also are identified which are relatively large. They may have been ignored or neglected. Groups also are identified which are being served, and service to them may be improved.

Commonly used methods for collection of information that is useful in program planning are analysis of census data and existing studies, face-to-face or telephone interviews, self-administered questionnaires, surveys, and in-depth studies. Guides such as Warren's *Studying Your Community* are helpful to planners of a community study.[2]

---

[2]Roland L. Warren, *Studying Your Community* (New York: Free Press, 1965); *Studying the Community: Basis for Planning Library Adult Education Services* (Chicago: American Library Assn., 1960); Priscilla Gotsick, *Assessing Community Information and Service Needs*, Public Library Training Institutes, Library Service Guide no. 2 (Morehead, Ky.: Appalachian Adult Education Center, Morehead State Univ., 1974. ERIC ED098982).

The study of the community and its resources is advisably paralleled by an assessment of the library situation and its resources, along with other communication resources in the community. The regular daily records can yield pertinent data where a systematic collection of facts is made. Such records should be relevant to the objectives and purposes of planning and an aid in evaluation of services.

Significant data for analysis include the number of users, answered and unanswered requests, social characteristics of users, their interests and preferences, their problems and needs, materials borrowed and wanted. The readers' opinions and evaluations of service, as well as the impact of service and programs, can be obtained through special surveys and interviews. Computerized records facilitate analysis where significant data are programmed. What material is most used? What information was not available? Who reads what? What is the quality and appropriateness of each part of the collection? What materials are lacking? Answers to this type of questioning become valuable guides to acquisition and interpretation. In addition, they serve to measure selection policy and principles.

The significance of the community study lies in the fact that this initial information enables the program planners to identify and describe reader groups and individual users—that is, the clientele, the audience, the potential users to be served—and to establish objectives. Long-range, intermediate, and short-range objectives are determined. Then and then only is it possible to decide upon what program to organize—the audience or clientele, the type of program or activity, the necessary resources (human and material), the physical facilities, the promotion, the costs, and the evaluation procedures.

Staff

The staff of the library—the librarians who are responsible for the selection and organization of reading materials, their interpretation and use, and reading development programs and guidance—is as crucial a variable as teachers, who are responsible for reading instruction and the use of reading in communication. Librarians need to attract readers, to be qualified, to be skilled readers themselves, and to have adequate understanding of the major aspects of reading and instruction. Librarians assist in creating appropriate learning conditions. They work with teachers and students to diagnose problems, identify interests, individualize reading, and choose materials that best serve the interests and needs of the readers or students. Librarians have the technical knowledge and technical services to organize and administer the reading collections and services. In brief, they have the "know how." They have a responsibility to initiate cooperative and coordinated efforts with adult education and reading programs of other agencies and organizations.

The staff for any public service needs to be one with which the clientele can identify. The attitudes, beliefs, and values held by the library staff are as influential as their professional knowledge in library science. Their attitudes and opinions toward the clientele, the community, the service, the program, and the materials are crucial to successful development of the program and the collection. They can make or break it. The dedicated believer who is directly responsible for service to adults and to ethnic reader groups needs the support of all the staff. The character of adult services in reading programs demands a knowledge of other disciplines, particularly social sciences and education. It demands a knowledge of cultures, other than the librarian's own culture, and their circumstances of cultural development. It necessitates that the staff keep up to date on current trends, not only in library development but also in society.

Gaps in previous library education and new professional interests and specialization require further study in library science and other disciplines. Opportunities and support for continuing education are necessary. Staff development programs, staff seminars in preparation for responsibilities in evaluating materials and providing reading guidance, workshops, and short courses are ways of gaining further professional competence. Self-education and individual reading programs are always open to the person who has the interest and persistence to pursue such a course. Librarians, more than many professionals, have the resources and means of access to the literature.

Material Collections and Resources

The development of successful reading service programs is dependent on the development of resource collections that are suitable to the community and the objectives of the program, and equally dependent on the staff's knowledge of a collection and other community resources. Emphasis has been placed in this book on the various aspects and the importance of careful analysis of reading materials to implement successful service. Nothing like the evaluative process described earlier is exercised. Evaluation, in general, is poorly executed. Nevertheless, change in policies and priorities and new conditions forces a reconsideration. The increasing number of publications every year, the imperative need to select and describe, accurately and in detail, all material pertinent to the use and choices of individuals and groups, stringent economic restrictions, the priority of educational and literacy goals, and the awareness of service to the library's entire community force attention to the problem of evaluation. It becomes more and more clear that evaluative, selective procedures of detail and sophistication, never before achieved except in advisory service for limited groups of individuals served by librarians in special libraries, tutorial media programs, and reading guidance service in public libraries, are necessary.

Analysis is not merely to select and acquire at the initial stage in developing reading collections but also, and perhaps most appropriately, at the stage of interpretation and selection for a specific service, program, or activity and for specific individuals or groups.

Who selects the books for libraries? Few studies provide concrete information on this question. Four major studies on selection are related to the negative rather than positive aspect of selection. Fiske,[3] Moon,[4] Busha,[5] and Pope[6] investigate the problem of censorship. Pope, in his recent study, analyzes the time librarians reported spent in selecting materials.[7] Among school, college, and public libraries, 12.3 percent of the librarians were not involved in selection at all. Nearly 80 percent of the librarians spent 30 percent or less of their time in selecting materials. Public librarians seemed to have selection responsibilities "a little more evenly divided." Pope, with some bewilderment, states: "One begins to wonder who selects the books for our libraries."[8] It may very well be that a national plan and computerized data are the solution to the problem. The materials analysis criteria procedure lends itself to such a use.

Traditionally it has been the professional role of the library staff to make decisions and implement the policies and functions of the library in regard to the kind of resources which are required. Change in this pattern is indicated by a trend toward inclusion of the reader or potential reader in these decisions. Of course, teachers, professors, and adminis-

[3]Marjorie Fiske, *Book Selection and Censorship* (Berkeley: Univ. of California Pr., 1959).

[4]Eric Moon, *Book Selection and Censorship in the Sixties* (New York: R. R. Bowker, 1969).

[5]Charles H. Busha, *Freedom versus Suppression and Censorship* (Littleton, Colo.: Libraries Unlimited, 1972).

[6]Michael Pope, *Sex and the Undecided Librarian* (Metuchen, N.J.: Scarecrow, 1974).

[7]Ibid., p. 147–49.

[8]Ibid., p. 147.

trators at various times and places have assumed this role in whole or in part. The responsibility must be a shared one to be productive and equable. Libraries are experimenting with other approaches. Children in fourth grade and adults select titles based on examination of collections at the Cooperative Children's Book Center at the Library School of the University of Wisconsin–Madison. Media selection centers are projected for schools, and central or regional libraries in public and school library systems provide examination collections and advisory staff.

Contacts during the Library Materials Research Project indicated that public librarians, as coordinators of adult services, directors of adult reading projects and activities, acquisition and branch librarians, and staff members with other major responsibilities in administration, are likely to spend some time in selection. In adult basic education programs, administrators, and possibly teachers, select materials. A better balance in the reading collections may be possible if selection is based on evaluative analyses of the materials by a group of selectors, such as professional librarians who may or may not represent reader groups, residents of the community, adult education teachers, representatives of interested groups, and subject specialists from inside or outside the library system.

Analysis of the reading resources and related audiovisual resources would seem to be essential to building suitable collections and to gaining knowledge of content. All reading service and reading guidance depend on such informed knowledge. The mature reader, as librarian, achieves maturity through study and experience. But how is this ideal situation to be achieved?

The conflicts between reading intensively and extensively, between a great deal of reading and little reading, are difficult to resolve. The demands of other responsibilities and limitations of time and budgetary restrictions erode selection responsibilities. They appear to prevent the solution of what ultimately is this different problem—finding ways for the librarian to know the elements which make up the resources with which one works. Generally, opportunities to know the material through careful examination, reading, and structured analysis are inadequate or nonexistent. Serious evaluative selection and study are abandoned. Selection becomes the prerogative of editors, publishers, wholesalers, and book sellers. To state the problem so bluntly and broadly does not deny or ignore the fact that many public and school libraries develop policies and establish priorities to make evaluative procedures possible.

The types and characteristics of materials for adult new readers (as defined in the present context) are diverse and are selected for readers who are developing maturity in reading. The resource collections that are needed to support the kind of program and activities that are envisioned in this context are many:

1. A general reading collection, in varied formats, for readers who wish to browse and borrow materials and to supplement reading programs
2. Specific materials to support courses and curricula
3. Ethnic and cultural collections of interest to reader groups in the community
4. Subject collections to meet other than instructional needs of the community
5. Consultation collections of materials for adult readers, teachers, and other agencies' staffs, such collections to be accessible at all times for examination, study, research
6. Professional collections for staff and personnel in other agencies are made available at systems headquarters, media selection centers, or state library agencies
7. Newspaper, magazine, "real world," and pamphlet collections which are easily accessible and visible
8. Deposit collections, selected to meet local situations
9. Collections in languages other than English, and bilingual collections.

In general, multiple copies should be acquired of authors, titles, and subjects that are in demand and worthy of promotion. Materials such as workbooks and free and inexpensive items (which may be considered consumable and expendable) should be acquired in necessary quantity. Special consideration should be given to recreational reading matter and materials to supplement courses and curricula and for self-education.

It may be desirable to consider the size of the book in view of the pleasure and appeal a short work has for beginning and advanced readers. Dudley Randall's Broadside Press publishes many short books because of this kind of appeal. As is well known to publishers and librarians, paperbacks have similar appeal and attract many readers.

Although few libraries may afford total saturation in acquisition of one title, a saturation of content may be achieved through use of various sources—paperbacks, hardcovers, magazines, newspapers, pamphlets, "real world" materials. The latter help to keep a collection abreast of current knowledge. Sufficient numbers of a popular or important title may prevent such problems as keeping materials or stealing. Problems increase where no ready access is possible because of limited copies or sources. It is a major criticism of libraries by users.

An example of a materials collection which has been defined in terms of purpose is the highly successful Langston Hughes Community Library and Cultural Center of Corona–East Elmhurst, Queens (New York). The materials have provided the community a type of collection that may serve as a model for neglected inner-city areas:

1. Materials to improve the self-image, to study the rich cultural heritage, to raise aspirations, and to give motivation for self-betterment
2. A basic African and black history collection
3. Information to assist with problems or concerning benefits poor people are entitled to and how to avail themselves of them, employment opportunities and training, scholarship opportunities, codes, laws and regulations affecting the area and the people living in it
4. Books for self-improvement and home study, how-to-do-it books, books of high interest and easy vocabulary for adult readers seeking to improve their reading ability.[9]

A major problem in developing the various collections is the source. The first source is regular commercial publishers. Much of the coping-skill materials are ephemeral and fragmented among a multitude of sources—business, industry, government agencies, and social agencies and organizations. Useful material that is published by commercial interests requires careful evaluation to screen out material with inordinate advertising, poor writing, and unacceptable biases and reading levels.

Libraries no longer need accept the limitations of the local area and usual trade channels of distribution. The problems of space and distance are more easily met with modern transportation and communication.

Wholesalers may be responsive to concerted demands and accurate specifications. Dealers' and buying trips are quite possible.

Bookstores that specialize in black literature and culture are major sources for a great deal of material. They are found in university towns, metropolitan centers, and ghetto areas of Chicago, Baltimore, Newark, New York, and Washington, D.C. Similarly, dealers in Chicano literature, Spanish-language material, and bilingual publications are found in Denver, Los Angeles, Mexico, South America, and Puerto Rico. Fortunately, although sources are limited, they are expanding.

In 1971 the fifteen black-owned book publishing houses in the United States published an average of five to six books each year. Over fifty

[9]See Langston Hughes Community Library and Cultural Center of Corona–East Elmhurst, "The Comprehensive Plan—August 26, 1968" (New York: Queens Borough Public Library, 1968), p. 2.

black-interest periodicals were published. More than forty bookstores sold Afro-American materials. Barrio and MICTLA publications, which were founded to publish Chicano and other minority-group writers, were only beginning to publish in 1971. Because acquisition problems will continue, excessive effort, time, and frustration are to be expected. Librarians must search out such material, and often institute new procedures in ordering and recordkeeping.

In some instances the only way the library can acquire the types of materials needed is to publish them. Publication may mean rewriting at the required reading level, and publishing, reprinting, or creating new material. It is necessary to identify what is needed, find writers, obtain financial support, and print and distribute. Successful ventures have been demonstrated in such library publications as the newsletter *Chicory* at Enoch Pratt Free Library in Baltimore, the bibliography of materials in *Pivot* at the Free Library of Philadelphia, and the latter's successful directory of colleges. However, the problems and limitations are likely to override this solution.

Programs and Activities

Programming ideas can be derived from consideration of the implications of communication and social theories in relation to the various stages of the adult's personal and social development. Stages of the Maslow hierarchy of needs, from basic survival, safety, and belonging needs to ego needs for recognition, achievement, and self-realization, correspond with age and stages in the life cycle. Erikson's stages of psychosocial development correspond to developing needs of adulthood. Implications of these conceptual theories of human development suggest the kind of programs and library resources that will correspond to stages of development and the needs and interests in the life cycle. The opportunities in which the institution, through its resources in staff and media collection, can link adults at critical stages in their lives with the information and ideas they require become evident.

In designing programs it is necessary to distinguish between programs that are to assist in rehabilitation of readers and those that are to help in developing continuing growth. Programs are designed not only to improve literacy competence and skill but also to integrate information and appreciation into daily survival and life skills.

From time to time choice and necessity will require limiting programs to certain groups and deciding on priorities. In general, attention should be directed to the total community and to all levels of reading. Appropriate materials and activities will be provided for various ages, interest groups, and ethnic groups.

Adults' orientations to the educational activities in which they join are as varied as each individual's purpose. The inquiring mind, as Houle has shown, has three major reasons for participation in learning activities. There are:

1. Goal-oriented adults who want to learn a specific skill, gain some definite information; "who [use] education as a means of accomplishing fairly clear-cut objectives"
2. Activity-oriented adults who participate because of the type of activity—discussion group, lecture—for whom the circumstances of learning have "meaning" rather than "content"
3. Learning-oriented adults who take part for the value of learning, who seek "knowledge for its own sake."[10]

Programs and activities the library may conduct or sponsor with other agencies are as unlimited as the interests and needs of the community of adults and the imagination, vision, professional competence of the library's staff, and the supportive communication resources. Recent studies have stressed the importance of autonomy for directors of such projects. In some instances the autonomy is entrusted to the reader group rather than the professional librarian. The Langston Hughes Community Library and Cultural Center of Corona–East Elmhurst (New York), which serves the black ghetto community, and the Akwesasne Library at Rooseveltown (New York), which serves native people of the Mohawk Nation, are administered by the communities' representatives. They have demonstrated how successful this pattern of management can be when supported by professional technical knowledge.

What are the kinds of programs, activities, and services that library systems may provide? The suggestions made here are limited to identifying types of programs. The program planning design is applicable to general programs and specific activities within the programs.

Reference and information services to answer questions that arise in an adult's life may be provided through personal counsel, advocacy, or referral. Information about vocations, careers, health, employment opportunities, legal aid, Social Security, and emergency aid are common areas of need.

[10]See Cyril O. Houle, *The Inquiring Mind* (Madison: Univ. of Wisconsin Pr., 1961).

Remedial reading and literacy programs are organized in adult basic education courses, in library reading programs, and by various reading instruction groups. Librarians and adult educators have demonstrated different and imaginative approaches to literacy programs: the Reading Development Program at the Free Library of Philadelphia, the Reading Improvement Program at Brooklyn Public Library, and the Library–ABE Project at Morehead State University. A successful program of English-as-a-second-language classes has been conducted at Lincoln Heights Branch Library, Los Angeles.

Reading guidance activities include a range of methods. It is possible to consider various reading attainment levels, individualized appeals and orientations. A homework assistance program provides tutorial aid in the home to adult illiterates. Equivalency programs to prepare older and young adults for examinations at secondary and higher education levels are available in many parts of the country. Libraries are making a particular contribution in resources and administrative support to independent study programs in Dallas, Denver, Portland (Maine), and other cities.

The traditional reading guidance techniques are reemerging as important activities, with more attention on book talks, storytelling, reading aloud, lectures, and panel discussions. They are adapted easily for transmission through media—radio, television, and phonodiscs and tapes. This potential is being explored in programs at public libraries in Denver, San Francisco, Madison (Wisconsin), Memphis, New York, and several smaller systems. Field trips, tours, and book and film discussion groups provide additional service.

Individualized reading services assist readers to become mature, independent readers. Individual consultations (whenever possible) between the reader and librarian and between teacher and librarian can assist in the readers' growth. The immediate response to the reading interests and needs of the users builds trust and provides wider choices.

Librarians, through outreach and programs which are focused on ethnic groups, have conducted various social and cultural activities. Festivals, dances, music, books, films, and historical presentations are ways of interpreting and using the contributions of ethnic groups' cultural heritage and individual skills. Such programs build understanding and appreciation. Photography, book and art exhibits, concerts, jam sessions, book fairs, recording sessions, and television and radio programs have been part of libraries' programs in various parts of the country, for example, folk music programs at Oxon Hill Branch Library (Maryland), Biblioteca Ambulante at Fresno County Public Library (California), reading and study centers of the Chicago Public Library, the Latin American Library at Oakland Public Library (California), and large Spanish-language collections at Miami and New York public libraries.

Instruction in the use of library and library materials may be individualized or group instruction. A rather neglected service is that of giving advice on buying and developing individual and family reading collections. Cooperative and coordinated programs with other agencies and organizations have many advantages. Clienteles have been recruited and specific reading interests have been identified. Resource persons work together.

Library deficiencies and inadequate resources are recognized. Residents in crowded housing conditions, with poor facilities for study and noisy environments, are much in need of improved library reading areas. These problems have been solved in spacious modern library buildings in many places. Such facilities are desperately needed in ghetto areas.

In many instances, programs begun with the best intentions waive strict regulations. Flexibility is the rule. But as programs become more permanent or continue over a period of time, the tendency is to eliminate flexibility. Also, new problems may be generated because of dissimilar rules within a system or negative criticisms from staff in other units and other system users.

Some specific staff activities for library reading development programs are suggested:

1. Work closely with each other's agency staff, with reading teachers or specialists, and with content or subject area teachers through formal committees, boards, and selected projects.
2. Prepare reading lists for students and readers in pertinent areas of interest, such as information about careers and jobs and selected titles for persons who are leaving high school and preparing for college or are participating in various literacy programs.
3. Present regularly scheduled book talks and reviews, lectures on reading comprehension, and demonstrations on reading materials.
4. Provide individual reading guidance, teach in groups or tutorial programs, and evaluate readability levels of subject materials and textbooks.
5. Organize and conduct discussions for groups of readers and classes that want to talk about their reading.
6. Prepare reading lists on cultural and ethnic themes.
7. Recruit, train, and supervise volunteer aides and community aides, and contract with students to teach library skills.
8. Develop programs for parents on reading with children and developing their own reading skills.

9. Set up selection study centers for teachers and librarians.
10. Set up reading resource centers, develop comprehensive collections for teaching and research purposes, and develop learning materials and media units.
11. Present exhibitions and displays of materials, and have sample copies for examination.
12. Promote (after careful analysis) important titles and authors.
13. Collect and preserve textbooks that have been published and used in the past, as well as current texts, for purposes of content and comparative analysis.
14. Analyze characteristics and identify changes in different editions of works pertaining to social, historical, scientific material which deal with ethnic populations. Prepare, on basis of careful analysis, lists with critical annotations, pointing out inaccuracies and prejudices as well as accurate, unbiased materials.

Procedures and Regulations

Procedural regulations in libraries tend to discourage, frustrate, and anger adults who are unaccustomed to institutional rigidities, especially where unreasonable restrictions are demanded. Frequently unhappy experiences, which may have happened at earlier ages, completely discourage adults. The result is intimidation, submission, or rejection.

Flexibility in rules is essential. Libraries where demonstration and outreach programs have been developed successfully have time and again permitted adults to borrow freely and easily. Fines are discarded. Exchange of borrowed books for other books has permitted the abolishment of circulation records. (In fairness it should be stated that some libraries, under pressure of heavy losses, have instituted more, rather than fewer, controls.) Silence is not demanded. However, it should be noted how important is the provision of quiet study and reading areas. A disadvantage, readily observed in some libraries, whether undergraduate college, branch, neighborhood center, central regional library or media center, is the lack of space and quiet.

Financial Support and Budgeting

Sufficient financial support is essential to sustain the types of reading collections, personnel, and supportive services which are necessary to meet the reading needs and interests of the adult community. Such collections and support are a basic part of any library's resources. Only by continuing allocations in the regular budget will the desired quality and effective use of the collection be achieved. At times, supplemental funds will be required.

Demonstration and experimental projects require an exact assessment of costs, capital outlay, and maintenance funds. A plan for gradual transfer of these costs into the regular budget and a farsighted procedure to achieve this changeover are part of any proposed project. Otherwise, and all too often, the new or experimental project is short lived, discontinued, or—what is even more serious—fails. Special monies for initiating or extending a program should be estimated for special purposes. Expenditures are likely to be needed for new kinds of material, duplication of collections, multiple copies of selected titles, consumable or expendable materials recruitment of staff, multimedia materials and equipment, publication or republication of materials, training of staff, scholarships, and evaluation and reporting costs.

The regular budget may be supplemented by funds from other sources. Major sources have been grants from state tax funds. The alert librarian, board of trustees, or concerned citizen will be able to identify and obtain funds from such sources as foundations, cooperating agencies, private gifts, local organizations, and even by transfers from other budgetary items. Support may be other than direct funds, such as resource persons, advisory help, and participation.

Evaluation of the Service

Evaluation of the service measures what is done by what is desired or desirable. Questions are asked about any service and program. What has been accomplished? What happened? What effect has it had? What impact has been made?

The methods for evaluation are decided during the planning. Although often neglected or instituted as an afterthought, evaluation is most useful when it is carried out at specified periods. The simplest evaluation is possible by looking at what has happened in relation to the function and objectives established for the service.

The bases for evaluation depend upon the philosophy "why something is done" and upon values and the theory of what is thought to be desirable.[11] Adult services have objectives of social and personal needs that require sociological and psychological research techniques in program evaluation. Statistics, special records, national standards, checklists, evaluation forms, formulas for collection development, and funding grant

[11]Sarah Rebecca Reed, ed., "Evaluation of Library Services," *Library Trends*. 23, no. 3 (Jan. 1974).

requirements provide useful measurements. Measurement of a program by objectives is possible. Program planning, which sets goals and objectives within a definite time schedule for achievement, establishes a framework for evaluation. Staff and participants are quite capable of carrying out informal evaluation. Formal studies may be made through outside consultants with special skills.

Ideally, objectives should be stated in quantitative terms. The main question would be to what extent were the objectives reached. What are the norms desired? What are the entry performances? What change occurs? In evaluating reading and reading-related programs, questions to be answered would include:

Was the collection used?
Were objectives realized? Goals attained?
What impact did the program have on the library? On the participants? On the community?
To what extent was the library used? In what ways?
What did it cost? Was it worth it?
In what ways was it successful? Unsuccessful?
What has been learned?
What is the new situation? What next?

Of particular significance would be the evaluation of the intellectual and emotional impact, if it can be measured scientifically and accurately. Such measurements can be made subjectively and through observation.

The Barss, Reitzel and Associates "Study of Exemplary Public Library Reading and Reading-related Programs"[12] provides a procedural pattern as well as useful and interesting evaluations in the thirty case studies reported; and, admittedly, the judgments are purely subjective. The following outline reflects the pattern that was developed for the evaluation of program effectiveness:

1. Summary of program effectiveness—an overview
2. Penetration—in terms of reader groups reached
3. Participant impact and summary of program goals and participant impact
4. Library impact
5. Community impact
6. Factors related to effectiveness.

[12]Barss, Reitzel & Associates, "A Study of Exemplary Public Library Reading and Reading-related Programs for Children, Youth, and Adults," mimeographed, 1971 (ERIC ED066197).

Table 6 is an outline of the responses given by participants regarding the impact of the Reading Improvement Program in Brooklyn (New York). The program provides instruction in reading for adults eighteen years of age and older.

Table 7 shows further data on program impact by participant status. The data provide constructive patterns for categories of evaluation.

In evaluating the impact on the library, the size and quality of the reading collections can be estimated. What changes occur in organization and administration among staff? What effect has the program had

Table 6. AREAS OF PARTICIPANT IMPACT

	PERCENTAGE REPORTING PROGRAM IMPACT
	YOUNG ADULT/ ADULT (N = 97)
General	
Affect:	
Like to read	84 (*N* = 83)
Feel good about yourself as a person	63
Like the library	78 (*N* = 83)
Behavior:	
Read books	76
Read magazines	51
Watch the educational TV channel	28
Finish books you start	63
Skills and Knowledge:	
Know where to get the information you need	72
Do well in school (if you are in school)	75 (*N* = 40)
Know how to use the library	68
Understand what you read	88
Program Specific	
Affect:	
Get what you wanted from the program	89
Want to learn about new things	82
Behavior:	
Read newspapers	63
Participate in group discussions	25
Go to bookstores	40
Read new kinds of things	73
Go to concerts	9
Go to lectures	13
Go to museums	22
Skills and Knowledge:	
Be critical of what you read	77

Source: Barss, Reitzel & Associates, Inc., Case Study No. 24, p. 24–29.

Table 7. PROGRAM IMPACT BY PARTICIPANT STATUS, RACE, AND PRIOR LIBRARY USE

CHANGE MEASURE	PERCENTAGE REPORTING POSITIVE IMPACT					
	PARTICIPANT STATUS		RACE		PRIOR LIBRARY USE	
	PROGRAM PARTICIPANTS	PROGRAM GRADUATES	BLACKS	WHITES	LESS THAN ONCE A MONTH	ONCE A MONTH OR MORE
Read books	74	77	82	69	84	66
Understand what you read	88	88	93	79	92	84

Source: Barss, Reitzel & Associates, Inc., Case Study No. 24, p. 24–11.

on staff relationships? On the staff's relationships with participants and with the community? What changes should be made?

The use of the reading collections and reading materials by the clientele is a clear indication of the validity of the selection. Through the self-selection process of what is accessible and advisory and reading guidance which generates the use, a final choice is made by the reader. Was the information wanted or the material requested obtained? Did participants achieve their personal objectives? What unanticipated successes or failures occurred?

The broad response to a workshop, The Adult New Reader and His Reading, offered at the Library School of the University of Wisconsin–Madison in the spring of 1973, is evidence of the range of librarians' interests and activities in service to adult readers who are achieving functional literacy and extending their use of print materials (as well as other communication media). During the last ten years, more and more services and reading programs for adult new readers have been developed. In 1966, when the MacDonald report on literacy activities provided by public libraries was made, fifteen libraries were active in this field.[13] Librarians felt limited knowledge and lack of knowledge created great obstacles to any service. From 1967 to 1971, when the Library Materials Research Project study was carried out, certain libraries were in the vanguard. Thirteen libraries cooperated in the investigation for the overarching Materials Analysis Study. Five libraries, where substantive adult reader services were coordinated with adult education programs, cooperated with the Population Study.

The extensive development of such programs was identified clearly in the interest expressed by over one hundred librarians and library

[13]Bernice MacDonald, *Literacy Activities in Public Libraries* (Chicago: American Library Assn., 1966).

educators for the 1973 workshop. The emphasis on special services is illustrated in the variety of descriptive program titles that were represented there: Project Outreach, Reader Development Program, Inner-City Services, Reading Centers, Learning Centers, Adult Education Program, Job Information Center, Adult Services Department, Readers' Bureau, Special Extension Services, and Outreach Department.[14]

Community agencies and group organizations involved in the programs were diverse: Job/Books, Operation Step-Up, Literacy Volunteers of America, Inc., Adult Basic Education, Laubach Literacy, Right-to-Read, Teach a Neighbor to Read, Halfway Houses, Project Crossroads, and Continuing Education Programs. Services were extended to adult new readers in various agencies, such as correctional and detention centers, prisons, jails, rehabilitation centers, industrial schools, technical institutes, homes and retirement places for senior citizens, apartment complexes, church organizations, other libraries, schools of library science, reading tutorial and remedial reading programs, and programmed learning centers.

The clientele, as characterized by one librarian, includes "the population who are educationally, physically, psychologically, culturally, or geographically handicapped." Specific identification of clients further points up the awareness among the librarians of many individual groups within the population. These groups are described as the beginning, retarded, unprogressive, latent reader; the underuser or nonuser; the unserved; the exceptional child; the young adult, dropout, and high school students who graduate; black, Spanish speaking, suburban white, Chicano or Mexican American, Indian or native American. Also identified are young married, preschool mothers, women, disadvantaged, homebound, lower middle class, foreign born, adults learning English as a second language, library school students, librarians, community workers, students in adult basic education in high school equivalency programs, preretirement, rural senior citizens, rural poor, poor Ozark hill people, rural-oriented conservatives, institutionalized, handicapped, and blind.

Brief phrases reflect favorably and unfavorably on librarians' attitudes and values: "learn from them," "want to understand," "what does it mean?" "low-level readers," "these people," "bad adjustment to white culture," "language and cultural barriers seem insurmountable."

[14]The information reported here about the responses of librarians—as identified in the workshop at the Library School, the University of Wisconsin–Madison—first appeared in the article by Helen Huguenor Lyman, "Reading and the Adult New Reader."

The services provided through these libraries and special programs include what seem in most instances to be traditional services. They may be distinctive in that they are operational and revitalized, having become moribund or limited to the few white middle-class users of the public libraries. The selection and organization of materials for adult new readers have priority with reading guidance methods, such as subject bibliographies, annotated reading lists, coordinated buying lists for libraries, advisory service to librarians, community group services (including program planning), cooperation with other educational institutions, persons and community planning groups, book talks and book discussions, book fairs, and group programs. Other services include program planning, counseling, public relations efforts, organization of community advisory groups, and special collections placed in institution and organization centers. Training and staff development are mentioned. Major problems center on evaluation and sources of materials, identification of new readers, contact and promotion, and failure to interest or reach these clientele.

It would seem that librarians are engaged in soul-searching efforts to clarify, understand, and articulate the role and function of the library in the community and in the lives of individuals and groups. Among many questions asked, some seem new: Is the role only informational? Is the advocacy role important or appropriate? Does the library support or assist? Does it exercise its own rights and powers, determine its own actions, or follow other agencies? How does the library collaborate with other agencies?

Problems and Responses

Library responses to problems have overcome obstacles and brought new solutions. The library is viewed as an information center, a cultural center, and a center for the diffusion of knowledge for groups hitherto "outside" the library. Librarians recognize the power of information and ideas, and in many instances respond with outreach programs and learning resource centers. The concept is embodied in the term *a philosophy of reaching out*—taking service to the community, rather than bringing clientele to the library or limiting service to those who come to it. There is recognition of a changing society and changing community. The creation of new programs and extension of existing services are evident in reports in the literature. The application of principles and policies of service to include the total community, and particularly less advantaged and deprived persons who have not been served, is given some priority in large and small units of library systems.

Attention is being given to educating and training library school students who are interested in these areas of professional service. Recruitment of library school students from minority groups by universities adds to the quality of library personnel.

The ultimate purpose of this book is to resolve the dichotomy between the dominant majority group and the less influential minority groups, without devaluing pluralism. Residents and citizens of the United States are part of the whole society. The values of our educational, economic, social, and political agencies impinge, to a greater or less degree, on the life of each person. To maintain a total separateness would appear to be impossible and is certainly undesirable. But from the perspective of librarianship, no group should be considered to be the same as any other group. Common characteristics such as heritage, language, and values make it possible to differentiate distinctive characteristics. These differences create a heterogeneous quality for each group.

This philosophy, or point of view, is the basis for establishing a library policy that results in service for the whole community. Neither the persons or groups served, nor the services and resources for them, are to be thought of or identified as special. Special publics, special programs, special materials tend to belittle and wrongfully describe hitherto neglected groups—in the eyes of the clientele so designated. To be considered special creates the impression that they are assumed to be not essential, not part of regular library service. Everyone likes to feel that service is equal.

Another consequence within the internal organization of the library is that the special program often is temporary, fragmentary, peripheral. Even a successful exemplary program may lack continuity and continuation. It would seem that a new program may fail primarily because it has been considered special, experimental, rather than a permanent responsibility or ongoing service that is the right of the residents.

Admittedly, service to an entire community may not be achieved all at once, but it should be possible when the planning design has such a goal with scheduled points and levels of achievement. The strong programs of service are given continuing support and priority during the initial stages. Reading development programs with continuous periods of service are the ones which survive.

Because of professional knowledge and media resources which are available today, librarians have an unparalleled opportunity to create libraries that are truly intelligence and cultural centers for all residents of the library community. Libraries can provide reliable, relevant, and responsible community resources of all types and can help adults become active users of those resources. With vision and active reading guidance service, librarians can create libraries where adults find community resources meaningful to their lives. Thus libraries will be human agencies, suited to the intellectual, educational, social, and cultural needs and interests of all readers and user groups in the total community.

Bibliography

Adler, Mortimer J., and Van Doren, Charles. *How to Read a Book*. Rev. and updated. New York: Simon and Schuster, 1972.

Barss, Reitzel & Associates. "A Study of Exemplary Public Library Reading and Reading-related Programs for Children, Youth, and Adults." Mimeographed, 1971. ERIC ED06-6197.

Bem, Daryl J. *Beliefs, Attitudes, and Human Affairs*. Basic Concepts in Psychology Series. Belmont, Calif.: Brooks/Cole Publishing Co., 1970.

Bormuth, John R. "Reading Literacy: Its Definition and Assessment." *Reading Research Quarterly* 9, no. 1 (1973–74).

Cabrera, Y. Arturo. *Emerging Faces: The Mexican-Americans*. Dubuque, Iowa: William C. Brown Co., 1971.

Childers, Thomas. *The Information-Poor in America*. Metuchen, N.J.: Scarecrow, 1975.

Deligdisch, Yekutiel. "The Reading Comprehension of Adult Readers in Relation to Their Ethnic Background." Ph.D. dissertation, Univ. of Wisconsin–Madison, 1972.

Deloria, Vine, Jr. "This Country Was a Lot Better Off When the Indians Were Running It." In *Red Power*, edited by Alvin M. Josephy, Jr., p. 248. New York: American Heritage Pr., 1971.

Ennis, Philip H. *Adult Reading in the United States*. Report no. 105. Chicago: National Opinion Research Center, Univ. of Chicago, 1965.

Erikson, Erik H. *Childhood and Society*. 2d ed. New York: W. W. Norton, 1963.

Federal Interagency Committee on Education. *Task Force on Higher Education and Chicanos, Puerto Ricans, and American Indians*. Washington, D.C.: Dept. of Health, Education, and Welfare, 1973.

Flesch, Rudolph F. "A Readability Yardstick." *Journal of Applied Psychology* 32:221–33 (June 1948).

Freire, Paulo. "The Adult Literacy Process as Cultural Action for Freedom." *Harvard Educational Review* 40:212 (May 1970; special issue, Illiteracy in America).

———. *Cultural Action for Freedom.* Monograph Series no. 1. Cambridge, Mass.: Harvard Educational Review and Center for the Study of Development and Social Change, 1970.

Fry, Edward B. "A Readability Formula That Saves Time." *Journal of Reading* 11:513–16, 575–77 (April 1968).

———. "A Readability Graph for Librarians," Part 1. *School Libraries* 19:13–16 (Fall 1969).

Getzels, J. W. "The Problem of Interests: A Reconsideration." In *Reading: Seventy Years of Progress*, pp. 97–105, Proceedings of Annual Conference on Reading at University of Chicago, 1966, edited by H. Alan Robinson. Chicago: Univ. of Chicago Pr., 1966.

Gotsick, Priscilla. *Assessing Community Information and Service Needs.* Public Library Training Institutes, Library Service Guide no. 2. Morehead, Ky.: Appalachian Adult Education Center, Morehead State University, 1974. ERIC ED098982.

Gray, William S., and Leary, Bernice E. *What Makes a Book Readable?* Chicago: Univ. of Chicago Pr., 1935.

———. *Maturity in Reading: Its Nature and Appraisal.* Chicago: Univ. of Chicago Pr., 1956.

Gunning, Robert. *The Technique of Clear Writing.* Rev. ed. New York: McGraw-Hill, 1968.

Haines, Helen E. *Living with Books: The Art of Book Selection.* 2d ed. New York: Columbia Univ. Pr., 1950.

Havighurst, Robert J., and Orr, Betty. *Adult Education and Adult Needs.* Chicago: Center for the Study of Liberal Education for Adults, 1956. Supplement, 1960: *Adult Education for Our Time.*

Houle, Cyril O. *The Inquiring Mind.* Madison: Univ. of Wisconsin Pr., 1961.

Klare, George R. "Assessing Readability." *Reading Research Quarterly* 10:64 (1974–75).

———. *The Measurement of Readability.* Ames: Iowa State Univ. Pr., 1963.

Knowles, Malcolm S. *The Modern Practice of Adult Education: Andragogy versus Pedagogy.* New York: Association Pr., 1970.

Kohl, Herbert. *Reading, How To.* New York: Bantam, 1973.

Latimer, Bettye I., ed. *Starting Out Right: Choosing Books about Black People for Young Children.* Bulletin no. 2314. Madison: Wisconsin Dept. of Public Instruction, 1972.

Lohrer, Alice, ed. "Research in the Fields of Reading and Communications." *Library Trends* 22, no. 2 (Oct. 1973).

Lyman, Helen Huguenor. "Library Programs and Services to the Disadvantaged." *Library Trends* 20, no. 2 (Oct. 1971).

MacDonald, Bernice. *Literacy Activities in Public Libraries.* Chicago: American Library Assn., 1966.

Maslow, Abraham H. *Toward a Psychology of Being*. 2d ed. Princeton, N.J.: Van Nostrand, 1968.

Reed, Sarah Rebecca, ed. "Evaluation of Library Services." *Library Trends* 23, no. 3 (Jan. 1974).

Schramm, Wilbur. "Why Adults Read." In *Adult Reading*, pp. 57–88, 55th Yearbook of National Society for the Study of Education, part 2, edited by Nelson B. Henry. Chicago: National Society for the Study of Education and Univ. of Chicago Pr., 1956.

————, ed. *The Process and Effects of Mass Communication*. Urbana: Univ. of Illinois Pr., 1955.

———— and Roberts, Donald F. *The Process and Effects of Mass Communications*. Rev. ed. Urbana: Univ. of Illinois Pr., 1972.

Shaw, Alison. "The Visually Handicapped Readers: Print for Partial Sight." *Libri* 19:249–53 (1969).

Sheehy, Gail. *Passages: Predictable Crises of Adult Life*. New York: E. P. Dutton, 1976.

Sherrill, Laurence L. "The Affective Response of Ethnic Minority Readers to Indigenous Ghetto Literature: A Measurement." Ph.D. dissertation, Univ. of Wisconsin–Madison, 1972.

Simpson, Edwin L., and Lovall, Philip W. *Preparing and Selecting Printed Educational Material for Adult New Readers*. ERIC CE007 631. 1976.

Smith, Helen Lyman. *Adult Education Activities in Public Libraries*. Chicago: American Library Assn., 1954.

Smith, Joshua, ed. *Library and Information Services for Special Groups*. New York: Science Associates/International, Inc., 1974.

Tinker, Miles A. *Legibility of Print*. Ames: Iowa State Univ. Pr., 1963.

Waples, Douglas; Berelson, Bernard; and Bradshaw, Franklyn R. *What Reading Does to People*. Chicago: Univ. of Chicago Pr., 1940.

————, and Tyler, Ralph W. *What People Want to Read About*. Chicago: American Library Assn. and Univ. of Chicago Pr., 1931.

Warren, Roland L. *Studying Your Community*. New York: Free Pr., 1965.

Whitman, Lois Emily. "Adult Developmental Tasks: A Study of the Writings of Erik H. Erickson." Master's thesis, Univ. of Washington, 1968.

Index

Reading and the Adult New Reader
was set by Modern Typographers, Clearwater, Florida,
in Lino Times Roman:
text 10 points on 12   extracts, bibliography 9/11
footnotes, tabular matter, index 8/10
The display type on the half-title page is 14/16; in order of appearance on the
title page it is 36-, 10-, and 12-point roman, and 10-point italic. The chapter titles
are 18 point and the accompanying numbers, 30 point.
The type used for the figures (illustrations) is Helvetica, a sans serif type face.